WHAT YOUR COLLEAGUES ARE SAYING . . .

By redefining roles and responsibilities, Whorton helps create more sustainable, effective systems that support both student learning and educator development. This book is an essential guide for building stronger, more resilient school communities.

—Sarah Beal
Executive Director, US PREP
Phoenix, Arizona

This practical book is grounded in deep and wide experience that will help every school system reimagine and remake leadership roles that are sustainable and effective. Whorton understands the complex realities that educators face and offers a compelling, accessible, and helpful antidote to the superhero myth of leadership.

—Elizabeth A. City
Senior Lecturer, Harvard Graduate School of Education
Cambridge, Massachusetts

Sustainable school leadership isn't about one hero at the top—it's about building a team of empowered leaders at every level. Rather than superheroes, schools need strong, collaborative structures that allow leadership to thrive beyond a single person.

—Chassie Selouane
Principal, MLS International Riyadh
Riyadh, Kingdom of Saudi Arabia

Lindsay Whorton knows how to make the most of educators' talents and time. Her clear-eyed goals, thought-provoking questions, and expert guidance make A New School Leadership Architecture *vital reading for anyone serious about improving education.*

—Susan Moore Johnson
Research Professor, Harvard Graduate School of Education
Cambridge, Massachusetts

This book offers a fresh, thoughtful approach to school leadership, providing a framework that balances the principal's role, distributes leadership, and creates meaningful opportunities for teacher growth. A must-read for educational leaders seeking inspiration for change and practical ideas to build a more sustainable and supportive system.

—Kristina Fulton
Curriculum & Instruction Specialist, Lancaster-Lebanon IU13
Lancaster, Pennsylvania

This book offers practical tools and thoughtful insights, redefining what leadership and leadership structures can look like in today's ever-changing educational landscape. It is a must-read for anyone striving to create transformative learning environments.

—Sammie Cervantez
Program Specialist: ELA/ELD/Literacy Program,
San Luis Obispo County Office of Education
Pismo Beach, California

This book is a practical guide to growing effective principals in our ever challenging educational landscape.

—Tanna Nicely
Executive Principal, South Knoxville Elementary
Blaine, Tennessee

This is a clarion call for school district leadership to redesign leadership architecture and provide essential support that will systematically build leadership capabilities. A New School Leadership Architecture *offers step-by-step guidance for how a teacher can move through the process of becoming a team member and eventually a school leader.*

—Jerry Jailall
Assistant Chief Education Officer, Ministry of Education, Guyana
Baldwin Harbor, New York

Lindsay Whorton offers an inspiring vision that challenges what we think we know about "how schools must work"—and empowers forward-thinking leaders with the real-life examples and practical guidance they need to convert vision to action.

—David Rosenberg
Facilitator, Coalition to Reimagine the Teaching Role
Leader-in-Residence, Teach Plus
Cambridge, Massachusetts

Lindsay Whorton's framework offers a practical roadmap for designing roles that are sustainable, scalable, and centered on impact. This book is essential reading for any system leader serious about transforming schools for the better.

—Janice K. Jackson
Former CEO, Chicago Public Schools
Chicago, Illinois

Whorton offers a refreshing blueprint for how we can redesign our schools to support what we know is essential: ensuring that every teacher receives the mentorship, coaching, and support necessary to grow and thrive. Whorton's synthesis of research and theory into a practical approach will help educators advance much needed change.

—Ellen Moir
Founder, New Teacher Center
Santa Cruz, California

A noteworthy combination of bold and practical, A New School Leadership Architecture *will spark the thinking of educators to redesign schools that unlock the potential of our teachers and students. A timely addition to the field, given today's challenges and tomorrow's possibilities.*

—Vicki Phillips
CEO, NCEE
Washington, DC

A New School Leadership Architecture

A New School Leadership Architecture

A Four-Level Framework for Reimagining Roles

Lindsay Whorton

CORWIN

FOR INFORMATION:

Corwin
A SAGE Company
2455 Teller Road
Thousand Oaks, California 91320
(800) 233-9936
www.corwin.com

SAGE Publications Ltd.
1 Oliver's Yard
55 City Road
London EC1Y 1SP
United Kingdom

SAGE Publications India Pvt. Ltd.
10th Floor, Emaar Capital Tower 2
MG Road, Sikanderpur
Sector 26 Gurugram
Haryana 122002
India

SAGE Publications Asia-Pacific Pte. Ltd.
18 Cross Street #10-10/11/12
China Square Central
Singapore 048423

Vice President and Editorial Director: Monica Eckman
Acquisitions Editor: Pam Berkman
Content Development Manager: Desirée A. Bartlett
Senior Editorial Assistant: Nyle De Leon
Production Editors: Tori Mirsadjadi; Amy Schroller; Neelu Sahu
Copy Editor: Colleen Brennan
Typesetter: C&M Digitals (P) Ltd.
Cover Designer: Scott Van Atta

Printed and bound by CPI Group (UK) Ltd, Croydon, CR0 4YY

Paperback ISBN 978-1-0718-7277-2

This book is printed on acid-free paper.

25 26 27 28 29 10 9 8 7 6 5 4 3 2 1

Contents

For downloadable resources related to *A New School Leadership Architecture: A Four-Level Framework for Reimagining Roles,* please visit the companion website:
companion.corwin.com/courses/newschoolarchitecture

Preface

We love hero narratives. The Marvel Cinematic Universe has become the highest-grossing franchise ever, bringing in a staggering $29.8 billion. The superhero industry emerged in the 1930s as we careened toward a second world war. Uncertainty, fear, and a sense of powerlessness were overwhelming. Captain America. Batman. Black Panther. Wonder Woman. These heroes reminded us that good people could stand up to and overcome evil. They showed us that individuals could make a difference. And they told us that we could harness our strengths and overcome our weaknesses. Superheroes provided encouragement and hope.

The chapters of history have turned, but we continue to have a sweet spot for heroes. We continue to wish that one person could save us. That the solution to our problems could be that simple, that maybe we can be that person. We see these dreams reflected in the stories we tell, including our stories about schools. The late 1990s and early 2000s churned out one hero-educator story after another. Even when they depicted true stories of educators working tirelessly and creatively to help their students achieve great things, they reduced the sustained, shared work to support students to a simple story of one person's ingenuity and effort.

Stand and Deliver, profiling the inspiring educator Jaime Escalante, illustrates the pattern. Escalante was a gifted math teacher who achieved remarkable results at one of Los Angeles's poorest high schools. His story deserves to be known and celebrated. But the film tells an untrue version of a true story. It tells the tale of one man working alone to elevate a cohort of high school students from seventh-grade math to mastering calculus in one year. The reality is that Escalante worked with a *whole team* of educators to change the sequence of the math curriculum across the high school and build a system of targeted support that helped students learn and achieve at high levels over many years. It's a remarkable achievement. But it isn't the story of a lone hero. It is the story of a team of leaders working together to create systems for students to thrive.

Our public schools are facing enormous pressures and challenges: financial challenges linked to declining enrollment and persistent inflation. Growing politicization of education and distrust of public schools. School safety. A crisis of student mental health, well-being, and belonging. The lingering scars of the pandemic show up everywhere, from student attendance and behavior to academic outcomes. Schools' and districts' ability to meet and overcome these challenges depends on their people. What is the depth and capacity of talent and leadership available to tackle these challenges? Unfortunately, most schools and districts are struggling to find and develop the talent and leadership they need. There have been worrying signals about the health of the education profession for decades. The challenges are now reaching crisis levels.

Across the country, schools struggle to find enough qualified educators to teach every class (Tan et al., 2024). Educators are burning out and leaving the profession (Diliberti & Schwartz, 2023; Doan et al., 2024; Learning Policy Institute, 2024). Young people's interest in the teaching profession is low and declining (Kraft & Lyon, 2024). New teachers are increasingly underprepared (Garcia & Weiss, 2019; Marder et al., 2024; Templeton et al., 2024). And many principals have headed for the exits (Diliberti & Schwartz, 2023; National Association of Secondary School Principals, 2022).

Many factors drive these trends—from pay to disrespect to chronic stress and discouragement (Walker, 2022). But we need to confront the reality that jobs in our schools are too hard, approaching impossible. Working in a school and sustaining high performance over time basically requires super heroism. This is true of every role in our schools, from the classroom to the principal's desk. In many schools across the United States, jobs have become increasingly undoable. When you have undoable jobs, *will* or *skill* is not enough to make them sustainable. Principals and assistant principals alone can't provide the coaching and support our teachers need and deserve, especially when more teachers are new and underprepared. Though there are many challenges facing the profession, there are reasons for optimism: Teachers have great leadership capacity, and we must unleash it, including giving them time to focus on leadership responsibilities. But we can't just add new roles to the existing structure. Doing so won't be coherent, and it won't be sustainable. We need to redesign the whole building.

We can't just keep doing the same thing and expecting different results. We must think *differently*. This book will help you do that by building mental models that will allow you to see school leadership and leadership development in new ways and to find the steps to move toward a new reality. We need a new school leadership architecture—a new "unifying or coherent structure" (Merriam-Webster, n.d.)—that sets leaders and schools up for success.

The school leadership architecture that we present in this book is inspired by *The Leadership Pipeline* (Charan et al., 2011; Charan et al., 2024). *The Leadership Pipeline* argues that in order for organizations to succeed and thrive, they must structure leadership appropriately and they must support every leader to build the capabilities they need to succeed in their role. They define a series of leadership levels, each characterized by what the authors call "the job to be done" (Charan et al., 2024, p. 33). This is the structural part of the work—appropriately organizing and distributing leadership work. Then, as individuals move between leadership levels, they navigate a "leadership passage," requiring them to embrace new skills, time applications, and work values (Charan et al., 2024, p. 22). This is the behavioral part of the work. This book puts these ideas to work for public schools. By clearly defining the work that needs to be done across four leadership levels (Team Members, Team Leaders, Bridge Leaders, and the School Leader) and outlining the transition in skills, time, and values that individual leaders need to make to succeed at each level, the school leadership architecture can help individual leaders and schools thrive. By improving structures and helping leaders build the skills to lead effectively within them, the new architecture can provide school leaders with the capacity they need to build capacity and get results.

This book is designed to support multiple audiences:

- District leaders: You play an irreplaceable role in designing and improving how school leadership is structured in your district and ensuring that sitting and aspiring leaders have the skills and capabilities they need to succeed.
- Principals: You are a critical partner for district leaders who are working to change district-wide systems and structures. You may not have the power to unilaterally change your school's organizational structure, but you can still work to improve your individual leadership practice or to provide stronger coaching to the leaders you support. Within your sphere of influence, you can embrace the most important work for your leadership level, and you can hone the skills, time applications, and professional identity that you need to succeed. And if you have the responsibility of coaching and developing other leaders, you can use these tools to sharpen your coaching.
- All aspiring school leaders: Whether you are a teacher aspiring to make a great impact on your campus, an assistant principal working to sharpen your skill, or any other school-based leader, this book is designed to be a resource for you to succeed in your current role and prepare for future leadership roles.

The book is organized in three parts. Part I introduces the framework, the school leadership architecture. Chapter 1 explains the four leadership levels, the distinct work at each level, and how they promote a thriving school. In Chapter 2, school and district leaders deepen their understanding of the framework by putting it into practice. Application exercises support readers to diagnose holes or weaknesses in their school leadership architecture. Then, the second half of the chapter compares their findings to common challenges. We encourage all readers to start with Part I.

Understanding the framework is critical to using the tools and resources offered in the rest of the book.

Part II lights the path to system-level, structural change. It is designed to help districts rebuild and redesign school leadership roles. Chapter 3 highlights concrete examples of how the school leadership architecture has and can come to life. It will also unpack common barriers and challenges that districts will need to navigate to prioritize this work. Chapter 4 provides a practical roadmap for this leading change—first through a small pilot project and then at scale. Part II will be essential reading for district leaders and for principals interested in rethinking how school leadership roles are structured.

Part III focuses on how to help leaders build the new skills that they need to succeed in new structures. Districts must do more than change structures. They need to support leaders to evolve their behaviors and lead differently. Chapter 5 dives deeply into how an individual experiences the change from one leadership level to the next, and how we can support leaders who are navigating these shifts. Chapters 6, 7, and 8 break down the specific shifts that each leader must make at a new leadership level. Chapter 9 identifies the key principles of a strong district-wide leadership development system that ensures a deep bench of leaders who are ready to lead at each level. In addition to informing districts' leadership development strategies, Part III provides concrete tools and strategies for all sitting and aspiring school leaders to use to inform their personal development and to coach and support the leaders around them.

Leadership is certainly not the only thing that must be addressed to build the system of public education that we aspire to and that our children deserve. But it is the core resources that we will need to meet each challenge that we face. And too often the strength of the people in our schools is the condition that is skipped over as we race to chase a long list of initiatives that schools need to drive. So while there are many steps that we need to take to build stronger, more impactful, more joyful schools, we offer the strong leadership architecture as a critical first step.

Acknowledgments

Books are made of hundreds of solitary hours. But writing one has been another reminder that we don't do anything entirely on our own. I am grateful to many people who encouraged me and helped bring this book to life. I never would have undertaken this project without the encouragement and support of the board of the Holdsworth Center, especially our founding chair, Ruth Simmons, who gave me the push to get started, and Robert Gates, who supported it across the finish line. Thank you for always pushing me and us to do all we can to fulfill our mission and support education leaders. To my Holdsworth teammates: I am lucky to work alongside such incredible colleagues. The ideas in this book are a product of our shared work and learning. All errors in thinking or presentation are mine, and any positive contribution this book makes will be ours.

Many people were generous in reading drafts of this book and helping me make it better. I want to give a special mention to Ellen Moir, Michelle Darling, Jordan Mercedes, Alessandra Zielinski, Barry Aidman, Jennifer Parvin, LeeAnn Rutledge, Lisa Lawrence, Amanda Siepiola, and Patricia McKee for powering through the entirety of an early, not-that-great draft. Listening to your reflections helped me see the path forward and to believe it was worth pursuing. I am also grateful to Marta Tienda, Rob Schwartz, Susan Moore Johnson, Jennifer Cheatham, Sarah Beal, Jenny McGown, and many others for your feedback and advice. Thank you to Mark Estrada, Stephaine Camarillo, Jamee Griebel, and the Plum Creek Elementary School team for allowing me to tell your story and helping me to get it right.

To the team at Corwin, especially my editor, Pam Berkman: Thank you for the care and attention you have invested in this project and your commitment to serving education leaders and students. To every classroom, school, and district leader who reads this book: thank you for your relentless pursuit of what is best for each and every one of our students. I know that you give so much of yourself to this work. Every citizen in this country owes you the utmost gratitude and respect. I am inspired by you every day.

PUBLISHER'S ACKNOWLEDGMENTS

Corwin gratefully acknowledges the contributions of the following reviewers:

Helene Alalouf
Instructional Coach, Educational Consultant, SOLVED Consulting
New York, New York

Brian Booker
Teaching and Learning Consultant, Social Studies
Lancaster, Pennsylvania

Sammie Cervantez
Program Specialist, ELA/ELD/Literacy Program,
Office of Education, San Luis Obispo County
Pismo Beach, California

Kristina Fulton
Curriculum & Instruction Specialist, Lancaster-Lebanon IU13
Lancaster, Pennsylvania

Jerry Jailall
Assistant Chief Education Officer, Ministry of Education, Guyana
Baldwin Harbour, New York

Marianne Lucas Lescher
Principal, Kyrene Traditional Academy
Chandler, Arizona

Louis Lim
Principal, Bur Oak Secondary School
Toronto, Ontario, Canada

Neil MacNeill
Former Superintendent and Principal, Ellenbrook Primary School
Scarborough, Western Australia

Tanna Nicely
Executive Principal, South Knoxville Elementary
Blaine, Tennessee

Chassie Selouane
Principal, MLS International Riyadh
Riyadh, Kingdom of Saudi Arabia

About the Author

Lindsay Whorton is proud to be a founding member of The Holdsworth Center, a non-profit organization in Texas dedicated to building educational leaders. She is proud to have led the organization through a period of significant growth, from serving seven school districts and 42 leaders in 2017 to more than 1,900 leaders in 89 public school districts through 2025. Lindsay is a teacher, writer, speaker, and advocate for public education and champion of the educators who make them great.

PART I

A New Architecture

Solutions-oriented readers will be eager to jump into the action. But before we can act in new ways, we need to think in new ways, and that is the work of Part I. Over the course of two chapters, Part I introduces a new way of seeing school leadership. Chapter 1 introduces and makes the case for the four-level leadership architecture. Chapter 2 offers readers an opportunity to apply the model to their own school or district and compare what they find to common weaknesses in the school leadership architecture. Equipped with a strong understanding of the four leadership levels, readers will be ready to revamp the structure of roles (Part II) and help leaders build the skills they need to succeed in new structures (Part III).

CHAPTER 1

A New School Leadership Architecture

Plum Creek Elementary is a single-story brick structure, squat and long, nestled between parks and a small neighborhood in Lockhart, Texas. Jamee Griebel has been the principal at Plum Creek, which serves just over 500 students, since 2016. But she will tell you that her job in 2025 is completely different from when she was first promoted from the assistant principal role.

"When I think back on my first few years as a principal, I felt like all the decisions had to come through me. It was my responsibility to approve everything, communicate everything, and be involved in every decision that was made across the entire campus," Griebel reflects. "I was working seven days a week, 10, 12, sometimes 14 hours a day trying to keep up with everything that needed to be done. I was coaching teachers, coaching assistant principals, and coaching aides. I was stretched so thin in terms of my time and my content knowledge. It is hard to know everything and every aspect of the work across the entire campus." She was discouraged: "Despite how hard I was working, I didn't feel like I was doing a really good job when I thought about everything I was responsible for. And I wondered how long I'd be able to keep the speed that I was going at, how long I could sustain in this role."

After Lockhart Independent School District (ISD) launched a process to overhaul school leadership structures in 2019, an effort called Shared Leadership, Griebel can hardly believe the change. "This shift with shared leadership has really allowed the time and space to really build the success of the school. Before Shared Leadership, I was in every aspect of everything across the campus. I was planning our in-service schedules, professional development, making the master schedules, being the sole person responsible for coaching all our teachers. Now, I have a team of people I trust with different expertise who are growing teachers in ways I never could have on my own. This allows me to focus on growing leaders across my school, getting out of the weeds of every decision, and truly leading from a balcony view."

Five-plus years into this new model, the results are evident. Lockhart ISD has a district-wide commitment to grow every student, no matter their starting point, at least 1.5 years in reading and math. "Prior to Shared Leadership," Griebel says, "20% to 30% of our students were growing 1.5. This year, 94% of our students grew by 1.5 years in reading. The impact of this change has just been huge."

Griebel's early experience will sound familiar to many principals, novice and experienced: the stress, the doubts, the relentless pressure. Too often, our advice to leaders like Griebel is simply work harder and be a better leader. But what if jobs in our schools are too hard, approaching impossible? If that is the problem, sending the message that all will be well if people just work harder or if we just train them better is irresponsible. It adds fuel to a fire that is already raging. It's another voice whispering in the ears of mission-driven educators: "This is your fault. If only you had worked a little harder, things would be better." What we need to be screaming is "This is unsustainable! Something must change!" This book argues that the challenges Griebel experienced are structural: we have layered on more and more without giving schools the leadership capacity they need to succeed. The story of Plum Creek Elementary reminds us that change is possible. We can build the leadership capacity that our schools need to thrive. Doing so will require us to change both how we structure leadership roles in schools and how we develop people for them.

The mission of this book is to support you to do that work. We can design roles that are doable, that allow the school's most important work to be done, starting with every teacher receiving the support they need to grow and thrive. The new school leadership architecture provides a framework for thinking about what this could look like. It is composed of four levels, each with a unique leadership mission: Team Members, Team Leaders, Bridge Leaders, and School Leaders. It is a framework, not a prescription. It is a lens through which we can see how to make things work better for both individuals and the organization. It can help us rethink how we structure roles in our schools. And it can help us improve how we identify, develop, and support leaders in those roles. After presenting the theory of the problem, this chapter will make the case for replacing our principal-centric leadership structures with a four-level leadership model.

THE THEORY OF THE PROBLEM: UNDOABLE JOBS

In the early 2000s, mental models about school leadership began to shift seismically. Pre-2000, many principals had seen themselves as "building managers." In that era, administrators kept the trains running on schedule, ensured smooth operations, and created a supportive atmosphere for teachers, who operated largely autonomously to deliver instruction. High-stakes accountability, which accelerated with the No Child Left Behind Act, signed into law in 2002, shifted the context and demanded a more proactive approach to managing instruction and driving results. The era of instructional leadership had begun.

In this new era, principals needed to do more than manage operations or work effectively with teachers and staff. They needed to understand what effective instruction looked like, monitor and evaluate the instructional program, and be able to coach and develop staff members to deliver against their instructional expectations. Ultimately, principals were responsible in a new way for the school's academic performance. This shift in focus was—and is—a great thing. Of course the leader of the organization should have a deep understanding of its core work and the skills to recognize and cultivate excellence. Of course they should be held accountable for the results the organization produces. So far, so good.

But here's the challenge. Being the "instructional leader" was communicated as a long list of things that the principal needed to *personally* do. What many principals heard was that they were the (only) instructional leader. The shift to instructional leadership added priorities to the principal's plate without taking much off. The job wasn't just different; it was bigger and harder.

Researchers and policymakers almost certainly didn't intend to send a message to principals that they needed to personally execute a growing list of tasks to be an instructional leader. Surely, the goal was to send the message that the principal was responsible for ensuring that these things occurred (in a high-quality way), not that they were personally responsible for executing them. But that's not what most principals heard.

The result? The implicit expectations we hold for our principals outstrip what is realistic for a single human being to do. Take just one aspect of their job—coaching and developing staff. According to a 2016 study, 96% of principals said they were responsible for the performance of teachers in their buildings; 82% said they were the primary person responsible (Bierly et al., 2016). An average U.S. public school serves almost 500 students and employs around 33 teachers (National Center for Education Statistics, 2022–2023). So, the principal of an average school views themself as the primary person responsible for the development of 33 teachers.

Even if developing teachers was the *only* thing principals did (and we know it is far from the only thing principals do), it would be an extraordinary expectation. The number of people a leader supervises is called their "span of control." For knowledge workers such as accountants, lawyers, and engineers, the average span of control is five people (Bierly, et al., 2016). Many principals are responsible for at least six times as many people. What happens when a principal views themself as the primary person responsible for the development of more than 30 teachers?

- Principals are less likely to delegate work to others, such as assistant principals and other school leaders.
- Principals experience a persistent sense of failure. There's never enough time to dedicate to developing teachers the way they would like to while still meeting all the other responsibilities they face.
- Teachers don't receive the coaching, feedback, and development they need or deserve.

It's simply impossible to provide consistent support and coaching to that many people. Wide spans of control force principals to make choices. One choice is to cut corners on observation, feedback, or evaluation. Another choice is for principals to triage, concentrating their efforts on the handful of teachers who are struggling the most, leaving other teachers who are still eager to grow, improve, and fend for themselves.

We all need to care about the principal's job being impossible. Not just because we care about principals, but because we know the impossibility of the principal's job impacts every other person in that school building. The challenges facing principals—they are stretched thin and forced to be reactive—are directly linked to the pressures teachers face—they are overloaded and under-supported. When teachers don't get the support they deserve, it generates a negative feedback loop. Teachers don't grow, improve, or become their best. They don't experience self-efficacy or confidence. Instead, they feel overwhelmed and discouraged as they pour everything into their teaching but feel like it is never enough. Eventually, beaten down and burned-out teachers leave the profession. As these dynamics churn, students are the ones impacted.

From the classroom to the principal's office, we have created jobs that require superheroes. While demands have steadily increased, school leadership and staffing structures have changed little. These jobs are too difficult—approaching impossible. That is why we have a human capital crisis playing out in public schools across the country. Ignoring that reality is a huge mistake.

There are close to 100,000 public schools in the United States (National Center for Education Statistics, n.d.). Let's say that you can prove that some percentage of principals have the skillset and capacity to do the job as currently designed. We say, "*Who cares!*" We *must* give up on the dream that we can build excellent, sustainable school systems through a superhero strategy. We have to build a system that can succeed consistently and at scale. Continuing to design a system with an "only the strong survive" logic guarantees we will keep getting the results we currently have—a system where many kids are not receiving the educational opportunities they deserve.

PAUSE AND REFLECT

- What is your reaction to this framing of the problem?
- How does it connect to your experience as a leader or to what you have witnessed?
- What questions does it raise for you?

THE WORK OF SCHOOL LEADERS: BUILD CAPACITY AND DELIVER RESULTS

In many schools, school leadership structures fail to create enough leadership capacity on two dimensions. The first is coaching and developing others—what we'll call *building capacity*. The second, which we'll summarize as *delivering results*, is the work of strategy, planning, and execution. Restructuring responsibility for building capacity starts with establishing reasonable spans of control—the number of individuals each leader is responsible for coaching, developing, and supporting. Spans of control need to be much closer to the average for knowledge workers.

The need for smaller spans of control is especially important as schools work to support and develop an increasing proportion of inexperienced and underprepared classroom teachers. Nationally, the shares of inexperienced (less than five years of experience) and novice (less than two years of experience) teachers, those teaching without a credential, were growing before the pandemic arrived. From 2011–2012 to 2015–2016, the share of inexperienced and novice teachers increased from 20.3% to 22.4% and 6.8% to 9.4%, respectively, and teachers without a credential grew from 8.4% to 8.8% (Garcia & Weiss 2019). In 2023, at least 41,920 positions were unfilled in 30 states and Washington, D.C., and an additional 365,044 classrooms were staffed by teachers not fully certified for their assignment across 49 states and D.C. (Tan et al., 2024). In Texas, these trends are particularly alarming. In 2013–2014, 10% of new teachers were uncertified; in 2023–2024 the share of new teachers who were uncertified had risen to 52% (Marder et al., 2024). Though schools may not be able to quite get down to 5 teachers, we should strive for leaders to be responsible for the growth and development of no more than 6 to 10 teachers (Kraft & Blazer, 2017).

When it comes to delivering results, the organization needs capacity to drive short- and long-term excellence. Every day, teachers must design and deliver lessons, assess learning, and respond to student needs. Every day, the school needs to be responsive to the needs and concerns of caregivers and community members and respond to unexpected events and needs within the school community. But these actions aren't enough to create an excellent school. School Leaders must build, refresh, and communicate an inspiring and aspirational vision for the school's future and prioritize the change agenda that will help it move closer to that vision in the next three to five years. And between the daily execution and the big vision and strategy is the medium-term work (one- to two-year time horizon) of building and improving systems and driving continuous improvement.

If principals are spending all of their time directly coaching teachers and constantly fighting fires, the organization is in trouble (Figure 1.1). On the building capacity dimension, we know that one principal can't provide the support that 30+ teachers deserve. But while they try, dedicating most of their capacity to teachers, assistant principals and other school leaders aren't receiving the coaching and support they need to succeed in their role and grow as leaders. In terms of delivering results, principals who are consumed with the immediate are neglecting their essential responsibility as senior leaders—to be thinking, planning, and acting with a long-term view in mind. That is the time horizon on which innovation, change, and improvement occur.

FIGURE 1.1 • In Many Schools: Impossible Jobs and Schools Struggling to Improve

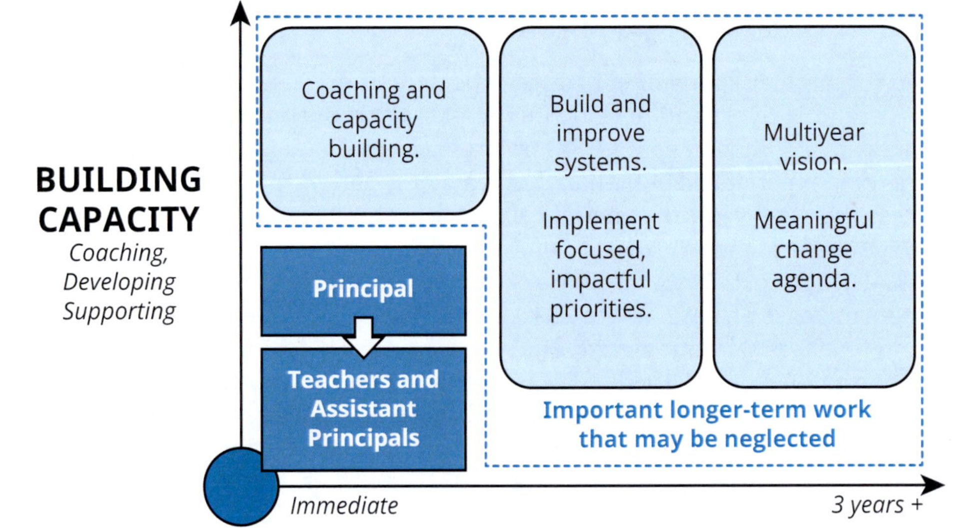

It is easy for (new) principals to get trapped in a cycle of responding to pressing problems. At first, they may think that if they just deal with the small stuff, they will eventually get to the strategic priorities. But this is an illusion. There is an endless supply of small, urgent things to respond to. An organization that is consumed with day-to-day problem-solving is an organization that will struggle to grow and improve. In short, when schools' leadership architecture is broken, several bad outcomes occur:

- The school is constantly in reaction mode. The most important work is not getting done consistently, especially long-term vision, strategy, and planning.
- The school does not deliver results. Or it delivers results it cannot and will not sustain.
- Teachers, assistant principals, and other staff members are not growing and developing as leaders.
- Jobs feel undoable. Leaders are exhausted, discouraged, and lose confidence.

A SCHOOL LEADERSHIP ARCHITECTURE THAT SETS LEADERS AND SCHOOLS UP FOR SUCCESS

The new school leadership architecture is composed of four distinct leadership levels: Team Members, Team Leaders, Bridge Leaders, and School Leaders. Each of the four leadership levels plays a distinct, essential role in building capacity and getting results (Figure 1.2). In terms of building capacity, each leadership level has a clear focus: the School Leader coaches and supports Bridge Leaders, who support Team Leaders, who develop Team Members. The work of getting results—vision, strategy, and execution—is also clearly defined. In strong school leadership architectures, this work is clearly assigned across the four levels, not owned exclusively by one person. Team Members and Team Leaders are primarily focused on execution, Bridge Leaders shift toward system-building and continuous improvement, and the School Leader drives vision and strategy, while monitoring continuous improvement and execution.

Figure 1.2 provides a high-level snapshot of how these roles fit together. But the unique leadership mission for each level provides a more detailed view (see Figure 1.3). Together, the leadership missions are focused on the heart of a great school—effective, engaging instruction available to every student in joyful classrooms supported by a vibrant, positive school culture.

FIGURE 1.2 • The Four-Level School Leadership Architecture Builds Capacity and Gets Results

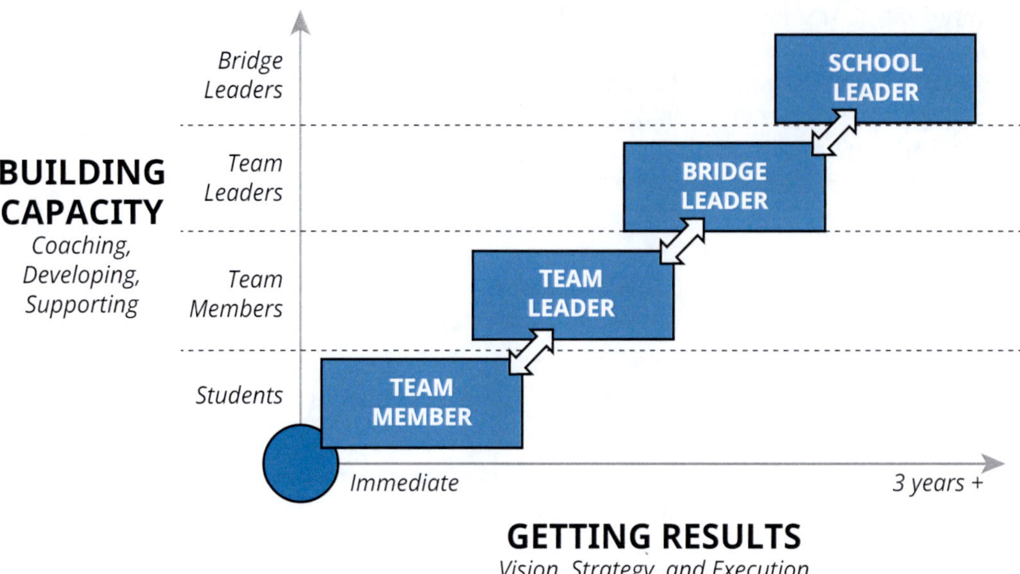

Before we summarize the unique leadership mission of each level, we want to explain why we use leadership levels instead of titles. The simplest reason is that there will often be multiple roles (and multiple titles) operating at each level. For example, schools will have many people operating at the Team Member level—teachers, librarians, custodial staff members, instructional specialists who work directly with students, and the list goes on. The more complex reason we use levels instead of titles is because *a leader's level is defined by their work, not their title or position in the organizational chart.*

A person can have a big title and still be operating as a Team Member. Many school districts use the same title to describe significantly different work. For example, an instructional specialist who works directly with students and does not coach or support other teachers is operating at the Team Member level. An instructional specialist who works primarily as a coach who delivers results through others (e.g., providing feedback on lesson plans, observing instruction and coaching teachers' practice) is operating at the Team Leader level. Same title, different role and different leadership level. Chapter 2 covers this in depth. For now, our focus is clearly defining the work of each leadership level.

TEAM MEMBERS

Team Members, often called individual contributors, deliver results through their personal knowledge and skills. Though they collaborate with others, most of their time will be spent working independently. In most organizations, especially larger ones, most staff will be individual contributors. In school systems, the largest group of Team Members is teachers. They are the heart of the school. They drive the day-to-day work and are responsible for responding to the needs of students from moment to moment. The quality of their work is what produces the school's results.

The other leadership levels are responsible for creating the conditions or building the capacity for Team Members to be effective and successful. Teachers, and other Team Members who may work on campuses or in the central office, derive their sense of pride and accomplishment from the quality and impact of their individual work. They develop and hone deep and wide-ranging knowledge and skills—from deep content knowledge to the skill of designing and delivering instruction, to the knowledge and skill to build relationships with students and create a vibrant classroom culture.

TEAM LEADERS

Team Leaders are directly responsible for coaching, developing, and supporting a group of Team Members. They build their team's knowledge, skill, and capacity to deliver the school's vision of excellent teaching and learning. They support their team to set data-informed goals, track progress and drive continuous improvement, and surface and address barriers to progress. Each Team Leader will have the following characteristics, which align to the National Institute for Excellence in Teaching's (2018) recommendations for formal hybrid leadership roles:

- They have significant time—50% or more—dedicated to their team leadership work. For classroom teachers stepping into a Team Leader role, that means they will have significant release time from their instructional duties. They won't just have leadership tasks layered on to their existing responsibilities without time allocated to complete them, as if they can magically generate more minutes in the day or additional capacity. They are "player-coaches"—like Bill Russell, who took on formal coaching duties of the Boston Celtics from 1966 to 1969 but continued to suit up and play.

- They are responsible—in their mind and according to other leaders in the school—for the results and student outcomes of their Team Members. If their team is not growing and improving, they are not succeeding as a Team Leader.
- Team Leaders have authority with their teams; for Team Members, engaging with the Team Leader isn't optional. This authority can take a variety of forms. In some schools, Team Leaders will evaluate their Team Members. In others, they will not (further discussed in Chapter 3). But what must be true—through shared expectations and the school culture—is that Team Members do not view the coaching and support they receive from their Team Leader as an optional resource.

What about "teacher leaders" who don't meet these three criteria? Most of the time, when we call someone a teacher leader, we are referring to situations where teachers are given an honorific title, more work to do, and minimal pay and time to complete it. The result is leadership-in-name-only opportunities that are not effective in improving teaching and learning (Suppovitz, 2017). These individuals are Team Members who provide leadership in a wide variety of ways to the school and the team. Team Leader roles are formal roles. Consultative, organic, and informal leadership is important and should be celebrated. But there is a difference between being a team captain and the team's coach (or player-coach). Team captains provide leadership as Team Members. They don't make decisions about who plays, what drills to run at practice, or what will be the focus of post-game analysis. That is the role of the coach, or Team Leader. Both are important forms of leadership, but they are distinct. And in most schools, we are confusing team captains with team coaches. We need more of the latter.

BRIDGE LEADERS

Bridge Leaders report to a School Leader and support a group of Team Leaders. The Bridge Leader is the glue of the school. They keep everyone connected—to each other, to the vision, to the most important priorities for students. The bridge that these leaders create isn't a single, one-way road with information flowing, top-down, from the principal to everyone else. A better analogy is the U.S. Interstate Highway System. The Bridge Leader's job is to build and maintain the structures, systems, and relationships that advance the mission and allow information and ideas to flow in all directions. Yes, the Bridge Leader keeps Team Leaders connected to the vision of the School Leader. But they also ensure that the School Leader knows what Team Leaders are seeing and benefits from their ideas and insights. They also keep Team Leaders connected to and aligned with each other—ensuring a shared understanding of the school's vision for excellent teaching and learning and consistent use of school-wide routines, structures, and practices.

Their role, as capacity builders, is to coach and develop Team Leaders. They must ensure that Team Leaders have the skills, knowledge, and resources that they need to effectively develop Team Members. They use data to identify where teams need additional support and coach and collaborate with their Team Leaders to provide it. Most of Bridge Leaders' time (75%–100%) is dedicated to delivering results through others or to building the conditions and systems that teams need to succeed.

Bridge Leaders play a critical role in delivering results. They connect and align teams to the vision and goals established and communicated by the School Leader. They must make sure that each team understands the vision and goals and has a plan to drive improvement and results in the short term (e.g., this semester, this year). Then, the Bridge Leader's role is to take a longer view and identify the systems and processes that must be put in place to set the school up for success in the future. They have time to act and think strategically, to plan projects and initiatives with an eye on one or two years versus one or two months. They lead their teams to build and implement these systems and to drive continuous improvement.

SCHOOL LEADERS

School Leaders are ultimately responsible for delivering results in all areas of the school—its culture and climate, the strength of its teachers and staff, and student outcomes. The School Leader sets the school's vision, short- and long-term goals, and strategy (the focused priorities that will enable the school to improve and succeed). The School Leader must communicate these priorities clearly because they set the direction for the team (Team Members, Team Leaders, and Bridge Leaders) that will drive day-to-day execution. Though the School Leader is ultimately accountable, they lean on a strong team to deliver results.

The School Leader must carry the vision and represent the school in all they do—with staff and the community. In terms of building capacity, the School Leader's focus is on developing and supporting their Bridge Leaders and any Team Leaders who report to them. In addition, they monitor the school's overarching efforts to develop staff capacity and provide direction and accountability to the leaders who design and implement those efforts to ensure that they are tightly aligned to the instructional vision and the school's priorities.

The unique leadership missions of each of the four levels are detailed in Figure 1.3. The figure shows how leadership responsibilities can be organized across a school to enable the most important work to get done in a way that is realistic and sustainable. It is *not* a set of job descriptions that comprehensively itemize the responsibilities and duties of every role on campus. If you look for that level of detail in Figure 1.3, you are going to find a lot that is missing. The bottom row, "Other duties & responsibilities," is a nod to this reality: every educator in every school has some duties and responsibilities that must get done because they're essential to how the school functions and how students get what they need. That's just part of the work. Chapter 3 will provide more detail on this. For now, what if there were different ways that we could staff schools to do the blocking and tackling that is currently done by certified administrators to free those leaders up to focus more on instruction and mission-critical work?

FIGURE 1.3 • Unique Leadership Missions, by Leadership Level

	TEAM MEMBER	TEAM LEADER	BRIDGE LEADER	SCHOOL LEADER
DELIVER RESULTS	• Work to consistently exemplify established standards of high-quality instruction. • Use data to drive instructional decisions. • Meet deadlines, fulfill responsibilities, and be prepared. • Demonstrate openness to new ideas and practices.	• Ensure every Team Member understands campus vision and definition of high-quality instruction. • Establish data-informed team priorities and goals. • Track progress and drive continuous improvement. • Identify barriers and make recommendations for school-wide improvement efforts.	• Track progress toward campus vision and successful execution of priorities. • Build Team Leader understanding of campus vision and priorities. • Ensure alignment between school-wide and team-specific priorities. • Remove barriers and create supportive conditions (culture, systems, etc.) for teams to thrive.	• Establish shared vision for the campus (including vision and definition of excellent instruction). • Ensure and manage alignment with district vision and priorities, including advocating for campus needs. • Establish short- and long-term campus priorities. • Through regular, purposeful communication, build understanding and ownership of the campus vision and priorities to all members of the campus community. • Use data to monitor progress and identify areas requiring attention.

	TEAM MEMBER	TEAM LEADER	BRIDGE LEADER	SCHOOL LEADER
			• Support Team Leaders to achieve data-informed goals and close identified gaps.	• Allocate resources (people, money, time) in alignment with vision and priorities. • Establish and maintain school climate and culture.
BUILD CAPACITY	• Demonstrate growth mindset and commitment to development and improvement. • Seek opportunities to build and deepen knowledge and skills. • Give and receive feedback. • Actively contribute to a productive and collaborative team.	• Coach and develop Team Members. • Build and maintain an effective team and facilitate collaboration. • Ensure coherence of support (professional development, coaching, evaluation, etc.) for Team Members. • Understand and use protocols in support of school-wide consistency and alignment.	• Coach and develop Team Leaders (as coaches). • Monitor Team Member results and development. • Identify priorities for school-wide professional learning—in pursuit of campus vision and driven by needs and gaps. • Drive school-wide professional learning (in partnership with Team Leaders and with input from School Leader). • Train Team Leaders in consistent and effective use of protocols.	• Coach and develop Bridge Leaders. • Monitor Team Leader results and development. • Establish protocols for feedback, team collaboration, etc. • Establish priorities for professional learning and ensure coherence of build capacity efforts and deliver results.
Other duties and responsibilities				

An editable version of Figure 1.3 can be found on this book's companion website.

You may be wondering—especially if you work in a smaller school—whether you need all four levels. Maybe not. If you have fewer than 18 to 24 teachers on your campus, you probably only need three levels: Team Member, Team Leader, and School Leader. (In a three-level model, most of the Bridge Leader responsibilities are absorbed by the School Leader.) Some larger schools may ultimately decide to use a three-level model. But don't pick a three-level model just because it seems easier or because it seems to require less change. Go through the process (partnering with School Leaders in your district) to work through the best way to bring the model to life in a way that meets the needs of your community. Schools are incredibly diverse in their structure and organization, so we should expect incredibly diverse examples of the school leadership architecture. As you work to bring the school leadership architecture to life in your school or district, the details will inevitably vary. And they should! You need to respond to the needs of your community, build on your strengths, and navigate your specific constraints and challenges. The school leadership architecture is anchored in principles, with room to customize the details.

THE CASE FOR THE SCHOOL LEADERSHIP ARCHITECTURE

For most schools, shifting their school leadership architecture won't be an incremental change. It can't be achieved by tinkering with one or two positions or by changing someone's title or job description. It requires districts to comprehensively rethink how *all* staff members on a campus are deployed. It isn't easy, but it is work worth doing. If a school operated in alignment with the four leadership levels, several important benefits would occur.

1. **Teachers would receive strong, effective, and consistent coaching, improving their practice and increasing the likelihood they will stay in the role.**

   All teachers need to be coached, developed, and supported so they are highly effective in their current roles and prepared to step into positions of greater responsibility over time (Kraft & Papay, 2014; Papay & Kraft, 2016). Some of you may be thinking of schools with very flat hierarchies that appear to only have two layers—teachers and principals—and wondering whether it's possible for a school to have only two leadership levels. Yes, these schools exist, but omitting the Team Leader level is unlikely to be effective over the long term, particularly as the teaching ranks are increasingly made of new teachers with minimal preparation or training. Team Leaders—individuals tasked with building the capacity of Team Members and who have significant time dedicated to this responsibility—are essential to a sustainably successful school that delivers positive student outcomes year after year and retains its staff over time.

This conclusion is driven by the importance of coaching for a teacher's development. A school with 200 to 300 students will employ 25 to 40 teachers and many more additional staff. One principal simply cannot provide the level of coaching, feedback, and support that 25 teachers deserve. If turnover and the unattractiveness of the teaching profession continues to drive down teachers' average experience and new entrants to the profession are receiving less rigorous pre-certification training, the need for high-quality and high-frequency coaching and support—and the importance of the Team Leader leadership level in schools—will only increase. Historically, the United States' approach to teacher development has placed a big emphasis on pre-service preparation with lighter touch, less systematic supports for new teachers once they become teachers of record (Darling-Hammond et al., 2017). Regardless of our preferences or our view of the ideal model, this is our reality: new teachers are less and less likely to have completed a rigorous pre-service preparation program (Garcia & Weiss, 2019; Ingersoll et al., 2021; Marder et al., 2014; Partelow, 2019). How should we respond to this reality?

We can, and should, work to increase the number of rigorously prepared new teachers. Yes, this is about increasing the quality and strength of clinical experiences in both traditional and alternative certification programs. This is a long-term goal because the attractiveness of the teaching profession is at the heart of this challenge. If young people and career changers are motivated to pursue teaching long term due to low wages, low prestige, working conditions, or any other factor, it is going to be hard to convince them to spend more money, more time, or more effort on a more rigorous pre-certification experience.

We can't afford to sit idly by, clutching our preferred strategy, waiting for these trends to turn. We must embrace a *yes, and* strategy: *yes*, we need to invest in long-term strategies, *and* we have to embrace an approach that will support the new teachers that we have today. We need to invest in rigorous support—mentoring, coaching, professional learning, and every form of scaffolding we can imagine—for new teachers in their first two years. The source of these supports are excellent, experienced educators with time, authority, and responsibility for building the capacity of new teachers. The school leadership architecture can unlock this resource. Coaching and developing others is a core leadership responsibility and one that most of our current school structures are not built to deliver.

2. **Schools would have the capacity they need to drive key initiatives and tackle their most important priorities.**

   The education sector is brimming with promising ideas to strengthen and improve schools that never get off the ground. The cycle repeats again and again:

   - A new hot idea gains a following.
   - Funders and policymakers work hard to create incentives and supports to drive change.
   - Schools and districts—often desperate for resources and willing to try anything to improve student results—jump in and give the new thing a try, piling it on as "one more thing" at the end of a long list of things for educators to accomplish.
   - Everyone inside and outside of schools knows that schools don't have the capacity to do one more thing. But no one wants to address the capacity issue—that work is too hard, too slow, too big to take on. So, instead, we create a special position, randomly inserted into the school or district to drive the initiative. Or we throw a bunch of technical assistance at schools and districts—a shot in the arm of capacity to get the initiative off the ground.
   - Time passes and before you know it the new thing is old news. By siloing the work in one position, it never got integrated and embedded in the work of teachers and staff. Or there wasn't enough technical assistance to build momentum or when the technical assistance faded, the work did too.

A debate carries on for a while sorting out why the thing didn't work or gain traction. Some argue vehemently that it was a wrong-headed idea from the beginning. Others point their finger at poor implementation. Everyone walks away more cynical. For educators, the experience adds to the accumulating "here we go again" attitude toward educational change. People outside of schools add the story to their mythology of the intransigent school system, becoming more and more convinced that things will never change.

Strengthening the school leadership architecture will expand the school's capacity to drive and sustain changes and can help us escape the loop of initiative fatigue. That's because the four-level architecture, through the unique leadership missions, provides capacity to drive any new initiative or change. At the risk of dating this text, let's take one current example—the implementation of a new curriculum.

Districts who have adopted a new curriculum know that achieving the promised outcomes, from improved student outcomes to saving teachers time, requires a big investment in implementation. Specifically, districts have realized the need for significant professional learning, coaching and feedback, and modelling and support to help teachers understand the curriculum, how to plan lessons, and what great instruction looks like using the new materials. The challenge for districts and schools is to find the capacity they need to do this work. Some try to deploy technical assistance providers or inject a boost of short-term instructional coaching to drive the change. Both efforts are hard to sustain long term and are likely to be experienced as "one more thing"—a barnacle tacked onto the system.

A school with a healthy and thriving school leadership architecture has more built-in capacity to tackle a strategic change initiative like curriculum implementation. Figure 1.4 illustrates how the specific work of curriculum implementation connects to the unique leadership missions framework.

FIGURE 1.4 ● How the Unique Leadership Missions Translate to a Specific Initiative—Curriculum Implementation

	TEAM MEMBER	TEAM LEADER	BRIDGE LEADER	SCHOOL LEADER
DELIVER RESULTS	• Work to consistently exemplify established standards of high-quality instruction. • Use data to drive instructional decisions. • Meet deadlines, fulfill responsibilities, and be prepared. • Demonstrate openness to new ideas and practices.	• Establish data-informed team priorities and goals. • Track progress and drive continuous improvement. • Identify barriers and make recommendations for school-wide improvement efforts.	• Track progress toward established milestones. • Build Team Leader understanding of curriculum and/or connect them to resources and supports. • Translate campus goals and milestones into team-level goals. • Remove barriers and create supportive conditions, both cultural and systemic, for teams to thrive.	• Communicate the case for change—build shared understanding and commitment. • Help teachers and staff understand how curriculum connects to the campus vision and why it is an important priority. • Define clear goals or milestones for curriculum implementation. (How will we make progress over time? How will we know that we are on track?) • Make choices about what work to de-prioritize or stop to be able to focus on curriculum. • Allocate resources—people, time, schedules, money—to support the work. • Use data to monitor progress and identify areas requiring attention, and drive continuous improvement.

	TEAM MEMBER	TEAM LEADER	BRIDGE LEADER	SCHOOL LEADER
BUILD CAPACITY	• Demonstrate growth mindset and commitment to development and improvement. • Seek out opportunities to build and deepen knowledge and skills. • Give and receive feedback. • Actively contribute to a productive and collaborative team.	• Coach and develop Team Members. • Use team meetings for shared planning, problem-solving, and internalization of curriculum. • Ensure coherence of support (professional development, coaching, evaluation, etc.). • Understand and use protocols in support of school-wide consistency and alignment.	• Coach and develop Team Leaders. • Monitor team member results and development (walkthroughs, etc.). • Identify priorities for school-wide professional learning. • Drive school-wide professional learning (in partnership with Team Leaders and with input from School Leader). • Train Team Leaders in consistent and effective use of protocols.	• Coach and develop Bridge Leaders' understanding of curriculum and key moves they need to make. • Establish and/or refine protocols for feedback, team collaboration, walkthroughs, etc., to support implementation. • Establish priorities for school-wide professional learning to close gaps and address needs.

3. **Educators would still find their jobs extremely challenging, but they also may find them more doable.**

   Being a principal is an extraordinarily complex job. But it would certainly be more doable if the work of the previous levels could be delegated and entrusted to a high-performing team of leaders, as described in this model. Without a strong team operating as part of an aligned leadership structure, a difficult job becomes almost impossible. The same is true for teachers. Without the coaching and support they deserve, a demanding but rewarding job becomes impossible and demoralizing. A strong leadership architecture can help us escape these traps.

4. **Educators would see a path for growing their impact and their careers. We would have a better chance of retaining our strongest teachers.**

   There is growing evidence that teachers want more opportunities for leadership and career growth (National

Institute for Excellence in Teaching, 2018). The idea of elevating teachers to leadership roles often produces anxiety. We may not want to encourage our most talented teachers to leave the classroom, and they may not want to either. When teachers describe career growth, they aren't necessarily talking about becoming a principal. According to one survey, only 16% of classroom teachers were interested in being a principal, and 69% were not at all interested. However, 51% were interested a hybrid role that combines teaching with other responsibilities, a finding that has been supported in other research (Johnson & Donaldson, 2004; MetLife, 2012). All evidence points to these trends, which have been in motion for decades and are accelerating as Gen Z, who place a high priority on career advancement, moves through the workforce (De Smet et al., 2023).

There is a way to design leadership opportunities that allow our strongest teachers to remain in the classroom and have time allocated to lead and contribute in other ways. We need to face the reality that we are *already asking* these exceptional teachers to lead beyond the walls of their classroom, for example, to lead professional learning communities (PLCs), facilitate staff professional development, or mentor new teachers. Yet, they aren't receiving the time they need to do things well or the compensation they deserve. Our current approach makes these jobs undoable, requiring teachers to work unsustainably or to make choices about where they will allow quality to slip. It's a surefire recipe for demoralizing our strongest classroom leaders. The new school leadership architecture proposed in this book allows us to unlock teacher's leadership in a more sustainable way.

CONCLUSION

Think of what could be possible if we could get this right. Think of the leaders who could feel a little bit lighter, finding the ability to focus on their most important work and leaning into the joy of empowering and supporting others. Think of the teachers who would feel more confident and equipped. They would have a strong coach to rely on and could see themselves getting better. Think of the students who would benefit—today and down the road—by a school that is built to be responsive and strategic, to solve today's problems and plan for bigger success in the future. A more effective and sustainable approach to school leadership is possible, and a different approach to leadership development is required. How do we get there? First, we must identify where we are: Where are the holes or breakdowns in our current leadership architecture? That is the topic of Chapter 2.

Big Ideas and Key Takeaways

- Leadership demands have steadily increased, but school leadership and staffing structures have changed little. The result is that jobs in many schools feel undoable.
- We need a school leadership architecture that sets leaders and schools up for success, enabling them to build capacity and deliver results.
- Most schools need four leadership levels in order to build capacity and deliver results: Team Member, Team Leader, Bridge Leader, School Leader.
- A leader's level is defined by their work, not their title or position in the organizational chart.
- Restructuring responsibility for building capacity starts with establishing reasonable spans of control, for example, the number of individuals each leader is responsible for coaching, developing, and supporting.
- A strong leadership architecture offers many benefits: more coaching and support for teachers, the ability to prioritize long-term vision and strategy, the capacity to drive key initiatives and priorities, and increased educator satisfaction and retention.

CHAPTER 2

Finding the Gaps in Our Current Architecture

Peter Senge's (2006) concept of creative tension is at the heart of successful change efforts. He describes vision and current reality as two hands held apart with a big thick rubber exercise band stretched between them. The top hand, at eye level, is the vision—where you want to go, who you want to be as a person or an organization. The bottom hand, at your belly button, is your current reality. Over time, if you keep those hands pulled apart, the muscles in your arms will begin to burn. What starts as a small, bearable tingle soon crescendos. Your arms shake, and the sweat starts dripping.

This burning is what Senge calls creative tension. And it won't take long before all you are thinking about is how to release it. The easy way out is to drop your top hand—to lower your vision and eliminate the gap between it and your current reality. The tension is gone, but so is your opportunity to change and improve. The path that takes courage is to stomach the tension for a bit longer, using it as a force to raise your current reality toward your vision over time.

In this chapter, we are going to focus on that bottom hand—our current reality. Two application exercises make up the first half of this chapter. Exercises 2.A and 2.B are designed to give you some practice at diagnosing flaws in the school leadership architecture. Exercise 2.A will invite you to practice with a hypothetical school called Typical High School. It is built from observations and analysis of real schools. We've found it helps leaders internalize the leadership levels and brings the architecture to life in a powerful way. Then, Exercise 2.B will give you an opportunity to begin identifying gaps or weaknesses in the leadership architecture of your school or district. The second half of the chapter analyzes common school leadership architecture flaws and their root causes. We need to understand *why* these flaws occur in order to develop sustainable solutions to address them. Grounded with an accurate view of where we are and why, we'll be able to use that creative tension to fuel the long-term work of moving toward a new vision.

EXERCISE 2.A

Putting It Into Practice

Typical High School Leadership Architecture

Typical School District enrolls 45,000 students in 50 schools. Over the past several years, the district has hired from five to seven new principals every year. District leaders have noticed that almost none of the internal applicants are truly ready to step into the principalship. This is especially true at the high schools, where the district has seen several vacancies in the last year. To analyze why their leadership architecture might be flawed, the district paused to analyze the roles in a high school and how they fit together.

Typical High School serves 3,000 students and employs 200 teachers. The following roles are present:

- **Department Chairs:** Teacher leader roles have not been a major focus in the past several years. All secondary schools have department chairs for core subject areas. There is a $500 stipend to serve as a department chair. Most teachers don't want to take on this responsibility, which means attending after-school meetings, compiling assessment data for use in professional learning communities (PLCs), and planning field trips. Typically, the role defaults to the most senior person on the team. Or, if they don't want it, teachers rotate whose turn it is to be the department chair. It is seen as a volunteer position.
- **Specialists:** High schools have several specialists who work with small groups of students who are behind in their reading skills, since literacy is a huge priority for the district and the school.
- **Dean of Culture:** Each high school has a dean of culture who is responsible for school-wide discipline and implementing the school's initiative on restorative justice. The dean spends most of their time meeting with students and in small groups for restorative justice circles.
- **Facilitator:** Each high school has a facilitator who runs the PLCs. The facilitator plans and runs PLC meetings once per month for each content area.
- **Assistant Principal:** Typical High School has five assistant principals (APs). Responsibilities vary widely among APs. Each is assigned a set of projects and tasks for the school that mostly focus on operations, for example, managing the bus schedule

and overseeing lunch duty. Two APs directly manage and evaluate some teachers, while three APs do not. One AP serves as testing coordinator.

- **Associate Principal:** The large comprehensive high schools also have an associate principal. While this role is technically more senior to the AP and one step closer to the principalship, in practice there is little difference in the responsibilities assigned to an associate principal versus an AP. One difference is the associate principal manages a larger number of teachers than the two APs who also manage teachers.
- **Principal:** The principal at Typical High School spends most of their time doing classroom walk-throughs (usually alone), meeting with parents, supporting the dean of culture with discipline, and planning for the weekly professional development time faculty has on early dismissal days. The associate principal, APs, facilitator, dean of culture, specialists, and department chairs all report to the principal. In addition, because the principal is passionate about literacy, they supervise and evaluate all English language arts teachers in the building.

Architecture Analysis

Using the information provided, plot each role to the leadership level it is operating at (remember, leadership levels are based on time, professional identity, and skills, not titles). If there are multiple people with the same title but there's clear evidence some individuals are operating at different leadership levels, record that title in multiple boxes.

Note: If you've got a whiteboard or chart paper and a friend, you might have more fun doing this exercise together. You can put the roles on sticky notes and then debate and discuss your responses.

TEAM MEMBER	TEAM LEADER	BRIDGE LEADER	SCHOOL LEADER

When you're done, you can review our analysis of Typical High School in Appendix A.

EXERCISE 2.B

Putting It Into Practice

Now bring your learning closer to home by diagnosing the gaps or weaknesses in your own school leadership architecture. Hopefully Typical High School (which is common, not an outlier) has made you feel more ready to face whatever might be happening in your own backyard.

Step 1: Start by picking a school you know well.

Given the variation across different schools in the same district, we encourage district leaders to start by applying the model to a single school they know well. Selecting one of your larger campuses will give you the most to work with. If you're a principal, you can apply this to your school.

Step 2: List all teaching and administrative roles in the school and a brief description of what people actually do. Prioritize roles focused on instruction.

- Start by listing all titles of jobs related to instruction—teachers, department heads, coaches, specialists, APs, and so on, including roles that may be connected to the central office or work across multiple schools.
- Then describe the work of each role. What are their responsibilities? How do they allocate their time? Do they work alone or in teams? When describing the work executed by each role, you may need to develop different descriptions for individuals with the same title who have very different jobs (based on responsibilities, time allocations, etc.). This is very common with APs—though they share a title, they may do very different work—but may apply to other positions in the school as well.

ROLE/NAME	DESCRIPTION

ROLE/NAME	DESCRIPTION

Step 3: Assign each role to a leadership level—Team Member, Team Leader, Bridge Leader, School Leader.

Use your description of leaders' objectives, skills, time applications, and professional identity—compared to Figure 1.3—to match roles with leadership levels. It will be tempting to assign roles to the level you think they *should* be operating or to where they fall in a hierarchy. But that's not the task. It is about describing how they are *operating in practice*.

SCHOOL LEADER	
BRIDGE LEADER	
TEAM LEADER	
TEAM MEMBER	

(Continued)

(Continued)

Step 4: Reflect on the architecture challenges you've identified and their possible root causes.

What challenges did you identify? Why do these matter? What might be the cause?

LEADERSHIP ARCHITECTURE CHALLENGE	IMPLICATIONS *WHAT ARE THE CONSEQUENCES IF THIS CONTINUES?*	POSSIBLE CAUSES *WHAT'S YOUR HYPOTHESIS ABOUT WHAT'S CAUSING THIS CHALLENGE?*
1.		
2.		
3.		

COMMON SCHOOL LEADERSHIP ARCHITECTURE PROBLEMS

There are countless possible outcomes to Exercise 2.B. Having facilitated this exercise with many school districts, we have found that most people who complete the exercise find some significant gaps and holes. If you've found gaps and holes, know that you're not alone. Despite an almost infinite number of combinations of roles that have been designed and deployed in schools, we have found several common leadership architecture challenges.

PROBLEM 1: ARCHITECTURE IS MISSING SCHOOL LEADER

The principal should be operating at the School Leader level. Yet, many of us inevitably reach the conclusion that the principal is operating below the School Leader level, possibly as a Bridge Leader or a Team Leader (Figure 2.1).

FIGURE 2.1 • Principal Operating at the Wrong Level

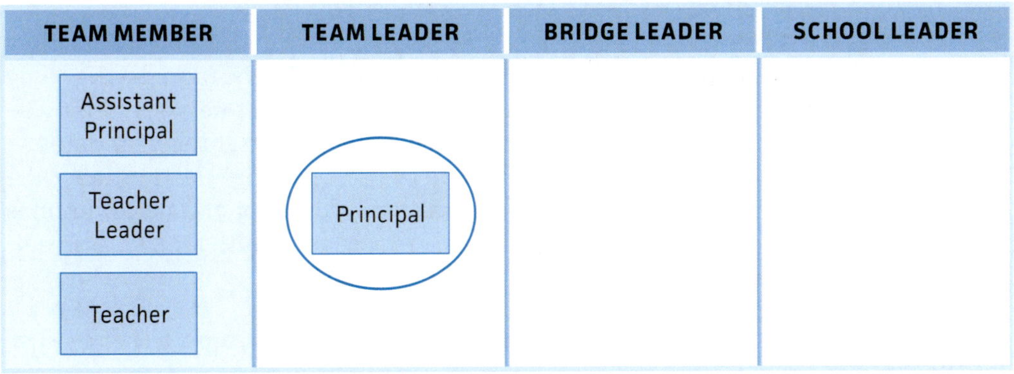

TEAM MEMBER	TEAM LEADER	BRIDGE LEADER	SCHOOL LEADER
Assistant Principal Teacher Leader Teacher	Principal		

Some principals may be operating closer to the Team Leader level. They are busy reacting and responding to pressing challenges. As a result, they can't focus on the long-term, high-leverage work that would make a difference for their school. They need to be allocating time to strategy and long-term planning and protecting time to think, reflect, and analyze. When that doesn't happen, it undermines their ability to communicate, set and drive strategy and goals, and facilitate the work of the team.

When the principal is operating as a Team Leader, everyone else in the building is prevented from operating at an appropriate leadership level. Who is doing the work of the Bridge Leader and of School Leader? No one. When this happens, the school will not succeed. Everyone will be in a reactive mode, and the principal will feel their job is impossible. Because it is. The other negative outcome is that the principal is stunting the growth of other leaders on campus. APs are being robbed of the opportunity to grow the appropriate leadership skills and will be unprepared to move into a principal role. What causes this to happen?

THE PRINCIPAL MAY NOT HAVE THE REQUIRED SKILLS OR CAPABILITIES

If the principal is new to the role, this is common. But it's important that the principal receives coaching and support in making the shifts to the new role (see Chapter 8). If they continue to operate below their appropriate level, the school's performance will suffer.

THE PRINCIPAL'S MANAGER (TYPICALLY A PRINCIPAL SUPERVISOR) MAY BE DOING THE PRINCIPAL'S JOB

When the principal's manager hasn't made the shifts they need to make in their new role (operating as a coach of principals, not an overactive copilot), they may be tempted to step in and do the principal's work versus coaching the principal to lead the school.

THERE IS LACK OF CLARITY OR SUPPORT FROM THE CENTRAL OFFICE

The role of the principal may be poorly defined. The principal may be doing exactly what they believe—or have been told—that they are expected to do. Or there may be conflict between what the principal understands their role to be and what they are empowered, in practice, to do by the system overall—most notably the various departments in central office that support and sometimes constrain their leadership. The root cause is different, but the outcome is the same.

THE PRINCIPAL IS RESPONDING TO OTHER LEADERSHIP ARCHITECTURE PROBLEMS, LOWER IN THE SYSTEM

Principals often operate at a lower leadership level because they are responding to other holes or gaps. They may be missing Team Leaders, Bridge Leaders, or both. This is true of every level of architecture. Because the work done at lower leadership levels is more immediate and urgent, if it is not being handled, leaders will drop down one or more levels to take it on; this is commonly called "firefighting." This reaction is natural and may be necessary at times, especially during a crisis. But this is not sustainable for the leader or the organization. If effort is not made to ensure that leaders are performing at the right level, the school is in trouble.

PAUSE AND REFLECT

Did you find the principal to be operating below the School Leader level in Exercise 2.B? If so, which root cause(s) might be contributing?

- ☐ Principal may have underdeveloped skills or capabilities.
- ☐ The principal's manager is doing their job for them.
- ☐ There is a lack of clarity or support from the central office.
- ☐ The principal is responding to other leadership architecture problems.

PROBLEM 2: A VARIETY OF ISSUES AND PAIN POINTS WITH ASSISTANT PRINCIPALS

For a principal to focus on School Leader work—dedicating time to long-term thinking and strategy, communicating with key stakeholders, building a strong team and organizational culture—they have to get out of the weeds. They can only do that if they can delegate many of their current responsibilities to other leaders. Team Leaders are responsible for providing the day-to-day coaching teachers need to succeed. But they aren't just left to their own devices. Bridge Leaders must be responsible for coaching, guiding, and supporting Team Leaders, and for executing the school's strategic priorities. On most campuses, this Bridge Leaders role *should* be the job of the APs, and yet, it rarely is. We have yet to encounter a district system that is not struggling with its AP role. Here are a few common themes.

MANY ASSISTANT PRINCIPALS (APs) ARE OPERATING LIKE TEAM MEMBERS: "DOING" VERSUS COACHING OR FACILITATING WORK

If APs are spending most of their time working to build a master schedule, manage testing, or address student behavior, they haven't moved to a new leadership level—they are still Team Members. If most APs are operating as Team Members, principals will struggle to operate as School Leaders. Like all architectural problems, there are a variety of possible root causes, including individual and systemic factors.

- Individuals may be struggling to learn new skills, capabilities, and mindsets (see Chapter 5).
- Inadequate coaching or development may be hindering individuals.
- Role definitions may be vague or unclear.
- Roles may be poorly structured, in which assigned work is incompatible with expected leadership level.

All of these may be in play with some APs. However, when we see a pattern across many APs in a district, we would be wise to look at structural or systemic causes—the latter three—versus focusing on individual skill or behavior.

We know AP roles are vaguely defined and poorly structured. We also have evidence that coaching and support from principals for APs and other leader roles is inadequate. One study found that less than 50% of APs and other leaders said they received frequent coaching or feedback on their performance from their principals (Bierly & Shy, 2013). As reflected in Figure 2.2, any time APs operate at a lower level, it will drag down the principal and draw them into more day-to-day, reactive problems. Long-term, these APs will be woefully unprepared to step into a principal role and navigate the breadth of leadership required.

FIGURE 2.2 • APs Operating at the Wrong (and Varying) Level of Leadership

TEAM MEMBER	TEAM LEADER	BRIDGE LEADER	SCHOOL LEADER
Teacher		Principal	
Teacher Leader			
Assistant Principal 1	Assistant Principal 3		
Assistant Principal 2			

THERE IS SIGNIFICANT VARIATION IN AP ROLES

In many districts, the AP role is not clearly defined in a way that is consistent across campuses. Commonly, principals divvy up the administrative work (yes, it's as uninspiring as it sounds) among their APs, resulting in a portfolio of projects or priorities for each AP (Goldring et al., 2021). Some principals assign work based on APs' strengths, others try to rotate portfolios over time to support APs' development, and some just give their APs work they don't want to do. The outcome is that people with similar titles have very different jobs and are often operating at different leadership levels.

In a model where everyone "helps" with everything, APs aren't empowered to lead, and principals are ultimately responsible for everything, an untenable approach that fails to acknowledge the importance of clearly defined leadership levels that are part of a coherent architecture. When APs aren't empowered to lead, principals are ultimately responsible for everything.

THE AP ROLE IS NOT ATTRACTIVE TO HIGH-PERFORMING TEACHERS AND NEGATIVELY IMPACTS HIGH-POTENTIAL LEADERS' INTEREST IN SCHOOL LEADERSHIP

Excellent educators are attracted to school leadership because they want to influence instruction and student outcomes beyond their classroom. Standing between their role as a classroom teacher and the principalship (where they see that work happening) is often the AP role. They watch APs spending all their time on student discipline, facility issues, testing, transportation, and other operational and compliance issues and think, "Why would I want that job?" The job includes more administrative work, less teaching, hard conversations with students and parents, and limited change in leadership or influence. In addition to deterring capable teachers from pursuing leadership roles, the structure of AP work has a second negative impact. Ultimately, many APs are unprepared for the principal role because they don't have opportunities to build the skills, professional identity, and time applications they will need to succeed (Bierly & Shy, 2013; Goldring et al., 2021).

PAUSE AND REFLECT

Did you identify challenges with APs? If so, which ones?

- ☐ Many APs are operating like Team Members: "doing" versus "facilitating."
- ☐ There is significant variation in AP roles.
- ☐ The AP role is not attractive and deters potential School Leaders.
- ☐ Other: ______________________________

What do you suspect are the root cause(s) of these issues?

- ☐ AP skill or capability gaps
- ☐ The way the central office defines the role
- ☐ The way the principal assigns duties and defines the role
- ☐ The principal operating at a lower level, taking away leadership opportunities from APs
- ☐ No one to delegate non-leadership responsibilities to
- ☐ The AP responding to other leadership architecture problems (no Team Leaders, etc.)

PROBLEM 3: VERY FEW TEAM LEADER ROLES

You will never be able to position APs (or anyone) to operate as Bridge Leaders if you do not have robust Team Leaders—roles that spend around 50% of the time delivering results through others. Many schools have a variety of experienced instructional staff with titles that imply Team Leader, but, in reality, many of these roles are operating as Team Members, leaving a big gap (Figure 2.3). They are loaded up with more responsibility for a little bit more pay and virtually no change in their teaching load. This honorific approach to teacher leadership is demoralizing and ineffective. We can't expect these results to shift by piling on more responsibilities and duties without adequate time to fulfill them.

FIGURE 2.3 ● Teacher Leaders in Name Only

TEAM MEMBER	TEAM LEADER	BRIDGE LEADER	SCHOOL LEADER
Teacher	Dean of Instruction	Principal	
Teacher Leaders	Assistant Principal		

As you completed Exercise 2.B, you probably identified a number of these roles. Some of these roles *are* designed to operate as Team Member roles—expert teachers who are deployed to work directly with students in a different way than a traditional classroom teacher would (like an interventionist). But others are intended to operate as Team Leaders, spending at least 50% of their time coaching and supporting teachers and facilitating professional learning and common planning. However, due to a variety of factors—lack of role clarity, the necessary skills, adequate time, authority, or other challenges—individuals in these roles operate like Team Members. You know this is the case when an instructional support staff member is spending the bulk of their time creating lessons or instructional materials, working directly with small groups of students, or covering duties across the campus.

Who is impacted when there are no, or not enough, Team Leaders? The short answer is everyone. New, inexperienced teachers don't have access to the coaching and support they need to develop and master their craft. Talented, experienced teachers are left to support their colleagues without having the time or resources to do so, which leads to frustration, discouragement, and burnout.

And don't be fooled. You can't just have a hole in the leadership architecture. That work—in this case the work of coaching, developing, and supporting teachers—must get done. Bridge Leaders and School Leaders, who should be operating at higher levels—doing other essential work, typically with a longer-term time horizon that will allow the school to thrive in the future—drop down to do the work that isn't getting done at the Team Leader level. In this scenario, their jobs become undoable, resulting in key work either not getting done or not getting done well. And anytime we have undoable jobs, we have a recipe for burnout and turnover.

PAUSE AND REFLECT

What issues did you observe at the Team Leader level?

- ☐ Not enough Team Leader roles
- ☐ Ineffective Team Leader roles (lack of skill, time, or authority)
- ☐ Many name-only "teacher leader" roles operating as Team Members

Synthesizing your reflections about principals and APs, how are weak or inadequate Team Leader roles impacting how other School Leaders are operating?

What would need to be different for the principal to be able to operate as the School Leader and one or more APs to be able to operate as a Bridge Leader?

STRENGTHENING AND REPAIRING THE ARCHITECTURE

Sometimes, a flawed leadership architecture is caused by an individual leader who is struggling to lead effectively. But if you see the same outcome again and again, you are looking at a systemic problem.

- *The system* does not provide clear, consistent, supportive leadership expectations to School Leaders.
- *The system* has not structured leadership roles consistently, coherently, and appropriately.
- *The system* is not set up to support new/future leaders to master the skills, time applications, or professional identity required to succeed.

As we all know, the system is perfectly designed to get the results it produces. Based on the results we see across schools and districts, the system of roles we have is designed to produce high levels of burnout and turnover and large numbers of new leaders who are not prepared to succeed in their roles.

Districts need to be willing to improve the leadership architecture—investing in all four levels of leadership and moving away from a model that is overreliant on principals. This work can't be offloaded to individual schools. The central office must play a leading role and ensure consistency in how roles are defined across all schools. There can still be flexibility at the campus level, but the central office must take the lead.

This statement is a direct affront to most districts' conventional practices. Most systems—even those that are centralized and don't provide significant autonomy to principals—have historically left decisions about leadership roles to principals. Given that tradition, it is easier to stay with the way things have always been done. However, as Bierly and colleagues (2016) framed the issue, "We don't ask principals to design the IT system from scratch or write their own textbooks. The school leadership model is no different—it is a tool that is best designed, with plenty of principal and teacher input, to serve the system as a whole with latitude for school-level customization" (p. 32).

Here's why districts *must* take the lead in addressing these structural issues:

- Deploying one shared model, with room for customization, allows the district to study what's working, share lessons and best practices across schools, and evolve the model over time.
- A consistent, clearly defined set of roles provides clearer career paths and supports a stronger, deeper, more diverse bench of future leaders at every level. A clearer pathway makes it easier for aspiring leaders to proactively pursue leadership roles and to receive the support they need to grow and succeed. For example, developing more consistent expectations for the role of the AP and ensuring that they are empowered to lead and given the opportunities to grow their skills are essential for ensuring that school-level decision-making doesn't produce "career cul-de-sacs" for some APs. The same is true for teacher leaders and any other stepping-stone roles.
- Greater consistency in leadership roles across schools will also make it easier for the district to build coherent systems to support leaders in those roles: professional development, well-designed compensation systems, evaluation, and knowledge sharing across schools. Ideally, by making the roles more doable and more focused on instruction, the revamped leadership roles also increase the attractiveness of school leadership for skilled teachers who want to have an impact on their school beyond their classroom walls.

Recommending a centrally designed leadership model does not mean that districts build and implement the model without the involvement of school-based staff. On the contrary, teachers, APs, and principals have critical insights and need to be at the table for all stages of the change process. Part II will illuminate the path.

Big Ideas and Key Takeaways

- When we see reactive schools, burned-out leaders, and campuses struggling to prioritize longer-term system improvement, we are probably seeing the symptoms of problems with the leadership architecture.
- There are common challenges experienced by most schools and districts. Many schools face one or more challenges. They can be rooted in weak structures, lack of clarity, or underdeveloped skills.
- When leaders are not operating at the right leadership level, other leaders have fewer opportunities to lead and grow.
- Leaders often operate at a lower leadership level because they are responding to holes or gaps in the architecture. Because the work done at lower leadership levels is more immediate and urgent, if it is not being handled leaders will drop down one or more levels to take it on. This is commonly called "firefighting."
- When the principal is not operating at the right leadership level, it impacts everyone. The school is more likely to be reactive and the principal will feel their job is impossible.
- AP roles are vaguely defined and poorly structured. You will never be able to position APs to operate as Bridge Leaders if you do not have robust Team Leaders.
- In many schools there are a variety of roles for experienced instructional staff with titles that imply Team Leader. But, in reality, many of these roles are operating as Team Members, thus leaving a big gap.
- When you observe the same problem, again and again, you are dealing with a systemic problem, not a problem of individual will or skill.
- Roles must be clearly defined, and they must be consistent across all schools in the system (i.e., at the district level). You cannot delegate this work to individual schools.
- Districts need to be willing to change the leadership architecture, investing in all levels of leadership and moving away from a model that is overreliant on principals. Then, districts must make shifts in how they develop leaders to more successfully navigate the shifts they face at each leadership level.

PART II

Changing Structures

As districts work to strengthen the school leadership architecture, they must tackle two specific systemic problems. First, they may need to change the way they structure campus roles across the district to provide clarity, coherence, and alignment. Second, they need to improve the way they develop individuals to be ready for new leadership roles, with an eye on preparing them to make the shift in skills, professional identity, and time applications required to lead at the next level. The structure of roles and the way districts develop and prepare people for them are two sides of one coin—they must attend to both. Improving the structure of roles is the focus of Part II.

Chapter 3 will highlight concrete examples of how the school leadership architecture has and can come to life. It will also unpack common barriers and challenges that districts will need to navigate to prioritize this change. Chapter 4 will provide a roadmap for redesigning roles—first through a small pilot study and then at scale.

CHAPTER 3

Rethinking Roles

Remember Senge's creative tension metaphor? Bottom hand is current reality, top hand is the vision, and the gap is the tension. Chapter 2 was current reality; this chapter is about building a vision of what's possible. The story of Plum Creek Elementary and Lockhart Independent School District (ISD), which you got a preview of in Chapter 1, provides one example of how it can be done. But it is just one example. After unpacking the story of change in Lockhart, this chapter will offer examples of how the model could come to life in other contexts, including small schools and secondary campuses. These examples won't capture all the ways the architecture could come to life on your school, but they illuminate principles you can build from. The second half of the chapter will outline ways of addressing common barriers that districts will work through. The heart of this work is navigating hard decisions and tradeoffs around finite resources. It isn't easy to change the school leadership architecture, but it is possible.

BRINGING SHARED LEADERSHIP TO LIFE

In 2019, Lockhart ISD superintendent Mark Estrada decided that the district needed to change its approach to school leadership. He knew this was a big undertaking. But he was convinced the most important thing they needed to do to achieve Lockhart ISD's commitment—1.5 years of growth for every student, every year—was to elevate the teaching profession. Teacher retention in Lockhart hovered around 78%, with many leaving the district for surrounding districts that could pay more. A survey of the Texas teaching profession deepened his conviction. It revealed three big reasons why teachers were fleeing the role: low compensation, lack of decision-making ability in their day-to-day work, and lack of career advancement opportunities (Charles Butt Foundation, 2020).

Estrada needed to retain his teachers and provide them with the support they needed to continue to strengthen their skills. And he knew leadership was a piece of the puzzle. But, at the same time, principals and administrators in Lockhart consistently reported that they did not have time to lead instruction on their campus and that their role was not focused on coaching and developing others. At the same time, he knew that they needed to do more to prepare future school leaders. The bench needed to be stronger, and roles needed to be more attractive.

Learning about Denver Public School's Teacher Leadership & Collaboration (TLC) initiative provided the inspiration for what would become Shared Leadership in Lockhart ISD. TLC started in 2013 with a focus on elevating the role of teacher leaders. Denver faced the same challenges as other schools and districts—undoable principal jobs, unattractive assistant principal (AP) roles, and inadequate coaching and support for teachers. In Denver, pressure on the typical leadership model (principal-reliant with a high span of control) reached a breaking point when a new, more ambitious teacher evaluation system was introduced. To implement the new system, the district needed more leaders to observe, coach, and evaluate teachers. The principal and one AP couldn't do it alone. Denver looked beyond the challenges to see an opportunity. Though principals and APs were overloaded, they knew they had hundreds of leaders in classrooms who had more to contribute.

Estrada was struck by the TLC theory of action. It was powerful and matched his assessment of the need in Lockhart:

- If we change the way schools are structured so that new teachers get more support and all teachers are members of strong teams,
- then we will grow, develop, and retain our teachers;
- increase the likelihood that "all students are taught by effective educators in joyful, rigorous, and personalized classrooms" (Denver Public Schools, 2019); and
- ultimately, support the success of every child.

As Estrada learned more, he became more convinced that tackling the way schools are structured might be a key part of the puzzle in Lockhart. Denver had launched the TLC initiative with a pilot group of 14 campuses. By Year 5, the model was in use on nearly all campuses. Early indicators were promising. On TLC campuses, 84% of teachers were glad their school adopted the model, and 85% of teachers said their team leader was successful in both evaluating and coaching them to improve (Bierly et al., 2016). The TLC model has proven enduring; it has become a crucial element of the district's DNA, essential to leadership sustainability, and ensuring that teachers receive the coaching, feedback, and support they need to grow.

What if Lockhart could provide leadership pathways, distribute leadership and empower great teachers, and ultimately improve instruction and student outcomes? After 12 months of planning and building a shared vision (see Chapter 4), Estrada and his leadership team were ready to pilot the new model. In the 2020–2021 school year, they started with one campus: Plum Creek Elementary School, led by principal Jamee Griebel.

The first move to launch Shared Leadership was creating new, robust Team Leader roles. In Lockhart, these positions were called Lever Leaders. Lever Leaders were highly effective teachers with a track record of driving student growth. They spent half of their time teaching and the other half leading a grade-level team, providing one-on-one coaching and support to their team members, and serving on the campus leadership team. In the first year, Plum Creek had four Lever Leaders, each receiving a $10,000 stipend in addition to their teacher salary. This was a step toward what would become the district's Pathway to 100K initiative—a commitment to paying excellent teachers $100,000 or more. Many questioned the size of the stipend for Lever Leaders, arguing for something more modest. Even Denver Public Schools had used a smaller stipend, coming in around $6,000 per teacher leader. But Estrada was adamant: It needed to be significant. It needed to attract great teachers, and it needed to match the significant increase in their responsibilities. So, he worked to find savings in other areas, so they could invest in teachers.

Like many schools that implement Team Leader roles, initially, the Lever Leaders were layered on with limited changes to other leadership roles. At Plum Creek, the four Lever Leaders each supported one grade level, with Griebel and her AP divvying up the rest. The Lever Leaders reported to Griebel and both Griebel and the AP continued to observe, evaluate, and coach individual teachers (Figure 3.1). In this configuration, the Lever Leaders added coaching capacity but didn't significantly change the way that leadership was distributed in the school.

FIGURE 3.1 ● Initial Implementation of Shared Leadership

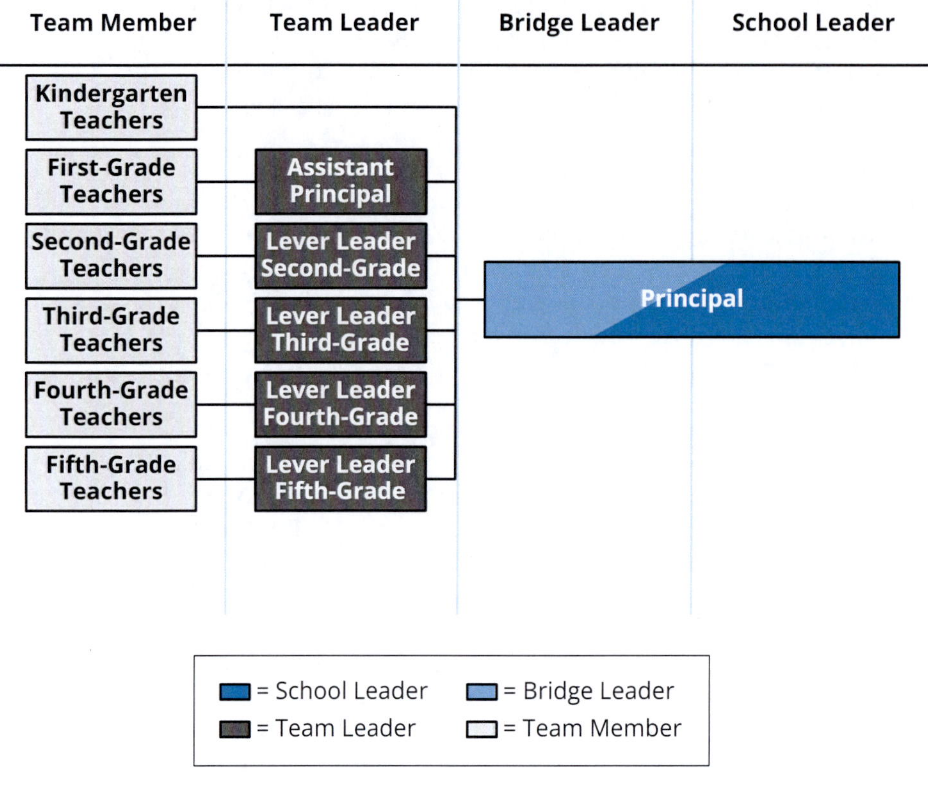

Effectively, it was a three-level leadership model with Lever Leaders and the AP operating as Team Leaders and Griebel continuing to do everything from Team Leader to School Leader. She found herself frequently bogged down in operations and discipline and continued to find it difficult to find the time to coach the grade level she was responsible for. After a year, Griebel made a shift—empowering her AP to coach and support the Lever Leaders—freeing her up to have the time and capacity to operate as the School Leader (Figure 3.2).

But they soon realized that sharing leadership was more than changing reporting relationships. Even with the change in structure, Griebel realized that they had to get to the point where Lever Leaders and her AP "don't need to come and ask me about every little thing." If she needed to be involved in every decision and action on campus, she wasn't maximizing the contributions and

FIGURE 3.2 • Evolution of Shared Leadership

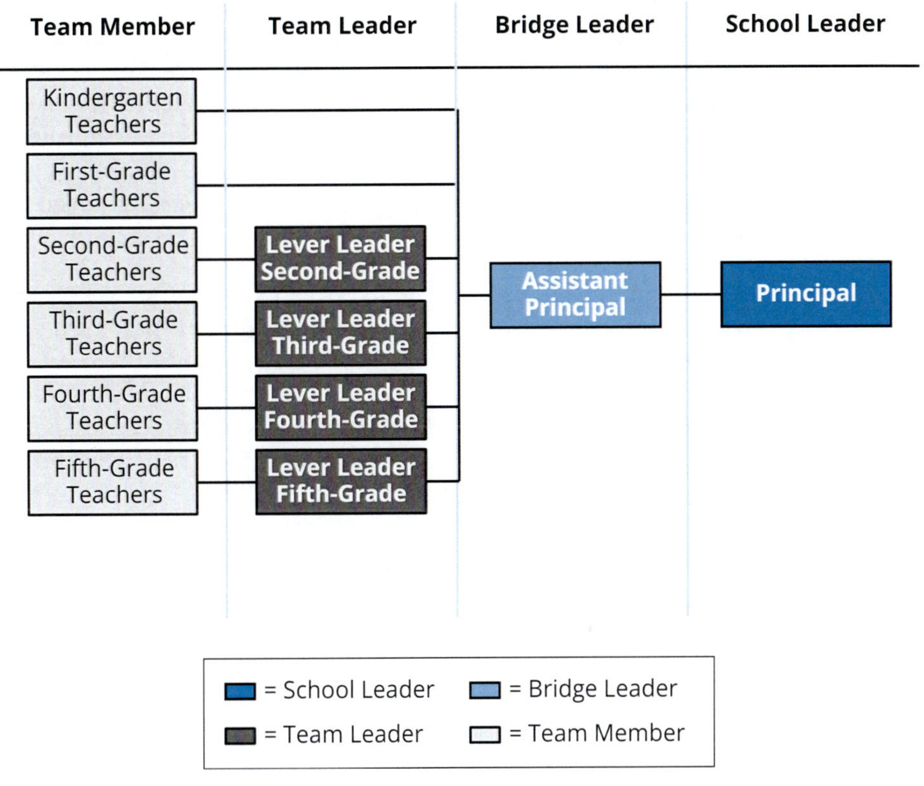

expertise of her team. And if she needed to be involved in everything, Griebel was going to continue to feel spread thin, unable to go deep on her most important priorities.

This is a key point. It's tempting for districts to shrink the change of roles work by identifying one role they want to create, evolve, or change while leaving everything else on campus the same. But it's not possible—or at least it is not a good idea. To effectively change one role in a school, districts must evolve *all* the roles on a campus. That's because, as Chapter 2 made clear, changes to one role have a cascading impact on other roles in the school. When a system creates Team Leader roles to support and coach teachers, the role that previously supported those teachers—either an assistant principal or principal—needs to change. And if a leader is going to *stop* doing something, someone else will likely have to *start* doing it, either through creating a new role or adding responsibilities to an existing portfolio.

As the Plum Creek team got clearer about their roles and Griebel released more responsibility to her team, it eventually led to bigger conversations across the district, particularly as the model scaled to more campuses. (By 2024–2025, there were 29 Lever Leaders working across seven of the district's nine campuses.) As principals worked to shift structures on their campuses, they started raising questions about roles and responsibilities at the district level. They couldn't empower Lever Leaders if they were getting micromanaged by the central office.

Dr. Stephaine Camarillo, the deputy superintendent, recognized that if Lockhart wanted to realize the promise of shared leadership, leaders needed to get on the same page about how they would distribute responsibilities. And then, they had to be disciplined in empowering people to make decisions and drive their responsibilities. Camarillo used the leadership architecture model and a process they called "threading of responsibilities" to get clear about how responsibilities—from the classroom to the superintendent's office—would be distributed. You can think of this as another, more detailed example of the unique missions outlined in Chapter 1. Figure 3.3 provides a high-level example of how the missions could be fleshed out for professional learning communities (PLCs).

FIGURE 3.3 • Threading Responsibilities—Professional Learning Communities (PLCs)

LEADERSHIP LEVEL	RESPONSIBILITIES AND DECISION-MAKING
School Leader	• In partnership with leadership team, establish PLC protocols and routines. • Ensure master schedule has common planning time. • Analyze data. • Periodically observe and monitor PLC system for consistency and alignment with shared protocols and routines. • Attend PLCs as needed and/or requested by Bridge Leader(s).
Bridge Leader	• Provide coaching and feedback to Team Leader about PLC goals and progress. • Observe PLCs in order to be able to provide feedback and coaching to Team Leader. • Identify agenda items and priorities. • Track data.

LEADERSHIP LEVEL	RESPONSIBILITIES AND DECISION-MAKING
Team Leader	• Lead and facilitate PLC. • Plan agenda. • Bring data and track progress. • Vet assessments.
Team Member	• Come prepared. • Meet deadlines. • Establish and follow norms.

Adapted from and inspired by work in Lockhart ISD.

Five years in, the results of Shared Leadership gave Lockhart confidence that it was on the right track. In 2022, before Shared Leadership was expanded to other campuses, 81% of Plum Creek teachers agreed with the statement "I work with a leader who supports me in improving instruction," 12 points higher than the district average (Holdsworth Center, 2022). In 2024, with Shared Leadership active on most campuses, teachers across the district were feeling the difference (Holdsworth Center, 2024):

- I am proud to work for LISD: 94 (+13)
- I am satisfied with the work I do: 90 (+9)
- I see professional growth/long-term career opportunities in this school district: 76 (+16)
- I feel appreciated for the work I do: 76 (+25)
- My supervisor identifies opportunities for my professional growth and improvement: 76 (+16)
- My supervisor regularly provides me feedback: 78 (+12)
- There are leadership opportunities for me with my school or district: 73 (+57)

And the impact of Lever Leaders is evident in student learning—the percentage of students achieving 1.5 years of growth in both math and reading have increased every year since the Lever Leaders were introduced and at a faster rate than campuses without Lever Leaders. At Plum Creek, in the 2023–2024 school year, 94% of students grew by 1.5 years in reading, up from 42% in 2021–2022.

BUT WHAT ABOUT . . .

Plum Creek's story helps to make the school leadership architecture concrete. But it is only one example and may not resonate with leaders from varied contexts. What about schools with different characteristics? What about *my* school? Let's focus on the most common two cases that may seem overlooked by the example of Plum Creek Elementary: smaller schools and secondary schools.

EXAMPLE 3.1: A SMALL SCHOOL

Throughout this book, we have argued that many schools need a four-level school leadership architecture. But not all. If you have fewer than 18 to 24 teachers on your campus, you may only need three levels: Team Member, Team Leader, and School Leader (Figure 3.4). In a three-level model, most of the Bridge Leader responsibilities are absorbed by the School Leader.

FIGURE 3.4 • Three-Level Model for Smaller Schools

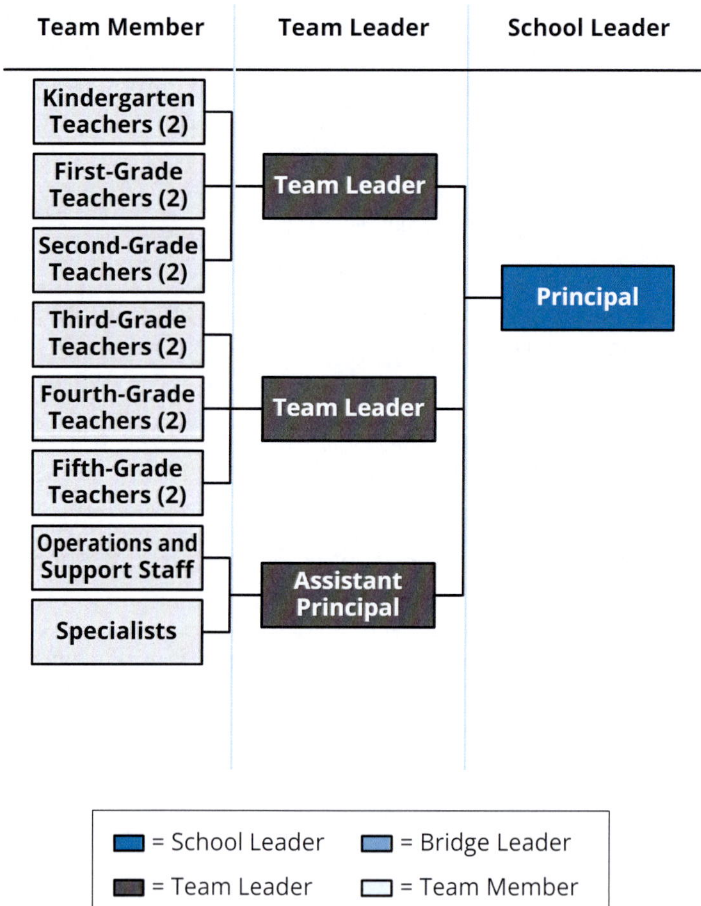

There is one big thing to watch out for in the three-level model—especially if all coaching shifts to Team Leaders and results in an AP role with a more traditional administrative portfolio. You need to think carefully about ensuring the AP role remains attractive—in terms of both duties and compensation. This is especially important if you view it as the primary training ground for future principals. In short, you need to consider your role design through the lens of both daily operations (short-term) and talent development (long-term). We'll return to these questions in Chapter 4.

EXAMPLE 3.2: A LARGE SECONDARY SCHOOL

Turning to secondary schools, this example is drawn from a larger, Grades 6–12 campus with a greater number of administrators. Figure 3.5 provides an overview of the organizational structure. This example highlights four key points that will inform districts' work with schools of all sizes and types.

FIGURE 3.5 • Organizational Structure With Differentiated AP Roles, Coded by Leadership Level

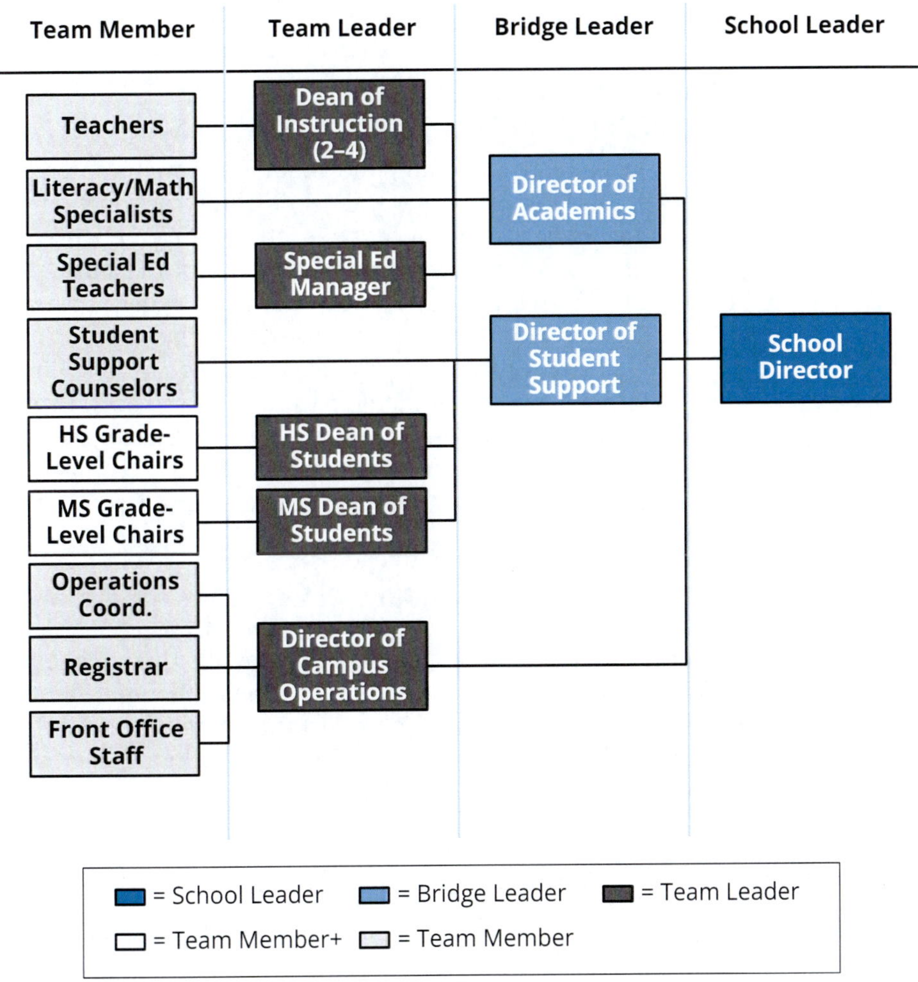

MANY SYSTEMS WILL NEED MULTIPLE, DISTINCT AP ROLES

Let's start by focusing on the AP roles—titled Directors in this school system. There are three distinct types of AP roles, defined centrally (the same across all schools): director of academics, director of student support, and director of campus operations. All three directors report to the School Leader, but only two (academics and student support) are operating as Bridge Leaders. They each lead a group of Team Leaders and a few Team Members. The third director (campus operations) is in a Team Leader role, managing a group of Team Members. As we've discussed, titles and leadership levels are not the same thing. This example also highlights another key point that will inform districts' work: as districts work to more clearly define AP roles, it is highly probable they will need to define multiple, distinct AP roles, not just one. While some will be Bridge Leaders, others may operate as Team Leaders. This variation in AP roles shouldn't be a surprise. There is simply no way the lone AP at a small elementary school is doing the same job as an AP at a high school who is one of a handful (or more) of APs on the campus. Furthermore, it's highly unlikely that all those APs at the high school are doing the same job. The key is to get clear and consistent about the differences in the roles.

NO ORGANIZATIONAL STRUCTURE WILL MAP PERFECTLY TO LEADERSHIP LEVELS

Returning to Figure 3.5, joining the director of campus operations at the Team Leader level are several deans of instruction or students and a manager of special education. At the Team Member level, it is important to clarify the role of grade-level chairs. In Figure 3.5, they are described as Team Members with additional leadership responsibilities. They are Team Members because they spend significantly less than 50% of their time delivering results through others. However, they do have meaningful leadership work—focused on student support and campus culture—and dedicate time to it. Ideally, the grade-level chairs are building skills and capabilities that will prepare them to move into a Team Leader role (dean of students, etc.) if they choose.

It is important to remember: leadership levels are not necessarily the same thing as titles or layers in the organizational hierarchy. It is unlikely that any organizational structure will perfectly map to leadership levels (i.e., a School Leader will only manage Bridge Leaders, or a Bridge Leader will only manage Team Leaders). And that isn't important. What is important is that the school has a robust leadership structure that allows the team to collectively do the work of all four levels of leadership.

ANOTHER BENEFIT OF CENTRALLY DEFINED ROLES? CAREER PATHWAYS

This example also reinforces one of the long-term benefits of centrally and consistently designed roles—clearer career pathways and better prepared leaders (Figure 3.6). In this model, teachers who aspire to school leadership often take on grade-level chairs before moving into dean positions (either academic or student support) before pursuing a director role. Though school directors can be drawn from any of the three director positions, they are most likely to have served as a director of academics or a director of student support as school directors are required to have a teaching/instructional background. When new school directors are named, they are required to prioritize hiring experienced directors in the tracks where they are less experienced.

FIGURE 3.6 • Career Path

	Academic	*Student Support*	*Operations*
School Leader		School Director	
Bridge Leader	Director of Academics	Director of Student Support	
Team Leader	• Dean of Instruction • Special Ed Manager	Dean of Students	Director of Operations
Team Member	• Literacy/Math specialists • Special Ed Teachers • Teachers	• Counselors • Grade-level Chairs • (Teachers)	• Operations Coordinator • Registrar • Front Office

Together, these examples only scratch the surface of the possible configurations that you might design. They are not exhaustive or prescriptive. They are designed to unlock and illuminate, to increase your sense of possibility. But getting there takes more than vision. There is real problem-solving to do.

PAUSE AND REFLECT

1. After reading the story of Lockhart and considering other examples, how has your understanding of the school leadership architecture changed or evolved?
2. What lessons might you take from these examples that apply to your own work?
3. What questions do they raise? What barriers are you thinking about?

ADDRESSING BARRIERS: NEED TO REPURPOSE AND REMOVE, NOT JUST ADD

These examples highlight what is possible. But they also raise as many questions as they answer. How do you pay for this? If APs are focused on coaching Team Leaders, who handles all of the other work they currently do? Many of these questions are about making the math work. How do we balance the ledger of limited resources in our context? Money. People. Time. The 100,000 public schools across the United States are astonishingly diverse. The school leadership architecture will inevitably look different in a 160-student rural district than it does in Lockhart or a district with 50,000 students and a 4,000-student high school. So rather than offer infinitely detailed answers for how one district navigated these questions, the rest of this chapter will highlight principles that districts can use to find answers for their context.

The barriers are real. But they aren't insurmountable. As we work through questions about people, time, and money, one big principle will guide our thinking. In a world of limited resources, districts can't just focus on what they will add (money, people, time, responsibilities). They must think about what they will repurpose.

GETTING *ALL* THE WORK DONE

The way we describe the school leadership architecture may sound like a utopian dream. The focus on building capacity and getting results may feel out-of-touch with the reality of many school leaders' experience—where they are spending time on all sorts of other responsibilities. Trying to support an AP to be more focused on supporting Team Leaders can feel like a never-ending game of whack-a-mole. All of the "other duties" just keep falling onto someone else's to-do list, the work doesn't get done, and everyone is frustrated. Building a sustainable, realistic leadership model will require thinking creatively about operational responsibilities, avoiding duplication of efforts, streamlining administrative and compliance activities, and using systems thinking to escape negative feedback loops.

THINK CREATIVELY ABOUT OPERATIONAL AND ADMINISTRATIVE RESPONSIBILITIES

Instructional leadership has added many responsibilities and time commitments to principals' plates, but we haven't systematically *removed* any of the responsibilities they carried in their building manager era. We've done what we often do: piled more on without taking anything off. As we work to improve the school leadership architecture, we have an opportunity to rethink how we tackle some of the important operational and administrative aspects of school leadership. We need to ask again: Which work requires the skill and expertise of a trained educator or administrator?

The idea that *all* the work of operating a school doesn't fall to educators and administrators isn't a new idea. We don't ask classroom teachers to conduct building maintenance or prepare breakfast or lunch because it doesn't align with their skills and would take time away from their instructional work. But we need to revisit where we've drawn the lines. Why does a teacher or administrator need to supervise lunch or recess? Do all the current responsibilities of an AP require the skill and expertise of an instructional expert with advanced degrees? Why couldn't some of these duties be carried out by non-instructional staff members with different skills and the ability to form strong relationships with students?

We don't have to start from scratch. We can draw inspiration from school systems across the country. Many charter schools have developed school leadership models that separate operational leadership from instructional leadership. The UnCommon School network uses a co-leader model: a principal, focused on instruction, and a school-based director of operations (Tooley, 2017). Other systems, like Achievement First and YES Prep Public Schools, stick with a single school leader but differentiate assistant school leader roles, with some dedicated to instruction and school culture and others focused on operations. Though the details vary, these models all produce a common advantage. Because there is a leader who is clearly designated and empowered to lead operations, the central office can streamline its communication and support for operational priorities. Rather than funneling every piece of information to the principal, who quickly becomes a bottleneck, support and guidance can go directly to the person who needs it.

Charter schools aren't the only school systems thinking creatively about ways to get operational responsibilities off principals' plates. The District of Columbia Public Schools created new strategy and leadership roles to allow principals to spend more time leading instruction and less time on a range of operational responsibilities (Tooley, 2017). The School Administration Management (SAM) Project helps principals spend more time leading instruction by delegating non-instructional management responsibilities (Tooley, 2017). The SAM project is more than a staffing model—it is a disciplined approach to changing how school leaders spend their time that relies on a disciplined approach to scheduling and systems and processes that help protect school leaders' time, identifying "first responders" to key issues and structured communications protocols. The Aspen Institute recently advocated that policymakers mandate (and fund) a director of operations role (Bennet & Cox, 2024). But schools and districts don't need a policy change to think more broadly about how to creatively deploy the talents of both instructional and non-instructional staff and enable school leaders to focus more on the work that only they can do.

AVOID DUPLICATION OF EFFORT

If districts add roles to increase support without revisiting existing responsibilities, they are at risk of duplicating efforts and wasting resources. Imagine if a School Leader, Bridge Leader, and Team Leader all believe that they are responsible for a teacher's development. Each leader spends significant hours observing, giving feedback, and coaching the teacher. They often find themselves all in the same classroom doing the same thing. Now imagine that you are a teacher who walks into your colleagues' classroom and sees a School Leader, Bridge Leader, and Team Leader all there, observing. How would you react? Would you think, *Wow, look at all of that support!* Or would you be more likely to wonder, *How do all of those administrators have time to be in there at the same time?*

There is too much work that needs to be done to double up on the same work. And there is a real risk that double investment doesn't produce double impact. If one teacher receives different coaching from multiple people, they may feel overwhelmed or confused, not supported. There are many decisions that a district will need to make as they work to maximize resources and avoid duplication of effort. But one big one will be who evaluates teachers—Team Leaders or Bridge/School Leaders?

In most school systems across the United States, performance evaluations are conducted by certified administrators—principals or assistant principals. In contrast, internationally, in many high-performing countries, teachers play a primary role in feedback and evaluation (Darling-Hammond et al., 2017). Many factors contribute to our default model of principal/AP-led evaluation, including the fact that many states' policies require evaluations to be completed by a certified administrator.

But beyond policy requirements, this is simply how we have always done things. The dominant view in most schools is that coaching and evaluation should be kept separate and can't be combined in one person. Here's the basic rationale:

- Coaching and support are about growth and improvement.
- Evaluation is about judging your performance in order to apply consequences or rewards.
- My relationship to the person who evaluates me is one of fear and/or distrust. I want to hide my weaknesses and vulnerabilities from them so that I will not be viewed as low performing.
- If the person who evaluates me is also the one who coaches me, the coaching won't be effective because I won't be able to be vulnerable with them and will be performing versus learning.

If you accept the premises, the logic holds. But what if, instead of focusing on carrots and sticks, rewarding the highest performers and exiting the lowest, the first purpose of evaluation was teacher development? You could make the case that it *must* be in our current context. When the supply of ready, willing, and able teachers is desperately low, you can't fire your way to success. Who is going to replace the teachers you drive out? No, we are going to develop and support our way to success. If that is the purpose, then the strongest, most valuable approach to evaluation (to teachers) could be one where the formal evaluation is a summary of *all* the observations and coaching conversations that a teacher has had over the course of the school year—not a rating based on 75 minutes of instruction over a few visits.

The most efficient and effective way to do that *might* be to integrate evaluation and coaching. Ultimately, this approach could make evaluation less of a high-stakes test and could empower Team Leaders in their work as ongoing coaches and supports. Making this shift would also free up Bridge Leaders' and School Leaders' time to focus on responsibilities that only they can do. What *if* Team Leaders were empowered to *both* evaluate *and* mentor/coach their team members? It's been done before—in school systems around the world and in the United States. Some models, like Toledo's Peer Assistance and Review (PAR), have even been union led or endorsed (Natale et al., 2013).

Making this shift requires real considerations, especially in school systems where evaluations carry high stakes, including teachers' pay. Team Leaders will need support and coaching to grow into this role. And it may make sense to phase the transition gradually, introducing Team Leaders as coaches first, pilot a Team Leader as evaluator, and then introduce more broadly. But we must weigh those risks and complexities against this reality: The current model of principal-led evaluations isn't working very well in most places (Kraft & Gilmore, 2016; National Institute for Excellence in Teaching, 2018). Whatever a district decides—combining coaching and evaluation or keeping it separate—they must think through how the supports will be coherent. They must avoid duplication of effort.

STREAMLINE ADMINISTRATIVE AND COMPLIANCE WORK

In addition to asking who does what, one of the first questions we need to ask is whether there are opportunities to work smarter instead of working harder. Are there tasks or activities that we can outsource to technology? In general, we should expect that many repetitive or routine non-manual tasks could be automated, saving teachers and staff time. School districts should take responsibility for finding, vetting, and introducing these efficiency-enhancing technologies. And it seems safe to assume that the opportunity to outsource less strategic work to technology will only accelerate in the coming decade.

School districts must also do all they can to streamline and simplify compliance activities. It is important to acknowledge that many compliance requirements are rooted in efforts to guarantee protections and access for students who have been consistently underserved in our schools. Laws were passed to remediate decades of poor or unequal results, and reporting requirements were established to ensure accountability and consistent implementation. We shouldn't gloss over the reason why these compliance measures were deemed necessary.

Though their impact on educators' time is significant, the reality is that, to some degree, compliance requirements are largely out of district or school leaders' sphere of control or influence. However, there are two things that educational leaders can do. First, they can work to develop systems to fulfill compliance requirements as efficiently as possible. And second, they can find ways to fulfill them with as little impact on instructional staff time as possible. In short, they can ask: How can we use technology? And how can we deploy non-instructional staff?

USE SYSTEMS THINKING TO ESCAPE NEGATIVE FEEDBACK LOOPS

On too many campuses, responding to behavior issues becomes close to a full-time job for many APs. When that is a school's current reality, it can be hard to imagine a different future. And yet, we know that one of the best strategies for promoting positive, engaged student behavior is offering excellent, rigorous, and engaging (fun!) instruction. The challenge for many schools is that they are locked into negative feedback loops. These loops keep their capacity tied up while schools react to symptoms versus investing in root causes.

The bet is that improving the school leadership architecture enables the school to have more capacity to invest in the root—whether that's teacher capacity and engaging, rigorous instruction or creating cultures of belonging and trusting relationships or providing students and staff with more robust mental health supports. It will likely take time to see the results. The school leadership team must stay focused and persistent.

EXERCISE 3.A

Getting *All* the Work Done

- Where do you see opportunities to rethink operational responsibilities?
  - How could existing positions (on campus or at the central office) be repurposed to decrease the amount of time instructional leaders spend on operations?
  - What questions or challenges might you need to work through?
- Where do you see opportunities to avoid duplication of effort?
  - Do you see any duplication of effort in the current leadership structure (including central office roles and supports)? What is the root cause?
  - Is your district open to combining evaluation and coaching responsibilities? Or is there a strong commitment to keeping them separate? What do you see as the strengths and weaknesses of each approach?
  - If you are committed to separating coaching from evaluation, how do you ensure alignment between coaching and evaluation? Do teachers experience evaluation as developmentally focused and helpful to them?
  - If you empower Team Leaders to be both coaches and evaluators, how will you train and support them to be effective, rigorous evaluators?
  - What are other examples where duplication of effort might exist and/or occur? These may be areas where you want to formally define roles and responsibilities like Lockhart did.
- Where might you have opportunities to streamline administrative and compliance work?
  - Are there bright spots in your district where you used technology or other systems to save school leaders time?
  - Where might there be additional opportunities to streamline or systematize this work?
- How could the school leadership architecture help you interrupt negative feedback loops? Where could investing leaders' capacity in addressing root causes alleviate some of the symptoms that consume significant time and attention now?

FINDING A SUSTAINABLE FUNDING MODEL

One of the most complex technical aspects of revising the leadership architecture is figuring out how to fund new leadership positions. Unfortunately, there isn't a simple formula that will spit out an answer to the question "How do we pay for this?" Each school system will find a unique answer, tailored to its needs and context. But if school systems attempt to strengthen the school leadership architecture through addition only—adding people, adding salaries, adding work to be done—they will quickly find the math difficult to balance. The key is to rethink and repurpose, not just add. These are hard decisions. They require leaders to evaluate trade-offs with care for all involved and with students at the center. Figure 3.7 summarizes where to look for savings in order to invest in a stronger school leadership architecture.

FIGURE 3.7 • Fund Through Repurposing, Not Adding; Save to Invest

SAVE MONEY BY . . .	INVEST MONEY IN . . .
• Maximizing the impact of classroom teacher positions, including strategically deploying paraprofessionals and teacher residents • Reducing or repurposing non-classroom instructional support roles • Reviewing stipends (department head, etc.). • Shifting positions from central office to schools	• Robust Team Leader and Bridge Leader roles • Developing future teachers and paying residents • New positions that shift operational/compliance responsibilities away from instructional leaders

THINK CAREFULLY AND CREATIVELY ABOUT CLASS SIZE

In a world with unlimited resources—a deep supply of excellent, well-trained educators and abundant financial resources—we would all want smaller class sizes for all grade levels, higher teacher pay, and more time for teachers to collaborate, plan, and learn. But unfortunately, we face a world of limited resources that forces us to make choices and negotiate trade-offs. From this perspective, even if we would *prefer* smaller class sizes, we may need to *accept* incrementally larger class sizes to prioritize something more important: higher salaries to help retain teachers or more time for teachers to learn, grow, and improve.

Across the world, school systems have navigated these trade-offs differently (Schleicher, 2018). Globally, teachers deliver 19 hours of instruction per week (Darling-Hammond, et al., 2017). This translates into a little over 700 hours of instruction per year for each teacher, compared to more than 950 hours for U.S. teachers (Organisation for Economic Co-operation and Development, 2022). These differences are stark and have huge implications for how teachers experience their jobs and the time that they have for learning and development. That's 250 hours that U.S. teachers don't have to plan, collaborate, and develop. It means that classroom teachers simply don't have time to take on meaningful leadership roles coaching and mentoring their colleagues. And it is part of why all the work of leading the school tends to drift toward the principal (Hargreaves, 2017).

But you don't have to leave the United States to find school systems that have made big investments in teaching planning, collaboration, and development. Achievement First, a charter network in the northeast, provides 725 non-instructional hours to teachers every year, compared to less than 400 hours in Duval County and District of Columbia Public Schools (Education Resource Strategies [ERS], 2013). Achievement First creates this additional time primarily by offering a longer school year with more contracted hours versus through fewer instructional hours. But, in addition to having *more* non-instructional time for teachers, Achievement First uses the time differently with 23% of it dedicated to intentional, formal professional growth (ERS, 2013).

Our context may force more school systems to take a hard look at class sizes. In the United States, we don't have enough well-prepared teachers to fill all our existing positions. We may need to accept larger class sizes as a necessity, in response to a limited supply of qualified educators where the real trade-off is often between smaller classes taught by less developed teachers and larger classes taught by more skilled ones. In an era of big, and potentially chronic, shortages, this is a question about how we most effectively deploy and retain the strong and developing teachers we have. If we can figure out how to reduce the number of teaching positions we need, that will release some of the pressure we are experiencing. And it may be the only way that we can build robust, financially sustainable career pathways for teachers.

This isn't a binary choice between small (14 students) or huge (38 students) class sizes. The choice may be between 22 and 25 students in a class. And there isn't one right answer. Systems must make choices based on their strengths, needs, and priorities. What do class sizes look like across your district, at each school, and by grade level or subject? Low (and declining) class sizes may be a sign that there is an opportunity to repurpose some classroom teacher positions.

For example, if an elementary school has six sections of first grade with class sizes of 20 students, one role could be repurposed as a Team Leader position. The result would be five sections with class sizes of 24 students. Or let's take a different example. Consider an elementary school with four sections of first graders and four sections of second graders and class sizes of 20. This school decides to do the following:

- Elevate one teacher role to a Team Leader position.
- Repurpose one position to a full-time teaching position who will *only* teach reading across all sections in first and second grade. Note: this role will create additional release time for the other six classroom teachers.
- Divide the first- and second-grade students into three homerooms for each grade. One of the homerooms for each grade level will be larger (32 students) and will be taught by an excellent teacher (who receives additional compensation) and works with a full-time paraprofessional or a teacher resident. The remaining sections will have 24 students.

These examples scratch the surface of possibilities, highlighting the ways we can think creatively about how we are designing teaching positions:

- Class sizes do not have to be identical across all sections. More experienced and effective teachers may be given larger groups of students and greater compensation.
- Groups of teachers can share responsibility for the learning of a group of students, including dynamic, team-based instructional strategies.
- Teachers-in-training, including teacher residents, can be incorporated into the model by being paired with strong teachers and larger classes. Paraprofessionals and aides can be strategically utilized to support the staffing model. They do not need to be allocated consistently across all classrooms.

The key idea is that we are not just tacking on new positions—we are repurposing positions in ways that expand teachers' impact, maximize our limited financial resources, and create career pathways for educators.

REVIEW INSTRUCTIONAL SPECIALIST, INSTRUCTIONAL COACH, AND OTHER NON-CLASSROOM INSTRUCTIONAL POSITIONS

The teaching workforce in the United States has been growing at a faster rate than the number of students in public schools. Between the 1987–1988 and the 2017–2018 school years, the number of teachers in public schools grew by 53% while the student population grew by 27% (Ingersoll et al., 2021). As a result, the teacher-to-student ratio has declined from over 30:1 in 1955 to 16:1 in

2012, a number that has remained steady in the past decade (Kena et al., 2015; National Center for Education Statistics, 2022). There are many drivers of these trends, but one is a significant increase in the number of instructional support roles. Bierly and colleagues (2016) found that for every principal, school systems had created, on average, 12 additional "leadership" positions. One to three of these positions were APs or instructional coaches. The rest carried a variety of titles—PLC lead, model teacher, mentor teacher, department chair, grade-level chair. One system had 40 different roles. Some roles report to the central office and work across multiple schools; others are campus positions selected and deployed by the principal. According to a recent study by Instruction Partners (2024):

> Between 1950 and 2018, the percent of overall education staff who are district staff, principals, or assistant principals didn't change, but the percent of non-teaching "support staff" grew from 23% of the education workforce to 31%. This increase was driven by an increase in staff focused on "instruction" or "student support." The growth in these roles has been linked as one driver of recent increases in per pupil spending. (p. 13)

Though well-intentioned, many of these roles were one-off creations designed to support a specific activity or initiative without any vision for how the roles should work together to advance the mission of the school or how leadership could be effectively and coherently organized. In short, there was no attention to the overall school leadership architecture. As you strengthen the leadership architecture, you will need to review these positions and consider one or more of the following actions:

1. Eliminate positions that are unnecessary, redundant, or not adding value.
2. Simplify the number of positions or titles that you use so that everyone understands what the role is and why it exists.
3. Repurpose and/or elevate one or more existing positions to a Team Leader role.
4. If needed, keep one non-classroom instructional expert Team Member role. Clearly define what this position does and who it reports to in the campus leadership structure.

TAKE A LOOK AT STIPENDS

If you have one or more leadership-in-name-only positions that receive stipends—like department head or grade-level lead—you will have to decide how they fit into your leadership architecture. A good place to start is evaluating whether these roles are impactful leadership positions: Are they consistently filled by your strongest teachers? Are they filled through rigorous selection processes (as opposed to a rotating position that people take turns doing)? Do they have meaningful time to focus on the leadership responsibilities that they've been assigned?

If the answer to these questions is "yes," they are meaningful leadership roles and may be a part of the leadership architecture like the grade-level leads in Figure 3.5. If the answer to one or more of these questions is "no," you may have an opportunity to repurpose these roles and the funds associated with them.

CONSIDER REPURPOSING CENTRAL OFFICE POSITIONS

When system leaders look at examples like the ones presented in this chapter, they are likely to notice all the new roles they don't yet have in their systems. They are less likely to notice what's missing—the roles that exist in their systems that may be omitted from these models, including central office–based positions.

Any system that pursues changes to leadership roles will have to prioritize. Both Denver and Lockhart funded positions on their campuses by eliminating central office positions. Denver subsidized the cost of release time for teacher leaders during the pilot phase but then asked campuses to find sustainable funding sources from within their budgets (reviewing all positions and identifying which could be consolidated and better deployed). As Lockhart's shared leadership model took root, it realized that it needed fewer central office roles now that it had empowered experts on campuses. It funded the expansion of the model, in part, by streamlining roles in the curriculum and instruction department. Regardless of the details for your district, here is the big picture: To achieve coherence across roles and financial sustainability, *all* roles must be on the table, not just some.

EXERCISE 3.B

Save to Invest

Maximize the impact of classroom teaching positions.

- What are your instincts, preferences, or convictions when it comes to class sizes? What experiences inform your views?
- How do you think about trade-offs between smaller classes and
  - higher pay for teachers?
  - fewer preps or hours of instruction for teachers?
  - fewer vacancies?
- What conditions could make larger class sizes workable?

- Where are class sizes across your district? What is your average class size by level? What is each school's average class sizes? What is each school's largest and smallest class (by grade level)?
- Do you see any variation that surprises you?
- How many classes are taught by a substitute, an uncertified teacher, or someone teaching outside of their certified grade or subject?

Review non-classroom instructional positions.

- What instructional support positions has your district created?
- Is each position
  - a Team Member or Team Leader role?
  - school-based or central office–based?
  - consistently used across all schools or highly variable?
- What questions do you have about these roles? What do you need to learn more about?
- Do you see a path to simplify or repurpose any of these roles?
  - What opportunities might you be able to unlock?
  - What challenges might you face?

Take a look at stipends.

- What stipend-compensated positions exist across your district?
  - How large is each stipend?
  - How much money does your district spend per campus on these positions? In total?
- For each position, use the following questions to evaluate if these roles are impactful leadership positions:
  - Are these roles consistently filled by your strongest teachers?
  - Is this position filled through a rigorous selection process (as opposed to a rotating position that people take turns doing)?
  - Do these positions have meaningful time to focus on the leadership responsibilities that they've been assigned?

Consider repurposing central office positions.

- Imagine that you had leadership roles on campus with the time and capacity to coach and develop teachers and with the instructional expertise to make sound decisions about curriculum and instruction. What work is currently done at the central office that might shift to schools in this new model?

BEYOND BARRIERS, OPPORTUNITIES

There are real challenges to work through with a change this significant. It can feel like too much risk. But the work is worth taking on because of the opportunity to

- make everyone's jobs more doable and increase the school's capacity to support students and staff,
- create elevated leadership opportunities for teachers to grow their impact and their careers, and
- provide a clearer path to principalship with stronger job-embedded development opportunities for all roles.

That's a lot of opportunity. But this work won't happen overnight. The key is to go slow to go fast, testing and learning with a small group of campuses before trying to scale any new models. Chapter 4 will provide a roadmap to that work.

Big Ideas and Key Takeaways

- There are many ways to bring the school leadership architecture to life. The details will vary across schools of different sizes and levels. What is important is that the school's leadership structures allow leaders to build capacity and deliver results.
- If school systems attempt to strengthen the school leadership architecture through addition only—adding people, adding salaries, adding work to be done—they will quickly find the math difficult to balance. The key is to rethink and repurpose, not just add.
- We need to think creatively about how to accomplish *all* of the school's most important work. Building a sustainable, realistic leadership model will require thinking creatively about operational responsibilities, avoiding duplication of efforts, streamlining administrative and compliance activities, and using systems thinking to escape negative feedback loops.
- Funding changes to the leadership architecture will require districts to look for opportunities to repurpose or save money—including at the central office—in order to make new investments.
- A world of limited resources requires us to make choices and weigh trade-offs creatively—between higher teacher pay, smaller class sizes, and the amount of time teachers have to collaborate, plan, and learn.

CHAPTER 4

Big Change Starts Small

Both Lockhart Independent School District (ISD) and Denver Public Schools drove a systemic change, not an isolated technical adjustment. Changing the school leadership architecture impacted every job in the school. But neither system "rolled out" a district-wide change in six months. They started small, engaging ready, willing, and able principals as partners. They tested and learned. And then they scaled.

This approach is key to successfully improving the school leadership architecture: To lead big, impactful, sustainable change, start small with the willing and eager. These committed and engaged leaders will stay with you when you hit bumps and challenges. They will help you solve the problems to make the new model successful. And ultimately, their success is what will fuel rapid scaling. Their endorsement and the positive experience of their staff will persuade doubters and be the strongest antidote to resistance.

This chapter is organized into two sections. In the first, we'll walk through the process to bring the school leadership architecture to life on one or more pilot campuses—a seven-step process. In the second section, we'll highlight four steps to incorporate the work of multiple schools into a coherent district-wide system that is scalable and sustainable.

PHASE I: STRONG PILOTS

This book argues that talent—finding, developing, retaining, and deploying people—must be a district-level responsibility and priority. Districts cannot delegate their responsibility for ensuring a coherent district-wide talent system and for removing barriers and providing the resources that campuses need to do this work. But the district must *partner* with schools. They need School Leaders' (including teachers') buy-in. But more importantly, they need their wisdom and perspective. And, engaging school-based leaders as partners builds goodwill and trust (Johnson et al., 2015). The first step in initiating this partnership is building supportive conditions at the district level.

STEP 1: ENSURE SUPPORTIVE CONDITIONS AT THE DISTRICT LEVEL

The culture of the central office and the mindset of district leaders are critical to the success of this work. Their approach matters. This work will be most successful when district leaders view themselves as a part of the work and a part of the system that is being worked on. Yes, the focus is the *school* leadership architecture, but, as we saw in Lockhart ISD in Chapter 3, changing the way schools are structured will have implications for the central office and how it operates—if district leaders are open to it.

When a principal shifts responsibility and decision-making to other Team Members, they may notice some friction with the central office. *Why does all the information about math curriculum come to me if I have a team empowered to make those decisions?* Or *How can I support a Bridge Leader to lead in that area if you are micro-managing me on the details?* Districts need to be ready to listen to feedback and willing to consider changes to how they operate. And that's the easy stuff. The harder part is being willing to look at central office positions and consider whether all the existing roles are necessary when campuses have more leadership capacity.

If districts only focus on changing schools but don't consider themselves part of the change, the result will be a shallower, more limited set of improvements. The most transformative work will occur when district leaders

- have a mindset that embraces delegating and distributing leadership, where they truly, personally embrace sharing leadership; and
- view this work as something that requires investment and sacrifice and change from them too.

This starts by taking real stock of the central office culture and being clear-eyed about what needs to change. Big structural changes are great opportunities to change schools' daily experience of the central office and to build trust *if* districts bring a real interest in hearing feedback and follow through with promised supports (Johnson et al., 2015). Exercise 4.A offers reflection questions to assess district mindsets and readiness.

EXERCISE 4.A

Assessing District Conditions and Mindsets

1. What evidence do we have that our district team has a partnership mindset (we exist to support schools and work together vs. doing things *to* schools)?

2. Do campus leaders experience our district team as bringing a partnership mindset? How do we know?
3. What evidence do we have that senior district leaders and the central office as a whole embrace distributing and sharing leadership and power?
4. In what ways might changing the school leadership architecture require sacrifice or change at the central office?
5. What conversations might we have to build shared understanding of those changes and prepare our team for them?
6. In what ways is our district culture likely to facilitate this work? In what ways is our district culture likely to be a barrier to this work?
7. How could this work create opportunities for us to improve or strengthen our district culture?
8. What specific moves do we need to make to drive these shifts and changes?
9. What might be warning signs that our culture or mindset has become a barrier to this work? How will we respond if we see those signals?

STEP 2: DEFINE LOOSE AND TIGHT

A true partnership between district leaders and schools can be a tricky balance to strike. District leaders can delegate too much, abdicating their responsibility or setting up campuses to invest time in decisions that will eventually get overturned or discarded. But district leaders can also hold on too tightly, failing to give campus leaders the autonomy that they need to think creatively and contribute. Clearly defining what is loose (up to the campus) versus tight (defined by the district and consistent across all schools) regarding the school leadership architecture is essential to a healthy, effective partnership between the central office and schools.

In Denver Public Schools' Teacher Leadership & Collaboration (TLC) effort, the principals of the 14 pilot campuses had flexibility in deciding the number and types of roles they wanted to deploy on their campus based on need, staff members' strengths, budget flexibility, and other factors. But several parameters were tight: they had to choose from five centrally defined roles, set release time for Team Leaders between 33% and 66%, and all new Team Leader roles had to be filled by classroom teachers (Denver Public Schools, 2019).

We recommend that the first "tight" parameter be a clear definition of the four leadership levels. Each campus should not independently define what it means to be a Team Leader or Bridge Leader. The expectations should be consistent, anchoring School Leaders as they design and refine their campus model. The unique leadership missions for each level should be held tight across all schools. Exercise 4.B walks you through this work.

EXERCISE 4.B

Refine the Unique Leadership Missions for Your District

You can find an editable version of Figure 1.3 at the companion website. As you contemplate tailoring or adjusting the framework, consider the following:

1. The leadership missions articulated in Figure 1.3 were high-level and general: Are there opportunities to make them more specific for your district?
2. Does anything need to be added or edited to ensure the unique leadership missions are comprehensive of the most critical instructional leadership work?

FIGURE 1.3 • Unique Leadership Missions, by Leadership Level

	TEAM MEMBER	TEAM LEADER	BRIDGE LEADER	SCHOOL LEADER
DELIVER RESULTS	• Work to consistently exemplify established standards of high-quality instruction. • Use data to drive instructional decisions. • Meet deadlines, fulfill responsibilities, and be prepared. • Demonstrate openness to new ideas and practices.	• Ensure every Team Member understands campus vision and definition of high-quality instruction. • Establish data-informed team priorities and goals. • Track progress and drive continuous improvement. • Identify barriers and make recommendations for school-wide improvement efforts.	• Track progress toward campus vision and successful execution of priorities. • Build Team Leader understanding of campus vision and priorities. • Ensure alignment between school-wide and team-specific priorities.	• Establish shared vision for the campus (including vision and definition of excellent instruction). • Ensure and manage alignment with district vision and priorities, including advocating for campus needs. • Establish short- and long-term campus priorities.

	TEAM MEMBER	TEAM LEADER	BRIDGE LEADER	SCHOOL LEADER
			• Remove barriers and create supportive conditions (culture, systems, etc.) for teams to thrive. • Support Team Leaders to achieve data-informed goals and close identified gaps.	• Through regular, purposeful communication, build understanding and ownership of the campus vision and priorities to all members of the campus community. • Use data to monitor progress and identify areas requiring attention. • Allocate resources (people, money, time) in alignment with vision and priorities. • Establish and maintain school climate and culture.
BUILD CAPACITY	• Demonstrate growth mindset and commitment to development and improvement. • Seek opportunities to build and deepen knowledge and skills. • Give and receive feedback.	• Coach and develop Team Members. • Build and maintain an effective team and facilitate collaboration. • Ensure coherence of support (professional development, coaching, evaluation, etc.) for Team Members.	• Coach and develop Team Leaders (as coaches). • Monitor Team Member results and development. • Identify priorities for school-wide professional learning—in pursuit of campus vision and driven by needs and gaps.	• Coach and develop Bridge Leaders. • Monitor Team Leader results and development. • Establish protocols for feedback, team collaboration, etc.

(Continued)

(Continued)

	TEAM MEMBER	TEAM LEADER	BRIDGE LEADER	SCHOOL LEADER
	• Actively contribute to a productive and collaborative team.	• Understand and use protocols in support of school-wide consistency and alignment.	• Drive school-wide professional learning (in partnership with Team Leaders and with input from School Leader). • Train Team Leaders in consistent and effective use of protocols.	• Establish priorities for professional learning and ensure coherence of build capacity efforts and deliver results.
Other duties and responsibilities				

Then, the district elaborates further parameters that must be consistent across all campuses (Figure 4.1 and Exercise 4.C). It is important to note that we are focused narrowly on the loose–tight parameters that will set the course for changing the school leadership architecture. These parameters are a subset of the broader central office–school relationship, which can range from highly centralized (most decisions about budget, academic programs, and staffing are made by the district) to highly decentralized (most decisions are made by campuses) (Johnson et al., 2015).

FIGURE 4.1 • Considerations for Loose Versus Tight Parameters Specific to the School Leadership Architecture

ESTABLISHED CONDITIONS	• How (de)centralized are decisions about instructional vision, curriculum, benchmark assessments, supplemental curriculum, and educational technology? • How (de)centralized are decisions about staffing and budget?
RECOMMENDED TIGHT PARAMETERS	• All teachers receive coaching and support from a Team Leader. • Team Leaders have at least 50% release time relative to their full-time teacher colleagues. • Team Leaders support between 6 and 10 teachers with a common goal. • Team Leaders should not be used as emergency substitutes or interventionists. • Team Leaders have influence over all of the supports that produce team success they are responsible for (typically a grade level or content area): paraprofessionals, classroom aides, tutors, and instructional specialists or coaches.

MONEY	1. Does the campus model need to be budget neutral? Or is the district willing to invest additional funds? If so, how much and for how many years? 2. Who will set salaries or stipends for new roles? When will those decisions be made? (Note: The "tightest" approach would be to establish a menu of roles/salaries at the outset and clarify any parameters on stipends.)
POSITIONS	3. Is the campus tasked with building a four-level architecture or a three-level architecture? 4. How much flexibility does the campus have to tailor duties? For example, are there any responsibilities that *must* be assigned to a Team Leader (vs. a Team Member), etc.? 5. Any parameters on who evaluates (teachers, etc.)? 6. Are there any positions that a campus *cannot* eliminate or repurpose? Or that a campus *must* eliminate or repurpose (including central office–based positions)? 7. How will (new) leadership roles be filled? Is a formal selection process required? What role, if any, will the district play in the selection process?
OTHER FACTORS	8. Are there any upper or lower limits on class sizes? 9. Are there any non-negotiables in the master schedule? (E.g., We are implementing a new curriculum that requires 90-minute instructional blocks in science.)

Equipped with these parameters, the district is ready to identify and engage with pilot campuses. It is important to articulate these parameters up-front, but that doesn't mean they need to be set in stone. As the work progresses and learning happens during the pilot, the loose and tight guardrails may be modified. As pilots gain traction and the system prepares to spread the change, it is likely that more components will tighten.

EXERCISE 4.C

Define Loose and Tight Parameters

Use Figure 4.1 as a guide to define loose and tight parameters.

1. First, identify your overall established conditions. How (de)centralized is decision-making about instruction, staffing, and budgeting? This will give you a baseline.
2. Then, review our recommended tight parameters.
    - Which are you adopting?
    - Which are you modifying or adapting? (For example, we recommend Team Leaders have *at least* 50% release time. You might choose to be more specific, prioritizing full-release, for example.)

(Continued)

(Continued)

3. Finally, work through the nine questions related to money, positions, and other factors.

For a write-in template of Exercise 4.C, see Template B.1. You can also download the write-in template for *Define Loose and Tight Parameters* from the book's companion website.

STEP 3: IDENTIFY AND SELECT PILOT CAMPUSES

Big change starts small. So, we expect a district-wide change to begin with a few pilot campuses—anywhere from one to a dozen. Ideally, your pilot campuses will represent a cross-section of your district (grade level, school size, etc.). But what is most important is that every pilot campus is ready, willing, and able to do this work. (If you are opening new schools, another way to get started is to test a new leadership model on a new campus with a strong founding principal.) Figure 4.2 recommends six non-negotiable criteria.

FIGURE 4.2 • Recommended Starter List for Non-Negotiable Criteria for Pilot Campuses

READY	1. The principal's leadership approach demonstrates a comfort with and willingness to share power and empower others. 2. The principal has credibility and influence with peers and colleagues.
WILLING	3. The principal and their team are enthusiastic about the opportunity to change the school leadership architecture. 4. The principal and their team have a demonstrated track record of embracing change. They are hungry to try new things.
ABLE	5. The principal and their team have demonstrated their skill and capacity to lead complex change on their campus. 6. The school has the capacity to invest time and energy in the change process. It is not engaged in too many other major change initiatives.

Beyond these non-negotiable criteria, seek to maximize two enabling conditions: campuses with (1) a supportive, developmentally focused school culture and (2) a clearly defined instructional vision and campus direction.

DOES YOUR SCHOOL HAVE A HEALTHY SCHOOL CULTURE AND SHARED BELIEFS?

There's no shortage of books about school culture, with a kaleidoscope of dimensions highlighted. When it comes to evolving the school leadership architecture, there are a few elements of a school's culture or shared beliefs that are significant enabling conditions:

- Does the school have an established collaborative culture? Or is there a "close my door and maintain my autonomy" mindset?
- Do teachers and staff embrace learning and continuous improvement? Is there a mindset that at this school we are always working to improve and get better? Or are we self-protective and afraid to make mistakes or be seen as having opportunities to improve?
- Do teachers and staff view feedback and coaching as a support that helps them get better and be excellent? Or do they view feedback and coaching through a deficit-based lens—such as a negative experience, something to defend yourself against, or an attack on your credibility?

A school whose culture represents more of these elements may experience faster traction and deeper success in evolving its school leadership architecture.

DOES YOUR SCHOOL HAVE A CLEAR VISION AND DIRECTION?

Every day, on every campus, dozens of educators make thousands of decisions. How does a School Leader make sure that these decisions add up to something that moves the school in the right direction? There are two basic strategies. One approach is to centralize decision-making. In this school of thought, one person making or approving all the decisions is the only way to ensure that the "right," aligned decisions are made. Guided by this implicit strategy, people are often nervous to share power or redistribute leadership responsibilities. They're terrified of the chaos that will result when each individual drives off in a different direction, guided by their own priorities and ideas.

The second approach is to establish a clear, shared vision and direction that is understood by all leaders and staff across the organization. In schools, a shared vision and direction will include the answers to the following questions:

- What promises does the school make and aim to keep to students and their families?

- What does great instruction look like at this school? If you walk into any classroom, what are the essential things that you always expect to see? What are teachers doing? What are students doing?
- What are the most important priorities the school is focused on in terms of improving their results?
- What values is the school committed to? How are people expected to treat each other?

In this model, you don't need a single person to make or review all the decisions because a wide number of people can make effective, aligned decisions guided by the vision and direction. Schools that have a strong vision and direction in place will find the work of reorganizing leadership much easier (National Institute for Excellence in Teaching, 2018). That's because a clear vision and direction scale. You can double or triple the number of leaders coaching teachers and have confidence in the consistency and alignment of their moves, as long as you ensure they understand the vision and direction.

NON-NEGOTIABLE CRITERIA ARE DIFFERENT FROM ENABLING CONDITIONS

What about a school that hasn't established these mindsets? Should they work on changing their culture before they initiate any changes or improvements in their leadership architecture? Many might say "yes" believing that you have to build the right conditions for change to stick. This is one way to think about driving change, but it isn't the only approach.

An alternative is to change the context first (the structures, roles, and routines) and then to use the changed context to facilitate a change in mindset and culture. Let's take clear vision and direction as an example. Ironically, the limitations of the school's existing architecture—where the principal is trying to do too much on their own—is likely part of the reason why a clear vision hasn't been established. The principal is fighting fires and can't prioritize the time to operate at the School Leader level. So, if this enabling condition isn't in place at the beginning, it just means that establishing the vision and direction—and concrete routines, practices, and protocols to guide and support leaders' work—has to be a top priority for the School Leader and their coach.

The same is true for school culture and shared beliefs. Changing the school leadership architecture will be more challenging on a campus where teachers don't demonstrate openness to feedback or where there isn't an established culture of collaboration. This can be overcome, and the new structures may help, but Team Leaders will need to overcome resistance. They will need to work to evolve the culture of the school and the mindsets of staff. And those Team Leaders are going to need ongoing support to make it happen. In short, a culture that embraces feedback, learning, and collaboration has real advantages in embracing a new leadership architecture. But the absence of these conditions isn't a reason to not act. Leaders will just have to develop a strategy to tackle structure and culture together.

Think of these conditions as the weather that you are sailing into: they can make your journey easier or harder. When these conditions are present, it is like having the wind at your back: they will fuel and accelerate your progress. The absence of these conditions is like headwinds: you may still set sail, but you need a plan for how you will contend with them.

EXERCISE 4.D

Planning to Identify and Select Pilot Campuses

1. How will you identify pilot campuses? Why are you choosing that method?
   - Share information with all campuses, invite them to express interest, and run a formal selection process.
   - Hand-pick campuses.
   - Use some other method.
2. What are you looking for in prospective pilot campuses?
   - What are your non-negotiable ready, willing, and able criteria? (Figure 4.2 can provide a starting point.)
   - What enabling conditions will you prioritize?
   - Leaders have at least 50% release time. You might choose to be more specific, prioritizing full-release, for example.
3. How will you evaluate these criteria and/or conditions?
   - What data or information will you review?
   - What information will you gather through an application?
   - What information will you gather through an interview or conversation?

For a write-in template of Exercise 4.D, see Template B.2. You can also download the write-in template for *Planning to Identify and Select Pilot Campuses* from the book's companion website.

STEP 4: GROUND YOURSELF IN CURRENT REALITY AND PROVIDE INSPIRATION

Once you've selected your ready, willing, and able campuses, it's time to get them together and begin building shared vision. The energy that will fuel the hard work of changing the school leadership architecture is campus teams knowing that they are solving problems that matter to and resonate with them, problems such as School Leaders who are stretched too thin, teachers who are undersupported, jobs that feel undoable. So don't gather your pilot campuses and hard-pitch a solution. Get them together and sell the problem. Exercise 4.E provides a template for planning this kick-off.

EXERCISE 4.E

Plan a Kick-Off Session With Pilot Campuses

1. Pre-work: Read Chapter 1 and Chapter 2 up until Exercises 2.A and 2.B.
2. In live session, complete Exercise 2.B.
3. Then, ask each team to draw an organizational chart that shows the following:
   - Who provides direction to each Team Member
   - Who is responsible for developing each Team Member
   - Note that this may include some lines to the central office
4. Give individuals time to read the rest of Chapter 2 (or facilitate a discussion about key lessons, highlighting what is most relevant to your district).
5. Discussion questions:
   - What did you notice as you completed these exercises?
   - What did that make you think?
   - Where is our campus facing challenges?
   - Where might there be opportunities for our campus if we could strengthen the architecture?

Note: This is not a complete session outline. It does not include detailed scripts for opening and closing (anchoring in goals, building community, etc.). It is designed to provide the bones for you to build on.

Selling the problem or grounding in current reality provides the initial momentum to take on the work, but providing a concrete vision of a different way of operating provides the final ingredient—a sense of possibility, an injection of belief. We have found site visits to be one of the best ways to do this. They make change concrete and make it feel a bit closer, a bit more achievable. As you look for potential inspiration visits, remember that you don't need to see a perfect model, that is, one that exemplifies your vision or addresses every element. What matters is that your campus teams get an opportunity to see something different than their current reality. Seeing a different model increases our sense of possibility and gives us an opportunity to identify what resonates and what doesn't fit from the new model—an opportunity for campus teams to begin building shared vision.

There are examples throughout this book that you may want to investigate further. Realistically, you'll probably want to find an inspiration visit close to home to save money and time. Be creative in thinking about where you might find inspiration. Maybe there's a specialty school in a neighboring district or a charter school that uses a different staffing model. Consider using Chapter 3 as a pre-read before the visits.

STEP 5: PILOT CAMPUSES DEVELOP MODELS

Armed with their diagnosis of their current reality, the loose versus tight principles, and the guidance of Chapter 3, it is time for campus teams to develop the prototype for their new model. The prototype needs to include a description of roles classified by leadership level (titles with simple descriptions of responsibilities and commensurate release time), an updated organizational chart, and a master schedule that illustrates how teaching and leadership responsibilities will fit together. Collectively, these describe the positions that will be eliminated, repurposed, or added to strengthen the school leadership architecture. Appendix B provides a write-in template to guide prototype development. You can also download the editable "Template for Creating Prototypes" from the companion website.

There will be an infinite number of models that a campus could produce. Generally, if they are consistent with the loose versus tight criteria, the district should give the green light. Ideally, this first draft is completed in the third quarter of the school year. That allows the fourth quarter and the summer to be dedicated to bringing the new model to life by Day 1 of the next school year.

EXERCISE 4.F

District Checklist for Model Drafting

1. How will we communicate—at the district and campus levels—about this work through the design and launch phase?
2. What milestones will drive campuses' drafting process? How will we provide feedback?
3. Who will review campus plans and provide feedback and/or questions?

STEP 6: SELECT AND (RE)TRAIN LEADERS

Defining (and funding) the roles is hard work, but it is only the beginning. It would be a waste of the time and energy you've invested to change the leadership architecture and create new roles and then fill them with people who don't have the skills and dispositions to lead effectively. For any new role, or any role with a significant change in responsibilities, you need to run a formal selection process. The bar needs to be high, and it needs to be consistent across all campuses. So, recruiting and selecting these leaders need to be a partnership between the district and campuses. Chapter 9, which delves into leadership development systems, will go deeper on selection, but Figure 4.3 highlights a few criteria districts can use to identify strong people for new roles. The criteria are divided into two groups: a set that apply to all leaders, at all levels, and in all roles and a few that are role specific.

FIGURE 4.3 • Criteria for Leader Selection

Universal Criteria *(apply to all leadership levels)*	***Deeply grounded in a student-centered "why"*** Motivations for leadership are grounded in their values and a commitment to positively impacting students and ensuring that *every* child flourishes and fulfills their potential. Is grounded in a deep conviction that all students can learn. Their values, purpose, and convictions drive their actions and decisions.
	Consistently embodies organizational values Leaders' actions will shape the culture, so it is important to choose leaders who will be strong role models for the culture you want to have.
	Demonstrates a growth mindset Is eager to learn, open to feedback, and not afraid to try new things and make mistakes. Does not view feedback as criticism and isn't crushed by falling short of a goal—views both as opportunities to learn, grow, and improve.
	Listens well and has a track record of building strong, productive relationships with diverse colleagues Is this someone who their colleagues respect, trust, and follow?
	Learns quickly Can connect the dots and see how different systems, processes, and ideas fit together. Sees the big picture and can diagnose the root cause of an issue.
Role-Specific Criteria	***For instructional leadership roles, has a strong track record of effectiveness and impact in prior roles*** If a Team Leader role is responsible for coaching and developing a team of teachers in order to strengthen instruction and improve student outcomes, it is essential that candidates are considered for the role *only* if they have been excellent teachers.
	Exhibits the competencies required of the next leadership level/role This will be broken down further in Chapters 5–9, but, at a high level, your job is to look for evidence that candidates can do or will quickly learn the skills required for the next leadership level.

To be clear, this list is not exhaustive. You will have additional, specific criteria that are important for leaders in your district and you should add them. This is a starter list of non-negotiables—things that are fairly simple and somewhat obvious but easy to overlook. In addition to these criteria, let's address a few FAQs:

1. *So, you're saying that the principal can't just tap people on the shoulder or volunteer them for these positions?* Yes, that's correct.
2. *But that's how we've selected department heads in the past.* Have your department heads consistently been your strongest leaders? If not, why is that a practice that you would continue?
3. *But shouldn't our department heads have first shot at any new positions, especially if we are getting rid of department head stipends?* No. This is a different job and if the department head is the best candidate, they will demonstrate it through the process. (Also, it's more and different responsibilities. You need to make sure they even want that role.)

You've done all this work to create clearly defined roles with robust responsibilities, authority, and time. Give this the best chance of succeeding by placing people with the greatest capability in those roles.

EXERCISE 4.G

District Checklist for Selecting Leaders for New Roles

- When will we announce new positions and any changes to existing positions?
- How will we run selection processes? What role will the district play in selection?
- What are our minimum, non-negotiable requirements for new roles? What will we do if we do not have enough qualified applicants?
- How will we ensure that all campuses have access to the most qualified candidates? How will we balance the needs and preferences of applicants and campuses?

Even with the best role design and the most robust selection processes, leaders will still need development and support to thrive in roles. Denver discovered this early in its pilot phase, and Lockhart learned from its experience in how it designed and implemented its shared leadership model. Denver realized almost immediately that in addition to evolving structures—titles, responsibilities, compensation—it needed to help leaders build new skills, professional identity, and time applications.

One group it needed to support were teacher leaders who were moving into new roles that required them to level up from strong Team Members to Team Leaders. Denver quickly learned that this transition didn't happen automatically, a natural side effect of changing the structure. The district needed to formalize this professional learning and actively support newly appointed teacher leaders if it was going to successfully navigate this transition.

Leaders in new roles weren't the only people who needed to change their practices, because the introduction of new roles required *everyone* to level up their leadership. Principals and assistant principals (APs) also needed to make a shift. Principals who had been operating as Team Leaders—directly supervising, coaching, and evaluating teachers—needed to evolve their leadership practice. They needed to empower, coach, and support Team Leaders to do that work and take advantage of the opportunity to level up their leadership. They were entering a significant, but somewhat disguised, leadership passage and needed support to navigate it successfully. Eventually, Denver created comprehensive training for the Instructional Leadership Team (ILT) to help individuals and teams make shifts in skills, professional identity, and time applications needed to bring the structure to life. It is the district's role to be proactive in identifying the development and support that leaders—both new and existing—need to thrive in the new model.

EXERCISE 4.H

District Checklist for (Re)Training and Developing Leaders

- How will we onboard, develop, and support individuals taking on new roles? (See Chapters 5–9.)
- How will we develop and support existing leaders to evolve their leadership to embrace their unique leadership mission in the new model?
- How will we develop and support campus leadership teams?

STEP 7: IMPLEMENT AND LEARN

Throughout the first year of implementation, part of the learning process will be noticing what isn't working. How is this going differently than you expected? What did you overlook? District leaders' job is to listen to campus leaders as they share what is working and where there are pain points. Then, together, you can troubleshoot and change. There are a few areas where district leaders need to have a particularly sharp eye:

- Are leaders being overwhelmed with ad hoc demands? (From the central office? From their principal?)
- Where is there conflict or tension between the way that campus leaders are trying to operate and the way district-level positions have historically functioned?
- Now that schools have more robust leadership teams, are district-level leaders engaging *all* of those leaders appropriately? Or does all information and input still run through the principal?

Don't panic if things aren't perfect right away. Small, steady adjustments will move you in the right direction. Eventually, after a year or two (or more), you'll notice that you've found a groove. You've worked through the wrinkles; you're seeing promising results. You think you're ready to spread the work to more campuses across the district.

EXERCISE 4.I

District Checklist for Continuous Improvement

1. What formal touchpoints will you set up throughout the first year to discuss how things are going?
2. What data—qualitative and quantitative—will you collect to monitor implementation?
3. How will you make it easy for campuses to identify the changes and support they need from the central office?

PHASE II: BUILD SYSTEMS FOR SCALE

As you turn to the work of scaling, the role of the district is to synthesize and refine the details of the pilots into a coherent, simple system that can be scaled and sustained across the district. The purpose of the pilots was to explore variation, to give each campus the space to tailor the model to its individual strengths and needs. Why not continue to spread the model this way, allowing thousands of flowers to bloom?

Eventually, inconsistencies in how roles are defined and structured across campuses will lead to two problems. First, they will produce friction and inefficiency in how district teams support their campus counterparts. The more consistency and predictability there is in the structure of leadership roles across campuses, the easier it is for district teams to deliver the right information and support to the right people. In short, the easier it will be to build a successful system. Second, inconsistencies in titles, responsibilities, and compensation will create incoherent career pathways that are confusing to individuals and produce talent gaps for the district. The greater the variation in roles across campuses, the greater the likelihood that incentives will be poorly designed and misaligned with system goals. Individuals won't understand how they can grow their impact or their career. Without clear, coherent career pathways, the district cannot play its essential role of identifying and developing leadership. So, before scaling the great work of the pilot campuses, the district needs to refine the variation across the models to prevent them from spilling over into inconsistency, contradiction, and confusion. This is the work of building systems to support scale and sustainability.

STEP 8: CONSTRUCT PROTOTYPES

To reduce unproductive variation but harness the important lessons from pilot campuses, we recommend adopting a small number of leadership architecture prototypes. A larger district may have four to eight prototypes. Smaller districts may only have one or two. Each prototype should include

- all roles, classified by leadership level, with clear job descriptions;
- a sample organizational chart; and
- sample master schedules.

Each prototype will certainly involve different numbers and configurations of roles and it may even include one or more unique roles (defined as a title, job description, and compensation band). But any role should be consistent across all prototypes: one title should only mean one clear set of responsibilities, and one set of responsibilities should always carry the same title. For example:

- If you continue to use the title "assistant principal," it must mean only one thing—the role should always be at the same leadership level and should describe a similar set of unique leadership missions. If you see AP used in one prototype to refer to a Bridge Leader and in another to refer to a Team Leader, that is not internally consistent.
- You may see two prototypes deploying a similar role, but one calls it an Instructional Coach and the other calls it an Instructional Specialist. It will be simpler if the same job is always referred to with the same title. Just pick one.

Equipped with these concrete prototypes with consistently defined roles, the district will be able to scale the work in a more streamlined way. New campuses won't start with a blank sheet of paper. Their first move will be to select the prototype that best matches the structure and needs of their campus. From there, they have the flexibility to tweak the model using the district's loose versus tight parameters, which will inevitably be refined from the initial pilots. One tight parameter that will inevitably be added is the expectation that campuses do not deviate from the district-defined roles (titles, responsibilities, and compensation). For a write-in template to help in creating prototypes, see Template B.3 in Appendix B or the book's companion website.

STEP 9: DEFINE CAREER PATHWAYS

The prototypes provide the critical inputs to map out coherent, strategic career pathways—a holistic picture of how educators increase their impact and their compensation by taking on new roles with greater responsibility and wider reach. The leadership levels provide the framework we need to get started.

Figure 4.4 provides an example of what you will create. The rows in the table are the four leadership levels and the columns are different career tracks. Two things are likely to jump out at you right away. First, the three tracks: academics (all instructional staff and those who lead and support them), operations and support (including administrators who focus primarily or exclusively on operations), and specialists (counselors, librarians, etc.). You might define career tracks differently, and that's fine. What matters is that the tracks capture the work that is to be done and provide clarity about how roles grow in complexity, contribution, and pay. Every career track may not have a school-based role at every leadership level. Put differently, not all career tracks lead to a principal role. In this example, principals come exclusively through the academic track. If someone in a specialist or operations and support role aspired to be a principal, they would need to make a lateral move to develop and demonstrate academic expertise.

The second thing that likely stands out is the four distinctions within the academic track Team Member roles: emerging, developing, proficient, expert. What's going on there? As the share of novice teachers grows and as new teachers are, on average, less well-trained before entering the classroom, the four tiers provide us with a more concrete way to think about staffing our classrooms. *Expert teachers* are our strongest teachers and those who want to stay in the classroom full-time. They take on responsibilities that allow them to impact more students' learning and receive higher compensation. This could include teaching more students (larger class size, with support from a paraprofessional

FIGURE 4.4 • An Example Career Pathway

		Academic	Operations and Support	Specialists
School Leader		Principal		
Bridge Leader		Assistant Principal		
Team Leader		Director	Director	
Team Member	Expert	• Master Teacher • Mentor Teacher • Instructional Specialist	Various *(Custodial, Office, Food Service, etc.)*	Various *(Librarian, Counselor, etc.)*
	Proficient	• Classroom Teacher		
	Developing	• Novice Teacher		
	Emerging	• Resident • Apprentice • Paraprofessional • Aide		

= No school-based career pathway, next role for this position at district level

= Typical advancement pathway

= Lateral rotation

= Next role may be a district-level role

or aide). In Figure 4.4, these roles carry the title Master Teacher. Or expert teachers could support the development of one or more early career teachers—hosting a resident, co-teaching, serving as a model classroom, or acting as other forms of support. This role carries the title Mentor Teacher in Figure 4.4.

Proficient teachers are those who have built basic fluency in their role (likely after three to five years of teaching). They are still growing as professionals and may not be ready to expand their reach, but they are not targets of intensive support. *Developing teachers* are teachers of record, but they are novices who need significant support to grow into strong teachers. They may teach fewer lessons or fewer students, engage in co-teaching with an expert, or need other forms of coaching and support. *Emerging teachers* are not yet teachers of record, but they can support student learning in partnership with expert or proficient teachers. Ideally, many emerging teachers aspire to the role and/or are in the process of being certified.

Thinking about teacher roles in this way allows us to think more creatively about the challenges facing the teaching profession and how we deploy our resources (people, money, time). It also helps us move closer to a profession teachers deserve—one that maximizes the contributions of excellent teachers by creating pathways for them to expand their impact and grow their careers. Moving into a Team Leader role is one way to do that, but it doesn't have to be the only way.

WHAT IF WE HAVE A THREE-LEVEL LEADERSHIP PROTOTYPE?

As we discussed in Chapter 1, there are likely to be many schools—especially smaller ones—for whom a three-level model is more appropriate. In fact, it's possible that even in large school districts, at least one of their prototypes may be a three-level model. A three-level model can coexist with four-level models in the same school district. It just needs to be integrated coherently into the career pathway (Figure 4.5). The three-level prototype simply doesn't use all the roles. In this case, it doesn't have a Bridge Leader (assistant principal) and only uses Team Leader roles (director of academics, director of operations).

FIGURE 4.5 ● A Closer Look at the Career Pathway

		Academic	*Operations and Support*	*Specialists*
School Leader		***Principal***		
Bridge Leader		Assistant Principal		
Team Leader		Director	Director	
Team Member	Expert	• Master Teacher • Mentor Teacher • Instructional Specialist	Various *(Custodial, Office, Food Service, etc.)*	Various *(Librarian, Counselor, etc.)*
	Proficient	• Classroom Teacher		
	Developing	• Novice Teacher		
	Emerging	• Resident • Apprentice • Paraprofessional • Aide		

= No school-based career pathway, next role for this position at district level

= Typical advancement pathway

= Lateral rotation

= Next role may be a district-level role

Gray = A role that is used in the district but not at this school

As discussed in Chapter 1, in a three-level model, the School Leader absorbs the leadership missions of a Bridge Leader. And the career pathway coherently describes the basic progression of all roles across the district. Obviously, one question that the district will consider is whether it requires individuals to progress through each level, without skipping steps. To be more concrete: Do directors on a three-level campus need to take a Bridge Leader role at a four-level campus before they would be considered for a School Leader role? Or can they skip directly to being a principal of a three-level school, potentially with some targeted development (like a residency or apprenticeship)?

To be clear, there are pros and cons of both approaches. More rigidity may shrink the pool of eligible future leaders; less rigidity could result in leaders moving into positions before they are ready. What matters is that the district is clear, that it is consistent, and that it has a robust strategy to ensure they have an ample supply of ready leaders for their schools. As you turn to the work of mapping your career pathway in Exercise 4.J, remember that the scaffolding in this section is intended to be supportive, not restrictive. It is also designed to be simple even though this work is very complicated! But complicated systems are hard to operate and sustain, so the simpler we can make this, the more likely we are to be able to actually do something with it.

EXERCISE 4.J

Defining Career Pathways

For a write-in template of Exercise 4.J, see Template B.4. You can also download the write-in template for Defining Career Pathways *from the book's companion website.*

Step 1: Confirm what pathways you want to have. We have recommended academic, operations and support, and specialist, but you can tailor these to fit your system.

Step 2: Take all of your prototypes (which should have roles/titles classified by level) and add them to your chart. Start by focusing on the four leadership levels.

Step 3: Take a closer look at Team Member roles. Consider whether you want to tier those roles to reflect different levels of expertise and contribution. If so, determine the number of tiers and classify those roles.

Step 4: Use arrows to indicate the likely progression between roles.

Step 5: Iterate between these steps and debate as needed.

STEP 10: IDENTIFY LEGACY ISSUES AND PLAN TO ADDRESS THEM

In most cases, your career pathways table from Step 9 describes your ideal future state and not your current reality. You stayed committed to the instructions, focusing on the unique leadership missions and leadership level, not the title or compensation. But you found yourself writing some big titles in some of the lower-level boxes. And though you didn't have all the salary data handy, you knew from memory that the level of these positions doesn't match how they are paid. You've got some Team Members making more than Bridge Leaders.

This is where the work gets messy, but it's important to tackle it. If you don't align those incentives, you are going to have a hard time identifying and developing the leaders you need for these roles in the future. And every dollar you spend overpaying for one role is money you don't have to fund the impactful positions you need. You may not be able to resolve all these issues immediately, but you need to formulate a plan (ideally working with a compensation expert) to close these gaps as soon as possible (Exercise 4.K).

Wherever possible, if you have a problem with an existing position—for example, it is overpaid, the performance of the incumbents is a level or more below target, or there is significant variation in how the role is currently performed—you may want to consider eliminating the position and replacing it with one or more new roles with different titles. Why?

- It's easier to explain and understand what is new and different by making a clean break from old roles versus trying to rebrand them.
- It allows you to open the position up to be filled by the most qualified person. It will get you the strongest candidate and it's fairer—to incumbents who may want to change roles now that they understand the new expectations and to others who may want to apply for the open position.
- It is a faster path toward a more coherent career pathway. The alternative is a multiyear process of resolving big legacy issues. And the risk is that you never get it done.

There will certainly be situations where you need to take a longer path, especially when dealing with positions that are part of collective bargaining agreements. But there are two actions that you can take to build trust with teachers and their unions and to generate the broadest set of possibilities for how this work can move forward. The first is including teachers' unions as partners from the beginning. The second is consistently anchoring this work in the way it is good for teachers: increasing the quality and quantity of support they receive, giving teachers more leadership and decision-making authority, and creating more opportunities for teachers to grow their compensation without leaving the classroom.

EXERCISE 4.K

Identify Legacy Issues and Build an Action Plan

For a write-in template of Exercise 4.K, see Template B.5. You can also download the write-in template for Identify Legacy Issues and Build an Action Plan *from the book's companion website.*

Step 1: Identify issues.

- Identify any roles/titles that currently exist in your district that are *not* reflected in your pathway chart.
- Identify any roles/titles on your pathway chart where the performance of incumbents is consistently below what is expected of leaders at this level. (Note: we are looking for systemic issues, not individual ones.)
- Plot the compensation bands of all positions. Identify any roles on your pathway chart that are currently compensated significantly above (or below) what you would expect (i.e., they make as much as or more than positions a level above them).

Step 2: For each identified issue, make a plan.

- Eliminate the role/title—all incumbents apply for new positions.
- Phase out the role/title over time—when vacancies occur, do not rehire for this position.
- Attempt to "level up" the position (keep all incumbents) by providing support and strong performance management.

STEP 11: SPREAD THE MODEL TO NEW CAMPUSES

Equipped with all you have learned, built, and refined from your pilots, you are ready to spread and scale to new campuses. Ideally, the buzz around the pilots—positive feedback from teachers and administrators at pilot campuses and leading indicators of impact—has spread, generating a growing number of campuses who are eager to get involved. Especially in the early stages, don't be afraid to spread and scale the work slowly; move at the pace of your capacity, ready campuses, and your confidence in the model and your systems. Go slow to go fast.

No matter how fast you scale, remember that you never graduate from listening and collecting feedback. How well you listen to, engage, and partner with campuses during the pilots is critical to building trust and investment in the new model. But it isn't just important at the beginning; you never graduate from being in listening mode.

> A district's strategy was only as good as the central administrators' judgment and ongoing interest in gaining more feedback and providing support. When they truly relied on school-based educators' experience and advice, trust grew within schools about the good intentions of central administrators. However, trust could quickly disappear if teachers and principals saw the district's request for feedback as no more than a symbolic nod to participation. (Johnson et al., 2015, p. 50)

TWO SIDES OF THE COIN: STRUCTURES AND PEOPLE

Ultimately, the work of strengthening the school leadership architecture is a two-sided coin. First, districts need to structure campus roles consistently across the district, providing clarity, coherence, and alignment to make each job doable. This is our focus in Part II (Chapters 3 and 4). But new structures without evolved, elevated leadership behaviors will accomplish little. If a principal still leads as if they are solely responsible for all the leadership work in the school, it won't matter that they have a robust team of Team Leaders and Bridge Leaders to support the work. Those leaders will be undermined and discouraged. Their effectiveness will be limited, and they won't grow and develop. It would be a tragic waste to do the hard work of improving the structure of roles to then neglect the other side of the coin—the need to develop individuals to be ready for new leadership roles. That is the focus of Part III.

Big Ideas and Key Takeaways

- Districts cannot delegate their responsibility for ensuring a coherent district-wide talent system and for removing barriers and providing the resources that campuses need to do this work. The district must *partner* with schools to build their buy-in and benefit from their wisdom and perspective.

(Continued)

(Continued)

- This work will be most successful when district leaders view themselves as a part of the work and a part of the system that is being worked on.
- Clearly defining what is loose (up to the campus) versus tight (defined by the district and consistent across all schools) regarding the school leadership architecture is essential to a healthy, effective partnership between the central office and schools.
- The energy that will fuel the hard work of changing the school leadership architecture is campus teams knowing that they are solving problems that matter to and resonate with them. So don't gather your pilot campuses and hard-pitch a solution. Get them together and sell the problem.
- It would be a waste of the time and energy you've invested to change the leadership architecture and create new roles and then fill them with people who don't have the skills and dispositions to lead effectively.
- Before scaling the great work of the pilot campuses, the district needs to refine the variation across the models to prevent them from spilling over into inconsistency, contradiction, and confusion. They must construct prototypes, define career pathways, and identify and address legacy issues.

PART III

Developing People

In Part III, our focus is on supporting leaders to build the new skills that they need to succeed in new structures. Chapter 5 will introduce a framework for thinking about how individuals experience leadership passages, or the transitions between leadership levels. It will offer advice on how individuals and the people who coach and mentor them can successfully navigate these important shifts. Then, the following three chapters dig into each of the school leadership passages, unpacking the new skills, time applications, and professional identity required to succeed and thrive at the new level. The chapters will also provide resources and tools that individuals can use for self-reflection or to coach leaders they support.

- Chapter 6 describes the transition from Team Member to Team Leader.
- Chapter 7 describes the transition from Team Leader to Bridge Leader.
- Chapter 8 describes the transition from Bridge Leader to School Leader.

Though these chapters will be most powerful when used in a system that has strengthened the way that roles are structured, they can be used in any system to grow and develop as a leader. Finally, Chapter 9 outlines how districts can build more intentional, coherent leadership development systems in order to identify, develop, select, and support strong leaders at every level.

CHAPTER 5

Making the Shift

"What got you here won't get you there." Marshall Goldsmith, a renowned executive coach, coined this advice and used it as the title of his 2007 book. It spread rapidly, a quip passed from leader to leader. Like most nuggets of wisdom, it's easier to understand than to practice. It is ironic that the very things that have made us successful and led to roles of greater responsibility can morph into our kryptonite.

It's like driving on a remote, windy road on a dark, moonless night. There are no streetlights, and only the dim glow of stars paints the sky a deep navy gray. The car's headlights extend the view to about 400 feet. Traveling at 70 miles per hour, you have four seconds of visibility. You lean forward, tightening your grip on the wheel. You're looking for those reflective signs that signal the road is about to veer sharply to the right or left, into the darkness.

For a leader moving to a new leadership level, success depends on their ability to see and respond to those reflective signs. They mark the ways in which this role is not just a continuation of the work they've always done. The new role doesn't ask for the same leadership with broader reach and more authority; instead, each new leadership level requires a 90-degree turn, what Charan and colleagues (2024) call a leadership passage. This chapter:

- Describes the three types of shifts leaders experience as they move to a new leadership level.
- Supports readers to apply the shifts to their own experience, including recognizing when they are stuck in a passage.
- Shares some key moves to master new skills, change time applications, or evolve professional identity. Offers key principles for individual leaders navigating a passage and for coaches supporting them.

LEADERSHIP PASSAGES REQUIRE THREE KINDS OF SHIFTS

In each leadership passage, individuals must make a shift in *skills*, *time applications* (both how they spend their time and how far out on the horizon they think and plan), and *professional identity* (what they think is important and choose to focus on).

SHIFTS IN SKILLS

There are distinct shifts in skills as leaders progress through the four levels, but in general, at each transition, leadership skills become more about

- interpersonal effectiveness, including delivering results through others versus managing and making things;
- the effectiveness and clarity of your two-way communication;
- planning and developing strategy versus doing; and
- greater breadth versus deeper specialization.

In the chapters to come, when we describe skill shifts you will notice that it is a relatively short list of skills. Some readers may wonder, *Surely, this isn't a comprehensive account of the knowledge and skills you need at this leadership level?* You are right. The skill shifts highlight the most important capabilities that will be new—and are most likely to be challenging at first—at that leadership level. The shifts build on the skills and capabilities that a leader has already developed and demonstrated at previous leadership levels. They depend on the deep foundation of technical knowledge and skills that instructional leaders at all levels will need—child development, pedagogy, curriculum and instruction, adult learning, and data fluency, to name a few. In short, the skill shifts are not intended to replace professional standards or other more comprehensive accounts of leaders' knowledge and skills.

Have you experienced these shifts as you've transitioned between leadership levels? Exercise 5.A is designed to give you an opportunity to reflect on your leadership experience through the lens of the key shifts.

SHIFTS IN TIME APPLICATIONS

Each leadership passage requires leaders to make two shifts related to their time. First, they need to *allocate* their time differently. As they transition to a new leadership level, they have a new job to do. They need to stop doing their old job and dedicate their time and attention to their new responsibilities. We'll get into the specific details in the chapters ahead, but we can generally expect that the closer a leader is to the School Leader level, the more of their time will be used to deliver results through others (versus getting things done directly). As leaders progress, we should expect more of their time to be spent communicating, working with people (individuals, teams, stakeholders), and on planning and developing vision and strategy. If a leader has transitioned to a new leadership level and their calendar looks identical to their old role, something is off. On the other hand, a completely overloaded calendar is also a warning sign: It may mean that a leader has picked up new habits, practices, and responsibilities but failed to let go of the work of the previous level.

The second time-shift they need to make is in their *time horizon*. At each leadership passage, leaders need to think and act with an increasingly long-time horizon. On one end, Team Members' actions are generally going to be focused on the shortest time horizon—driving short-term planning and execution and responding to pressing needs. At the other end, School Leaders must think and act with a multiyear view. This distribution of time horizons is part of what enables a school to accomplish its most important work, from being responsive to daily needs and emergent issues to driving long-term improvement. If a School Leader is planning, thinking, and acting day to day, week to week, or even month to month, the school is in trouble.

SHIFTS IN PROFESSIONAL IDENTITY

Each day, we shut off the lights in our classroom or office and we head home. As we walk down the hallways and begin our commute, many of us have subconsciously graded our day and are silently ruminating on what made it great or awful. The A+ days tend to be days where we found a flow—making progress and using some of our best skills and talents—or where we had big wins. At the other end of the spectrum are the days when we struggled, with few signs of progress and maybe even some big losses.

Humans are pattern-finding machines. Before you know it, without even trying, we find the patterns in our best and worst days and start attaching them to our professional identities.

> *I'm an executor, someone who gets things done.*
>
> *I'm a behind-the-scenes person. I do my best work out of the spotlight.*
>
> *I'm an expert. I love having the opportunity to share what I know.*

To be clear, this is a subconscious process. It's not like we slap stickers on our shirt with our prized professional identities. But when we move into a leadership passage, these unspoken professional identities begin to surface. Shifting to a new leadership level is sometimes about what we *start* doing—new skills, mindsets, habits—or about a *change* that we need to make to an existing practice. But our ability to successfully evolve or adopt a new practice will often depend on being disciplined in what we *stop* doing—our ability to leave old practices, habits, or mindsets behind. And that's where professional identity comes into play.

Each of us builds up a professional identity over the course of our careers. We develop an image of who we are at work. It's a highlight reel of the things we're good at. When we excel at something—when we stand out as uniquely talented, maybe even better than most of our colleagues—we feel good. We feel like what we're doing really matters, that *we* matter. We feel a sense of purpose in our work.

Then comes the call: "What got you here won't get you there." This new role isn't just an extension of our previous role—bigger, broader, more. It is a completely different job, requiring us to embrace new responsibilities and leave others behind. The hidden calculus goes something like this: to succeed in this role, we need to stop doing a bunch of things that we love and are excellent at—the things that make us feel good, that give us a sense of accomplishment when we go home to our family each night, that make us feel proud and competent. Meanwhile, we need to add new and different things that we haven't done before, aren't comfortable doing, and, maybe, aren't very good at (yet).

After the shine of novelty has faded, many leaders struggle with their professional identity when they transition to a new leadership level. They bristle at the new requirements—not necessarily because they *can't* fulfill them but because they aren't sure if they *want* to. As leaders move to a new leadership level, they may hear a little voice that says, "I'm not the person who does *that*." Or it might sound like one of the following:

- *I didn't realize this is what the job would be. It doesn't have very much to do with working with students. It's all about dealing with adults and solving their problems.*
- *If I had known this was how I'd be spending my time, I never would have taken the job.*
- *I hate some parts of this job. But I am just going to put up with them and try to limit how much of my time they consume so I can focus on the things I know are important.*
- *I will never feel comfortable having difficult conversations with colleagues or "being in charge." This isn't who I am.*

These are signals of a professional identity shift—a need to see yourself in a new way so that you can embrace new skills and time applications.

EXERCISE 5.A

From Ideas to Practice

Think back to when you transitioned from being a Team Member to a Team Leader.

- *You can choose a different transition if you prefer. We recommend the first passage because it tends to be vivid and memorable.*
- *If you haven't navigated this leadership passage, you might use the case study in Appendix C as an alternative way to unpack and apply the key shifts.*

When did you make this "turn" in your career? What role were you moving from and moving to?

____

What challenges, if any, did you face as you navigated this career passage?

____

____

____

____

How were those challenges connected to the key shifts in skills, time, and professional identity that are associated with this passage? (Figure 5.1 may spark your thinking.)

Skills ____________________________________

____

____

Time ____________________________________

____

Professional Identity ____________________________

____

____

What was most helpful to you in navigating these shifts?

____

____

____

Did you fully master the shifts of this passage before you entered the next one? If not, what shifts were left unfinished?

____

____

____

(Continued)

(Continued)

In what ways could better understanding the key shifts have helped you navigate this career transition?

____

____

____

FIGURE 5.1 • Snapshot View of Three Leadership Passages

	LEADERSHIP PASSAGE 1: FROM TEAM MEMBER TO TEAM LEADER	LEADERSHIP PASSAGE 2: FROM TEAM LEADER TO BRIDGE LEADER	LEADERSHIP PASSAGE 3: FROM BRIDGE LEADER TO LEADER OF SCHOOL
DEFINED IN BRIEF	Transition from an expert instructor with deep expertise and skills to leaders who spend at least 50% of their time delivering results through others.	Transition from Team Leader to leaders who deliver results across many teams by coaching and supporting Team Leaders, ensuring teams are aligned to the campus vision and priorities, and removing barriers and developing systems that facilitate the teams' work.	Transition from Bridge Leader to leaders who are accountable for organizational results—short and long term. Establishes and maintains the campus vision and priorities through clear, consistent communication with staff, families, and the school district.
SKILLS	• Build strong, trusting relationships. • Develop Team Members. • Build a strong team and ensure members work well together.	• Establish and improve systems. • Plan and prioritize for the long term. • Empower delegation. • Coach and support Team Leaders.	• Define long-term strategy and goals for the school, balancing future goals (3–5-year plan) with present needs and pressures. • Communicate clearly and effectively with all stakeholders. • Prevent and navigate crises.
TIME	*Time Application* • Managing > Individual work • Make time for others *Time Horizon* • Semesters or longer, not just days or weeks	*Time Application* • Managerial and system work (75% of time) • Organizational perspective vs. "own work" • Strategic and cultural issues *Time Horizon* • 1+ year planning horizon	*Time Application* • From primarily internal to significantly external focus • Protect time to think, reflect, and analyze *Time Horizon* • Long-term thinking and strategy (2–3 years)

	LEADERSHIP PASSAGE 1: FROM TEAM MEMBER TO TEAM LEADER	LEADERSHIP PASSAGE 2: FROM TEAM LEADER TO BRIDGE LEADER	LEADERSHIP PASSAGE 3: FROM BRIDGE LEADER TO LEADER OF SCHOOL
PROFESSIONAL IDENTITY	• Others' success • Discussing, not just doing • Comfort with authority	• Connector and facilitator • Dial up trust, dial down control	• Accept attention/ scrutiny that comes with being highly visible • Organizational culture

Note: The key shifts are an attempt to describe what is commonly experienced as challenges for many leaders. They are not designed to comprehensively describe all the knowledge, skills, and dispositions a leader needs (they are not professional standards). They are designed to be a tool for self-reflection, not a universal prescription. Some leaders, because of their experiences, may not experience all the shifts as significant challenges. Others may have "skipped a level" and may be struggling with a skill, time application, or professional identity shift at a previous level.

NAVIGATING LEADERSHIP PASSAGES—GETTING UNSTUCK

When leaders engage with Exercise 5.A, we notice common themes. Almost everyone can identify one or more shift where they were facing a steep learning curve and struggled. Most of the time, they figured it out eventually. But many think, *I wish someone could have told me this back then.* Or *I could have been so much more impactful in that role if I had understood this.* And *I could have avoided some painful mistakes.*

Feeling some friction when we navigate a new leadership passage is normal and healthy. It's a signal that we're veering from a familiar course, and we need to adjust our steering to stay on track. Here's what is concerning: Too many new leaders at every level are getting stuck. They're unable to successfully navigate the leadership passage. They decide the role isn't for them, so they quit and leave the profession or move back to a role where they feel more comfortable or fulfilled. Others persist but don't develop the new skills or time applications they need to really succeed in the role. They muddle along but make little progress toward the bold visions and aspirations that motivated them to take the job in the first place.

To help leaders get unstuck, we need to avoid a common mistake: the tendency to treat every leadership challenge as a skills problem, overlooking issues with time and professional identity. Why is this our instinct? One reason is that skill problems are the easiest to see. Time applications and professional identity are more subtle. The second reason is that we're most confident addressing skill issues. They respond to our go-to solutions: knowledge-building, training, practice, and mentorship. There's a saying that when you only have a hammer, all you see is nails. If we treat all leadership challenges as skill issues (nails) because they match our tools, we will misdiagnose what is going on and leaders will continue to get stuck. We need to match our intervention to the root cause (Figure 5.2).

FIGURE 5.2 • Interventions for Skills, Time Applications, and Professional Identity Shifts

SHIFT	INTERVENTIONS
SKILLS	• Knowledge-building and training • Mentoring/modeling • Focused practice (job-embedded attempts with coaching and feedback)
TIME APPLICATIONS	• Calendar audits • Prioritization and calendar discipline • Delegation or coaching others (to release responsibilities) • For time horizon—likely to rely on some skill-building interventions, especially modeling and focused practice
PROFESSIONAL IDENTITY	• Intentional "trial period" • Job crafting • Anchor in purpose

Sometimes, what looks like a skills gap is rooted in something deeper. Maybe a leader has all the knowledge and skills they need but just isn't shifting their time to prioritize the right work. In this scenario, the intervention must help the leader change how they spend their time. This might be as simple as sitting down and planning their time differently. But often, it requires more than just clear priorities and discipline. A leader may know what is most important and be committed to doing it. But they keep getting pulled into other essential work. They can't just drop it; they need to delegate it. And if there's no one to delegate it to, they need to invest time building someone's capacity.

Other times, what looks like a skill gap or time problem goes even deeper. The root cause may be a leader's professional identity. It's not that they can't (skill) or don't have time; it's that they don't want to. To diagnose a professional identity challenge, listen for discomfort, lack of motivation, and resistance. Once diagnosed, how do you respond?

Inspired by sports psychologist W. Timothy Gallwey's 1974 classic *The Inner Game of Tennis*, one intervention is to use a trial period. Leaders commit and go "all in" on the new skill, behavior, or time allocation for an extended period. This is a version of role-playing that might give the leader the opportunity to overcome a limiting story. Sometimes, especially when the leader has a strong skillset, a sustained trial period is enough to rewrite the leader's inner narrative. They notice they're better at this thing than they thought. It gets added to their professional highlight reel. After more and more at-bats, they notice their discomfort lessening. It isn't so bad after all.

The trial period tackles the challenge outside in. But some professional identity shifts may need to be addressed inside out, especially when a leader is dealing with motivation issues. Job crafting offers one approach (Wrzesniewski & Dutton, 2001). In cognitive job crafting, an individual focuses on changing how they perceive their responsibilities (Berg et al., 2008).

But there may be some aspect of the leader's job that they are just never going to like, no matter how they try to reframe it. It is never going to rise to the top of the list of things they want to do. In fact, it may be at the very bottom. In these situations, the leader must connect the responsibility to their purpose. They may never *love* public speaking or be naturally motivated to do it. But they are *extremely* motivated to lead in ways that advance excellence for the students they serve. They would do anything in their power and aligned to their values to fulfill that purpose. Through that lens, public speaking is just something they must do as part of that work. It is an opportunity to connect with and mobilize people toward that goal. The foundation of all of this is to be grounded in a deep sense of purpose. When we can see a task or a responsibility as a part of a larger purpose that we are committed to, it changes our motivation for that task.

As you work through the specific shifts of your current leadership passage in Chapter 6, 7, or 8, use Figure 5.2 as a reference to match your intervention to the root cause. But before you dig into that work, this chapter will close with a few general pieces of advice that are relevant to all leaders navigating a transition and to the coaches and mentors supporting them.

FOR LEADERS NAVIGATING A LEADERSHIP PASSAGE

If you are a leader who is navigating a leadership passage, this section offers eight pieces of encouragement for you. Each one is a lens through which leaders can see the transition with greater clarity. As you read, look for the two or three that resonate most as you navigate your current leadership passage.

EMBRACE AND ACCEPT DISCOMFORT

Making these shifts is going to feel uncomfortable, at least at first. But remember that discomfort is an essential ingredient to learning and growing. It isn't something to be avoided and it isn't a sign that you can't do it. According to Adam Grant (2023), growth requires the courage to lean into discomfort in three ways. We have to

- leave behind our old (comfortable) habits and skills,
- be willing to try new skills *before* we have mastered them, and
- be willing to make a lot of mistakes.

Grant (2023) reminds us, "Comfort in learning is a paradox. You can't become truly comfortable with a skill until you've practiced enough to master it. But practicing it *before* you master it is uncomfortable, so you often avoid it" (p. 33).

BE KIND TO YOURSELF

If you're a new leader reading Chapters 6 through 8, you might think, *Uh oh, there are several shifts that I don't think I've made.* The thought of operating in these ways may feel far from your current reality. If that's where you are, there's a risk that everything you read will feel overwhelming.

That is not the goal. In fact, it is perfectly normal when navigating a new leadership passage to have some areas where you need to embrace new mindsets and professional identities, change how you spend your time, and practice new skills. The purpose of outlining these shifts isn't for new leaders to give themselves a grade, especially one based on where they are 6 to 12 months into the role. Rather, the purpose is to give new leaders (and experienced ones) a clear marker of where they're trying to go. Maybe you have a skill gap or need to dramatically shift how you spend your time. The question is "What are you going to do in the next 6 to 12 months to set things up for greater effectiveness?" Instead of grading yourself, use the shifts to diagnose where you need to evolve or grow—just one or two things to start—and then take action to get there.

Think about a leader (or a student) who you have mentored or coached in your career, someone with great potential but who was really struggling to develop a new skill or mindset. They come to you, discouraged, not sure if they're cut out for this new challenge. What would you say to them? Stop and write it down before you keep reading.

What did you write?

That's the same advice that you should be offering yourself. Too often we say negative things to ourselves that we would *never* say to people who we believe in and care about. That has to change.

You deserve and need the same compassion and encouragement that you would offer anyone else. Keep your focus on getting better, not being perfect.

PICK A PLACE TO START AND CHIP AWAY AT IT

Odds are, at any one time, you have a long list of things that you'd like to learn or get better at. Have you ever tried tackling the whole list at once? New Year's Resolutions, maybe? How did that work out? For most people, the answer is "not very well." As you read through the subsequent chapters, you may develop a list of things that you want to work on or think about. Great—make your full list. And then, pick *a few* things that you are going to focus on. Once you make progress on one, you can come back to your list and pick another one.

COMMIT TO PRACTICE

We want there to be some magical, easy formula for learning new skills. We want to be able to read a book, sleep on it, and change. Unfortunately, that's not how it works. We have to commit to lots and lots of practice, and effective practice doesn't entail being comfortable or achieving immediate success. What Daniel Coyle (2009) calls *deep practice* starts with our being very uncomfortable. It requires us to be operating at or just outside the edge of our zone of competence. We must break the new skill down into small parts, repeated again and again. The work of learning a new skill doesn't happen in private, where no one will see us struggle or make mistakes. For best results, we need to practice with the support of a coach. We need people to help us see the corrections we need to make and to provide accountability and encouragement. Without this kind of practice, we won't get better.

RECOGNIZE AND NAME YOUR TRIGGERS

Linda A. Hill (2019), in her work studying leaders experiencing a career transition, observed that leaders tend to regress to old behaviors and mindsets in response to specific triggers such as insecurity and defensiveness. In these moments, they lean into old behaviors and mindsets because those mindsets provide comfort, a sense of mastery or control, approval, or instant gratification. As you begin scripting new behaviors, pay attention to the triggers that are most likely to trip you up. Naming the triggers can enable you to spot them and replace old behaviors with new ones.

In *The Coaching Habit* (2016), Michael Bungay Stanier uses a simple but powerful formula for building new habits. You identify the trigger and what habit it prompts. Then you define a new behavior. *When (insert trigger) happens, instead of (insert old habit), I will (insert new behavior).* The formula recognizes that building a new behavior or mindset isn't just about starting something new; it is also about leaving an old behavior or mindset behind.

WATCH OUT FOR THE "EXCESSIVE NEED TO BE ME"

This is another Marshall Goldsmith (2007) mantra. Here's what an "excessive need to be me" sounds like: *I can't do that (e.g., long-term planning). I'm not good at planning or anything that involves organization. My genius is my spontaneous creativity.* When we identify the essence of who we are with our behaviors, it provides a defensive moat "protecting" us from change and preventing us from changing and growing.

If you hear this in your mental narrative, remember that this is just a fixed mindset in disguise. You surely can learn new skills, build new habits, and change your approach. And you won't lose yourself in the process. You'll still have all the strengths that you love about yourself. You'll just have a wider range of ways of authentically expressing them and executing your leadership responsibilities.

RECOGNIZE WHAT'S TEMPORARY (I.E., MOST THINGS)

A leadership transition requires a few fundamental things: learning new skills, thinking in new ways, changing how you think about yourself, and building new habits. Those are taxing and stressful experiences. One of the most powerful tools that you have in finding a positive orientation to that stress is to remember that leadership transitions are temporary (Hill, 2019). You won't feel this way forever. In six months or a year, many of the things that are hard for you now will be easy. Many of the things that are unfamiliar now will be comfortable.

Navy SEAL selection and training (Basic Underwater Demolition/SEAL training or BUD/S) features prominently in Admiral William McRaven's many books on leadership. He describes it as a crucible experience. To those of us who haven't lived through it, the experience is hard to fathom, a relentless test of candidates' mental, physical, emotional, and spiritual strength and resolve. The candidates who enter BUD/S, called "tadpoles," are an elite group drawn from the best of the best. Only 20% complete the training, becoming Frogmen (or Frogwomen). In *Sea Stories* (2019), McRaven reveals the secret to successfully completing SEAL training: the people who finish just don't quit. When I read it, I thought, *That's completely unhelpful*. But then, he elaborated:

> Most BUD/S trainees dropped out because their event horizon was too far in the distance. They struggled not with the problem of the moment, but with what they perceived would be an endless series of problems, which they believed they couldn't overcome. When you tackled just one problem, one event, or, in the vernacular of BUD/S training, one evolution at a time, then the difficult became manageable. Like many things in life, success in BUD/S didn't always go to the strongest, the fastest, or the smartest. It went to the [person] who faltered, who

failed, who stumbled, but who persevered, who got up and kept moving. Always moving forward, one evolution at a time. (p. 38)

Approach this leadership transition with a "one evolution at a time" mindset. It will change the game for you.

STAY ANCHORED IN PURPOSE

It takes courage to learn. It takes energy to persist in doing hard things. The fuel to do both will come from your purpose. When you feel stuck or discouraged, remind yourself why you became an educator in the first place—the mission that led you to this work. And remember why you decided to take on this new leadership role. You did it because you believed that you could make a positive difference—could do more to advance that mission. That's your source of fuel and your compass. When you feel lost in the forest of this transition, come back to your mission statement.

EXERCISE 5.B

Reflection Questions for Leaders Navigating a Career Passage

With the eight practices or mindsets that help leaders navigate a transition in mind, answer these questions:

- Which do you see as your established strengths?
- Which one or two do you need to be more intentional about?
- Write down your commitment to yourself during this transition.

Consider how you can find support in this area as you navigate this transition.

- If you have a coach or manager, consider sharing this area of focus with them.
- If you don't have a coach you can lean on, is there a peer or another trusted person in your life who can encourage you and hold you accountable?

FOR COACHES AND THOSE SUPPORTING LEADERS NAVIGATING A TRANSITION

If you are coaching, managing, supporting, or leading an individual in a new role, you play a critical role in helping them make the shifts. There are four things that you need to do to help them succeed.

DEFINE AND CLARIFY

Your first job as a coach, manager, or supporter of a leader navigating a career passage is to help them understand the shift they need to make to succeed in their new role. We aren't talking about a job description or a long list of tasks. These well-intentioned documents tend to obscure the most important shifts. That's because

- they're a mishmash of new and existing responsibilities and skills;
- they don't explicitly name the underlying habits, mindsets, or approaches—especially time and professional identity shifts—that will enable a leader's success; and
- they're just way, way too long.

Instead, use the key shifts to help them understand the most important things that they need to stop, start, or change to succeed in their new role. This conversation should be an explicit part of a leader's on-boarding to a new role. Then, you can revisit how the leader is experiencing and understanding the shift on a monthly or quarterly basis. The goal is for a new leader to be able to articulate how this new role is different from their prior one. At first, they may just rely on the language that you provide. But, over time, the leader will be able to translate the ideas into their own words and generate their own insights about the skills they need to develop, how they need to shift their time, and the mindsets and professional identities that are holding them back.

FOCUS AND PRIORITIZE

Compared to a traditional job description, the key shifts are very lean. However, 8 to 10 things are still way too many things to ask a new leader to focus on. It's likely to be overwhelming and discouraging. It's also ineffective. Your role is to help the leader that you are supporting identify a few (one to three) things that they are going to focus on starting, stopping, or changing consistently. There are a few ways to prioritize, using your knowledge of the leader you are coaching and the specific shifts of the leadership passage they are navigating.

- Find the "high-leverage" shift—the one shift in professional identity, time, or skills that will make the biggest difference on its own or will unlock the rest—and focus on that.
- Address limiting behaviors or mindsets that put the leader's success at risk, could undermine their credibility, or could create early setbacks that are hard to recover from.
- Find a quick win that will generate momentum and build the leader's confidence.

ENCOURAGE AND ELEVATE

In *Hidden Potential* (2023), Adam Grant describes the influence that other people's expectations have on what we achieve. The expectations of credible people—people who we trust and admire, who have expertise and experience in our field—are especially powerful. Whether credible people believe in us or doubt us, those expectations tend to become self-fulfilling prophecies.

> When others believe in our potential, they give us a ladder. They elevate our aspirations and enable us to reach higher peaks. Dozens of experiments show that at work, when leaders hold high expectations, employees generally work harder, learn more, and perform better. . . . Whereas high expectations offer support for us to climb, low expectations tend to hold us back—it feels like our boots are made of lead. It's called the Golem effect: when others underestimate us, it limits our effort and growth. (p. 142)

Navigating a leadership passage is difficult. Individuals who are elevated to new leadership roles tend to have established track records of success and exceptional performance. Moving into a role that requires new mindsets and behaviors from them can be unsettling. It's uncomfortable. It's exhausting. And it can introduce self-doubt.

When that doubt creeps in, it's tempting to revert back to old behaviors and tasks: *I may not be confident doing that, but look how good I am at THIS. I'm still the best at THIS.* Though these reversions may be comforting, they aren't what the new leader needs. What they need is to persist in the new behaviors and to tolerate the discomfort that comes with growth and change.

You can help a new leader persist in this uncomfortable space. You can normalize their experience by saying things such as *I know this feels uncomfortable. But that doesn't mean it's bad or that you aren't cut out for this. This is a normal way to feel when we're navigating a leadership passage. This is what growth feels like.* You can help them see the progress that they are making. And you can express your belief in them: Give them the boost to believe in themselves and to do the hard work they need to do to succeed.

SCAFFOLD, BUT DON'T RESCUE

As leaders are working to establish new professional identities, evolve their time applications and horizons, and learn new skills, they will likely need scaffolding. But the scaffolding must be temporary. It is hard to watch a person struggle. But it's especially difficult when you're in a $2X + \frac{1}{2}Y$ situation: it is going to take you twice as long to coach this person (2X) as it would to just address the issue yourself and the outcome is going to be half as good ($\frac{1}{2}Y$).

In these situations, you really need to monitor your scaffolding to make sure that you aren't the one who's sliding down to a previous leadership level and reverting to old, comfortable behaviors. Is my support designed to help this person learn and grow? Or am I choosing expedience or what makes me most comfortable in the short term?

If you are intentionally choosing to take on leadership behaviors or responsibilities on a short-term basis in order to model, teach, or support a new leader, you need to clearly define when and how you will remove these scaffolds. If you can't do that, you are probably fooling yourself. And you're setting yourself, your team, and your school up for challenges.

EXERCISE 5.C

Reflection Questions for Coaches and Managers

As you support a leader navigating a career transition, we recommend working through these questions, using Chapters 6 through 8 as a resource.

1. Define and Clarify: Does the leader I am supporting understand what is different about this leadership role versus their prior role (skills, time, and professional identity)? Can they describe what they need to stop doing and what they need to start doing?
2. Focus and Prioritize: What are their strengths and growth opportunities in terms of the key shifts? If there are several growth areas, what is the most important one or two or us to focus on (high leverage, limiting behavior, or quick win)?
3. Encourage and Elevate: How can I normalize the tension and discomfort they may be feeling? How can I encourage them and help them see the progress they're making?
4. Scaffold but Don't Rescue: If I am pushing in support, do I have a plan for how I will release the work to the leader? Do I have a concrete date for when I will remove scaffolding?

YOUR LEADERSHIP PASSAGE

Leaders and coaches: With all of that in mind, you're ready to dive into the three school leadership passages. In each chapter, we will unpack the shifts in skills, the changes in time application and time horizon, and the shifts in professional identity required at each level. We have a gravitational pull toward the skill shifts—they feel concrete and tangible—but we can't skip over the essential changes in our mindset and how we spend our time.

You may be tempted to jump straight to your current leadership passage, and you are certainly welcome to do that. But, if you have the time, we encourage you to review the passages in order. You might notice that there are a few shifts of previous passages that you are still struggling with. That's not unusual, especially if leaders have skipped a passage or two. There's nothing wrong with working on a shift from a previous leadership passage if you need to.

At the end of Chapters 6, 7, and 8, you'll find a self-assessment. When you get to the chapter that reflects your current leadership level or transition, it will invite you to reflect on how you are navigating each shift in skills, time, and professional identity. Then, you will find a tool to help you prioritize your focus and action planning templates to map out your next steps. Throughout Chapters 6, 7, and 8, you will find reflection questions, exercises, and resources. Do not feel like you need to complete each one as you read the chapter for the first time. After you complete your self-assessment and prioritize your focus, your action planning templates will help you identify which reflection questions, exercises, or resources will be most useful to you. Embrace and accept discomfort, prioritize and chip away, commit to practice, and be kind and patient with yourself.

Big Ideas and Key Takeaways

- Feeling some friction when we navigate a new leadership passage is normal and healthy.
- It is often easier to identify where a new leader is "stuck"—struggling to make one or more key shifts—than it is to diagnose why.
- Skill issues are tackled with knowledge-building, practice, training, and mentorship.
- Shifts in time are about both time applications (what and how leaders spend it) and time horizons. Team Members have the shortest time horizons and School Leaders must have a multiyear view.
- If a leader is dealing with a professional identity shift—high levels of discomfort, lack of motivation, deep resistance—there are two ways to tackle it: prolonged trial period or reframe with purpose.
- As leaders navigate a transition, embrace discomfort, be patient, embrace practice, and chip away at it.

CHAPTER 6

Team Member to Team Leader

Most school-based Team Leaders are "player-coaches." Though more than 50% of their time is dedicated to delivering results through others (coach role), they continue to retain some teaching responsibilities (player role). The subtle transition from player to player-coach requires big changes in professional identity, time applications and horizon, and skills.

FIGURE 6.1 • Key Shifts for Team Leaders

LEADERSHIP PASSAGE 1 Team Member to Team Leader		
Unique Leadership Mission	**DELIVER RESULTS** • Ensure every Team Member understands campus vision and definition of high-quality instruction. • Establish data-informed team priorities and goals. • Track progress and drive continuous improvement. • Remove barriers and make recommendations for school-wide improvement efforts.	**BUILD CAPACITY** • Coach and develop Team Members. • Build and maintain an effective team and facilitate collaboration. • Ensure coherence of support (professional development, coaching, evaluation, etc.) for Team Members. • Understand and use protocols in support of school-wide consistency and alignment.
Shift in Skills	• Build strong, trusting relationships with and between team members. • Develop Team Members. • Build a strong team and ensure members work well together.	
Shift in Time	*Time Application* • Managing will take more time than individual work. • Make time for others. *Time Horizon* Think in terms of semesters or longer rather than days or weeks.	
Shift in Professional Identity	• Others' success is a priority. • Discuss, don't just do. • Be comfortable with authority.	

This chapter will support Team Members as they make the transition to Team Leader. For this transition, we'll start at the foundation—with professional identity—and then work our way up to shifts in time applications and skills.

SHIFTING PROFESSIONAL IDENTITY

As a Team Member, your professional success was driven by your expertise and personal effectiveness—your knowledge of curriculum and content, instructional skill, understanding of child development, and ability to build a joyful culture of belonging in your classroom. It was also rooted in your ability to get things done and produce results. You were a doer.

Now, to succeed as a Team Leader, you are going to adapt your professional identity in three ways—you must prioritize others' success; value discussing, not just doing; and get comfortable with having authority.

PROFESSIONAL IDENTITY SHIFT 1: OTHERS' SUCCESS

Imagine this scenario. You're on a grade-level team with five other teachers. Three of them are first-year teachers and the others just switched grade levels. In your Professional learning community (PLC) meeting, you review data from the latest formative assessment. First, you look at your class: They're on track for two years' worth of academic growth and the number of students who are demonstrating proficiency has doubled. Then, you scan the results for the grade level as a whole. Across the board, students are barely on track to make one year's worth of growth. Proficiency has stagnated. How do you feel?

If you're a Team Member, you feel great. You've worked hard to deliver those results. You spent the summer learning the new literacy curriculum, you've changed how you are approaching your lesson design, and you've used data to drive adjustments from week to week. You're proud of what you've accomplished. You're willing to help your colleagues if they're interested—but that's up to them. But, if you're a Team Leader, these data aren't cause for celebration. You're glad to see the growth that your assigned students are demonstrating, but you know that it's your job to help your team succeed with all your students. Clearly, you have more work to do.

I'm willing to bet that 99% of us identify as team players. We believe there's "no I in team" and we care about other people's success. But when we go home at night and talk about things that we are proud of, we don't tell our friends or loved ones about the awesome lesson our colleague delivered—we talk about the lesson *we* designed, the way *we* knocked your presentation out of the park, the smart thing *we* said in that team meeting.

There's nothing wrong with being proud of the great work you do. It's normal and healthy. But when you transition to a Team Leader, what matters the most is the success of the people around you. Your job is to set them up to be their best and to grow. If new Team Leaders don't make this internal shift, it will show up in how they spend their time: they will continue to prioritize their own work versus the team's work (more on that later). It will also show up in other little ways that can undermine their effectiveness as a coach and team leader.

When we are driven by a desire to be recognized for our individual contributions, how much we know, how skilled we are, and what our results are, it can perpetuate bad habits. Marshall Goldsmith (2007) highlights 20 habits that leaders often need to break to maximize their effectiveness. Three are likely to rear their heads when our identity is anchored in our individual contributions versus the success of our team: "adding too much value," "telling the world how smart we are," and "winning too much" (p. 40).

- *Adding too much value*—even when your colleagues have a good idea or suggestion, you think it's your job as the leader to make it even better. You think that's what makes you credible.
- *Telling the world how smart we are*—yes, you are in this role because you have insight and expertise to offer. But you don't need to constantly demonstrate it. Your job is to find and amplify the ideas and perspectives of your colleagues—to build their confidence.
- *Winning too much*—the need to be right, all the time. Watch out if you view discussions as competitions or a test of your leadership or authority. You might be right. But the question is do you need to win? Does it really matter? If it doesn't matter, let it go.

These habits may not have hurt you as Team Members, but they can be kryptonite in your efforts to lead others. If you find yourself struggling with these mindsets, it might be a sign that you are still navigating the shift from taking pride in having your own expertise and accomplishments recognized to taking pride in the capability and success of your teammates.

EXERCISE 6.A

Reflect and Commit on the Shift to Prioritizing Others' Success

- When you reflect on the accomplishments you're proud of, notice whether they are your individual achievements or the success of your team.
- Dedicate time to noticing your colleagues' success and growth. (This might take just 15 minutes a week!) After you celebrate your colleagues for their successes, take time, on your own, to reflect on the actions you took and time you invested to help them succeed.

PROFESSIONAL IDENTITY SHIFT 2: DISCUSSING, NOT JUST DOING

Meetings have a bad reputation. They're known as a waste of time, a lot of talk, no action, and no outcomes. Too often, you leave thinking, *There's an hour of my life I can never get back*, or *Think of all the lesson planning I could have done*. As an effective Team Member, you probably learned to protect and prioritize the time you needed to think, design, and plan. You lived by the mantra "Less Talk, More Action."

Well, I have some bad news for you. Sometimes, as a Team Leader, you're going to have to make time for some good old-fashioned talking. Now, there's good news too—you can make the meetings you lead and participate in effective and keep conversations kid-focused and action-oriented. But sometimes you're going to need to value *discussions* that aren't about making decisions or getting things done.

Discussions help to build shared vision. They help everyone understand what the destination looks like and how we're going to get there (Senge, 2006). They create the shared language and alignment that individuals and teams need to work effectively together. You must view leading and participating in discussions as part of your work—not a distraction from it.

PROFESSIONAL IDENTITY SHIFT 3: COMFORT WITH AUTHORITY

Many educators make the transition from Team Member to Team Leader without changing their school. They may not even change teams. Usually, consistency is a helpful condition for humans.

Constants provide comfort and stability. We can fall back on the familiar while we adapt to what's new. But in this case, consistency can be a trap. It hides a major change and can set us up for challenges. Everything may look the same on the surface, but the tectonic plates of our relationships are shifting.

Yesterday, you were "one of the teachers." Rolling your eyes or complaining about the "leadership" (or laughing at your colleagues while they did) helped you connect with your peers and sometimes made you feel better. Now, you're the leadership. Overnight, your relationships with your colleagues—even (especially) long-time friends—are different. You are now a person with authority. This is true whether you embrace it or not. You can't change how your colleagues react to this shift: Some may be more guarded or distant, some may challenge or test you, and some may pretend like nothing has changed. But you must think about how you will orient toward and enact your authority. Avoid being too hesitant or domineering (Green & Hauser, 2012).

Some new Team Leaders will be too worried about being nice or being liked, which will keep them from setting high expectations, having hard conversations, giving direct feedback, or making unpopular decisions. Some teachers may resist coaching, feedback, and support from a new Team Leader, especially if they were a colleague just a few months ago. Hesitant new Team Leaders will respond to this resistance by accommodating it. They will say things like "I'm not here to give you feedback or coach you; I'm just here to be a support" or "This is just a suggestion—you don't have to listen to it." Yes, there may be some situations where you offer suggestions and encourage your colleagues to prioritize what is most helpful for them. But if you frame your entire relationship as optional, you are undermining yourself and decreasing the likelihood that you will succeed in supporting your colleagues to improve their practice and outcomes.

Domineering leaders have the opposite problem. When they face resistance or challenges, they get defensive or may become aggressive. They don't listen to other people's perspectives and experience every question, comment, or challenge as a threat to their authority. They create a toxic, unproductive culture.

Domineering and hesitant leaders may look like polar opposites, but they have a few important things in common. First, they're not effective. Neither approach will help you achieve results with your team. Second, they both spring from either insecurity or a vacuum of how to embody authority in a healthy and values-aligned way. What's in between the two? Green and Hauser (2012) encourage new leaders to find a healthy assertiveness: direct, calm, open, fair, and comfortable with their role. They describe the best managers as people who "see their authority as simply one more tool for getting things done. It's neither something that makes them nervous nor something that they lord over others" (p. 191).

If you're feeling uncomfortable with all this talk about authority, there is good news for you. It is true that you have moved into a position with some authority and that this will change your relationships with your former colleagues. But the fact is that your authority alone won't help you get very much done. What will really matter is your ability to build and deploy your influence (Hill, 2019). It may take you some time to embrace and get comfortable with this new professional identity and that's OK. One of the best things that you can do to get off to a good start and accelerate your progress is to actively name your beliefs, commitments, and approach. Two different resources can help: crafting a Leadership Point of View and developing a User's Manual (see Exercises 6.B and 6.C).

Eventually, you'll want to share your story, beliefs, and way of operating with your team. It's a great opportunity for them to know who you are, what drives you, and what to expect. But this isn't a one-way exercise. By inviting them to share their Leadership Point of View and User's Manual at the same time, you also have an opportunity to get to know them better, build your relationship, and identify how you can tailor your approach to working together.

EXERCISES 6.B AND 6.C

Creating Your Leadership Point of View and User's Manual

A Leadership Point of View, a tool created by Ken and Margie Blanchard, is an invitation to craft and share your beliefs about leadership and your values. As you shape it, you will think about the stories and experiences that have shaped who you are and how you lead. A User's Manual invites you to get clear on how you operate and work with others. It isn't just an exercise where you talk about your ideals. It provides an opportunity to get real about some of your quirks and weaknesses.

As a new leader, spend some time drafting your Leadership Point of View and your User's Manual. Then, share them with a few people who know you well, who you trust, and who will be honest with you. Ask them "Does this read as truthful and accurate? Is this what I'm really like?" Use their feedback to refine what you've written and clarify, in writing and in your own mind, which elements are still aspirational. That doesn't mean you can't include them; it just changes the framing from "This is how I operate" to "This is how I aspire to be. I'm still working to get there, and I hope you'll help me identify how I can keep getting better."

EXERCISE 6.B

Your Leadership Point of View

Ken Blanchard (n.d.) describes a Leadership Point of View as a relatively short (ideally five minutes or less) elevator pitch that helps people understand who you are as a leader—your story, your values, what motivates you, and what you expect from others. Here are a few reflection questions that may help you refine and articulate your story:

1. What are your top three to five values as a leader?
2. What shaped these values? Who are your heroes? What key experiences or stories led you to these values?
3. What can people expect from you? What do you expect from others?

As you reflect on these questions, you'll likely identify more ideas than you can fit into five minutes. Spend some time editing and refining your thinking. Focus on what is most important for others to know about who you are and what your leadership is like.

EXERCISE 6.C

Your User's Manual

We were first introduced to the User's Manual by Hitendra Wadhwa at Mentora Institute. A quick Google search will turn up lots of results, forms, and questions. This is our take on the tool and some reflection questions to get you started:

1. What energizes you about your work?
2. What brings out your best work? What motivates you?
3. What is demotivating or hampers your ability to do your best work?
4. What is the most effective way for people to give you feedback? How do you prefer to share feedback?
5. How do you respond to conflict?
6. Do you have any pet peeves at work?

(Continued)

(Continued)

7. What do you see as your top strengths? What are your weaknesses or areas you're working to improve?
8. What else do you think people should know about you? Are there any misperceptions you want to clarify?
9. How do you like to communicate and collaborate with Team Members? How do you show up in meetings?

These questions are just a jump start. You don't have to answer all of them, and you don't have to restrict yourself to them. The goal is to identify the most important things that your teammates need to know about you and how you operate.

The transition from Team Member to Team Leader requires a significant shift in professional identity. New Team Leaders must embrace a focus on others' success; they must value discussing, not just doing; and they must develop comfort with having some formal authority. Making these transitions will allow new leaders to enjoy and embrace their new role. It also sets them up for success—creating the conditions for them to shift how they spend their time.

SHIFTING TIME ALLOCATIONS

New Team Leaders must be disciplined in prioritizing the work of leading others. They also must come to accept and embrace interruptions and the need to be responsive to the needs of their team. Over time, Team Leaders will work to extend the time horizon of their planning from weeks or months to semesters.

TIME SHIFT 1: MANAGING > INDIVIDUAL WORK

There is going to be a gravitational pull toward your old work over your new work. Returning to the player-coach analogy, you'll be drawn to your player duties over your coach duties. Your habits and routines will anchor you there, and you will gravitate toward it because it is comfortable. You are good at this work, and doing things we're good at bolsters our confidence. In contrast, your new Team Leader work may feel more ambiguous (*How do I get started?*) or more daunting (*I'm not sure I know what I'm doing*).

You will never figure it out, build the skills, or get more comfortable with this new work if you don't spend time on it. You must proactively commit to a time allocation that ensures your Team Leader work doesn't always come last. Establish an ideal time allocation up front, build your calendar around it, and actively reflect on whether you're sticking with it. You can lean on your manager or coach for accountability.

EXERCISE 6.D

Team Leader Calendar Audit

STEP 1: Do you use a calendar to plan and organize your time each week? If you don't, this is an important practice for you. If you need help getting started, check out Maia Heyck-Merlin and The Together Group.

STEP 2: Assuming you keep a calendar, does it reflect how you actually spend your time? If not, take a few minutes to reconstruct how you spent your time in the last week.

STEP 3: Color code your calendar to reflect your player-coach responsibilities.

- Delivering instruction, planning your lessons, grading student work, and all the things you do to directly impact student learning—mark those in one color.
- Then, mark all the ways that you spend your time executing your unique leadership mission as a Team Leader (see Figure 6.1) in a different color.
- What's the ratio of your time? Is it close to 50/50?

STEP 4: If you're spending most of your time as a Team Member, try proactively building a different calendar for the week ahead.

- Start with your non-negotiable responsibilities—instructional delivery, meetings you are committed to, etc.
- Next, add your Team Leader commitments. When will you plan for your grade-level meeting? When will you spend time observing and coaching each Team Member?
- If you're struggling, reach out to a coach or mentor for support. You may need to make this shift little by little.

TIME SHIFT 2: MAKING TIME FOR OTHERS

In her seminal book on first time Team Leaders, Linda A. Hill (2019) describes the shift as a personal transformation, one that she compares to parenting. To some, that might sound like a stretch. But it is an apt metaphor, particularly when it comes to how new Team Leaders experience their time. For most Team Leaders, like new parents, the transition is like a rupture—a clear divide between the old and the new. You may need to actively anchor yourself in your why—the bigger purpose and opportunity—until you come to enjoy the new things more and miss the old things less. And you may just need to give yourself space, as Hill encourages, to "learn to live with the pace, the brevity, and interruptions" (p. 180).

Now, this doesn't mean that you must always be available to your team. It is important for you to proactively plan your time. And some of your time blocks will likely be for focus time dedicated to planning. It is a good idea to be intentional about when and where you take this focused time. You might choose to schedule it during a time of day when you are less likely to be interrupted or to have a special location where you do this work so that your team understands when you are available and when you are not (unless it's a really mission-critical interruption). But you can't build a schedule that is 90% focused or unavailable time. Being available and responsive is part of your role. Expect it. Plan for it.

EXERCISE 6.E

Planning for Interruptions *and* for Focus

Go back to your calendar from Exercise 6.D (either your real calendar or your ideal planned calendar):

- Pay special attention to your work blocks, those times when you are not working directly with a teacher or a student. Count how many hours of work time you have in your schedule.
- What percentage of that work time do you think of as "office hours" (when you are prepared to be interrupted and responsive to your colleagues), and what percentage do you think of as focus time? If you are counting on 100% focus time, you are setting yourself up to be frustrated.
- Consider the work for which you need to be uninterrupted to do well. Consider when you schedule this work and where (physically) you work during these times. Is there a different time or place to schedule this uninterrupted time?
- Now, think about how you can reframe some of your work time as more flexible office hours. Consider being explicit with your colleagues about when you have these office hours, and work from an easily accessible location during those times.

TIME SHIFT 3: THINK IN SEMESTERS, MORE THAN DAYS OR WEEKS

Have you ever been on a team where meetings seem to lurch week to week from one random topic to a new pressing issue to another ad hoc agenda item, most of them requiring an immediate response or action? All the zig-zagging leaves you a bit dizzy. You never know what to expect, and you also don't feel like you're making any real progress. You're definitely not tackling the deeper work. Over time, most Team Members disengage or check out. You're all happy to be helpful when you can, but you don't really know what the point of these meetings are and they don't seem like a good use of your time and energy. Most of us have had this experience at some point in our working lives.

You are in a position to ensure that this isn't *your* team's experience. One of the most important things you can do to avoid this outcome is to think about your team's work and priorities over a longer time horizon—in semesters or even calendar years. Taking the long view will help you

- identify the most important work for your team,
- stage and sequence necessary work (yes, there are some things you just have to do) so that it doesn't feel like constant whack-a-mole, and
- help your team see how your regular meetings fit into the bigger picture and help the team progress and improve.

It's like a scope and sequence for adults. But don't be discouraged if it takes you a little time to consistently operate with this longer view. Part of the adjustment will be learning to incorporate some of the broader campus rhythms that may not have been as visible or prominent to you as a Team Member. Be patient with yourself and seek the context and missing information you need. But push yourself to see, plan, and think as far down the road as you can.

EXERCISE 6.F

Extending Your Time Horizon

1. Do you have a "scope and sequence" for your team meetings and professional learning times? If so, how far out does it go?
2. If you're still living meeting to meeting, set a realistic goal for where you want to be with your planning by the end of the quarter or the end of the semester.
3. Then, go back to your calendar. Have you dedicated enough time to doing this thinking and planning?
4. Are there any resources you can find to help you? Is there an experienced Team Leader who can share their approach to planning and tools they use?

As we have unpacked how time allocations shift, it is important to distinguish between quantity (*Am I spending my time on the right things?*) and quality (*Am I doing those things well and effectively?*). Our time allocations help us notice if we are prioritizing the right things. But we can have perfect time allocations and still miss the mark. That's where skills come into the mix.

SHIFTING SKILLS

With the shifts in professional identity and time in place, new Team Leaders must work to master a few big shifts in skills. Team Leaders have two major levers for delivering results through others. The first is to work with Team Members individually to help them grow, providing feedback, modeling or teaching new practices, and helping them drive improvement. The second is facilitating the work and collaboration of the team. Each of these levers requires new skills to be developed and put into practice. The foundation for both requires a third key skill—building trusting relationships. Because it's the foundation for everything else, that is where we'll start.

SKILL SHIFT 1: BUILD STRONG, TRUSTING RELATIONSHIPS

Building strong relationships can be boiled down to a three-part formula:

1. You (the leader) need to know them (your team).
2. They need to know who you are.
3. They need to know and believe that you care about them and their success.

It's a pretty similar formula to what great teachers use with their students. And yet, sometimes what we know to do with kids doesn't translate into our approach to working with adults. Why? For starters, we sometimes just take the relationship building for granted. We either don't think it matters very much (*Come on, we're all adults*), or we think we've already done it, especially if we're now leading a team of our former colleagues. We might think, *We know each other! They know me! They know I care!*

But how well do you really know your Team Members (Exercise 6.G)? Understanding your Team Members deeply is essential to figuring out how to work with them most effectively: how to motivate them, how to influence them, how to avoid getting off on the wrong foot. My guess is that even if you've been working with your team for a few years as peers, you may not know the answers to all of these questions (or at least you should double-check). And even if you spend some time asking these questions and confirm that you know *every single thing*, it still won't be a waste of time and energy. Why? Because it's a really easy first step to demonstrate that you care about them and their success!

EXERCISE 6.G

Knowing Your Team Members

For each of your Team Members, do you know the answers to the following questions?

- What is their professional story? What brought them to your school? How do their previous experiences shape their work and approach?
- What is important to them outside of work (family, civic engagement, hobbies, etc.)?
- What are their mindsets around feedback? Have they had good experiences with feedback? How do they prefer to receive feedback?
- What motivates them at work on a daily basis? What discourages them?
- What do they currently view as their top strengths, and which areas are they working to grow or improve?
- What are their long-term goals, aspirations, or motivations (professionally and personally)?

Turning the tables, even if your Team Members know you well *personally*, they don't know you *as a leader/manager*. Most new leaders understand intuitively that they need to establish themselves as credible. But they often focus on the wrong things, for example, on their *technical* competence, as the foundation of their credibility. To be clear, teachers *do* care about your technical competence: Do you know your content? Are you skilled instructionally? Do you build a thriving classroom community? But when evaluating your credibility as their *leader*, they want to know what your motives are and whether you care about them.

In the first few months of these new relationships, your team isn't trying to figure out if you're capable; rather, they're trying to figure out if they can trust you. Your team needs to know the answers to these questions:

- Why are you in this leadership role? What's your purpose? What motivates you?
- What are your goals? How will you measure success?
- How will you behave?

Your Leadership Point of View (Exercise 6.B) can be one way to formally share who you are with your team. But ultimately, your team will be listening and watching—because this will be about words and actions—for whether you care about them, believe in them, and want what's best for them.

SKILL SHIFT 2: DEVELOPING TEAM MEMBERS

At its core, your job is to ensure that each of your teachers delivers excellent results by helping them to grow and become more effective. To do this, you must

- set the destination—establish a clear definition for what excellent instruction looks like;
- find your blinking blue "You are here" dot—ensure each Team Member understands how their practice stacks up to that bar of excellence; and
- navigate the journey—help them improve.

SET THE DESTINATION

Resist the temptation to dive right in to helping your Team Members improve without taking the time to confirm where you are and where you're going. Setting the destination starts with you. Do you have a clear vision for what excellent instruction looks like in your school? When you walk into a classroom, what are you looking for or expecting to see? Ideally, this vision would be established at the school (or district) level and be shared by all leaders at every level. But, if you aren't sure if a vision has been established, this is a great question to ask the Bridge Leader who supports you. If your school hasn't done this work yet, you are going to need to get clear on the bar of excellence you are looking to build with your teachers. It anchors everything else you will do. Once you are clear, your job is to ensure that each Team Member, at minimum, understands and embraces the vision. You have a variety of tools in your toolkit from describing and defining, to showing (find a classroom where your teachers can see excellence in action), to modeling.

"YOU ARE HERE"

Now, where is each teacher relative to that target destination? You will assess this through your observations of each teacher's instruction, planning, and decision-making. Then, you will provide feedback, that is, concrete descriptions of what you are observing in their practice and how that compares to the bar for instructional excellence and student learning. In your conversations with each teacher, you will also be assessing their understanding and self-awareness of their current practice. If there is a significant gap between your assessments, you must work to close that gap.

NAVIGATE THE JOURNEY

And then the work of helping them improve begins. Many teachers, especially brand-new ones, may have a lot of miles to cover to get to the defined destination. Your job is to help them focus on the most important one or two things to start and then to keep progressing. No matter how much ground there is to cover, no one can improve if the list of things to accomplish is long. Attempting to do so is demoralizing.

It is easy to describe the process of setting the destination and navigating to get there, but it is hard to do. That's because the moves you need to make (the "how") will likely vary by Team Member. Most discussion of development strategies can be plotted on a spectrum based on how directive they are. The most directive development move is "telling"—sharing information or outlining what to do. In contrast, nondirective facilitation relies on listening, questioning, and playing back. To be clear, both—and the range of options in between—are important and helpful moves in developing others. However, in our well-intentioned efforts to define the work of coaching and developing our Team Members, we tend to oversimplify, sending the signal that there is one right way. Some resources are overreliant on directive strategies, implying that it's the one best way—it's fast, it's clear, and it can produce results and more consistency more quickly. Others glorify facilitative, nondirective moves as the ideal, highlighting their potential for capacity-building.

Presenting these moves as mutually exclusive—you are *either* directive *or* facilitative—does not set educational leaders up for success. Telling new Team Leaders that they should "only ask questions" sets them up for failure, especially if they are coaching a team of new teachers with limited knowledge, skill, or experience. It's like driving a group of seven people blindfolded deep into the woods, giving one person a map and a compass, and then dropping the group off with these instructions: *The person who has the map and compass is not to share it with the group. And they are only to ask the other six people questions, such as "Which way do you think we should go?" or "What do you want to try next?"* Directive moves—from teaching, explaining, and giving advice—will be powerful moves in Team Leaders' toolkits. But they aren't the only moves. We need to reframe this conversation. It isn't about one approach being the best in all situations.

The decision about which move to use isn't about the leader's preference or style. The decision is based on what is required by the task and the readiness of the person being coached or developed (readiness is defined as their ability and their willingness) (Center for Leadership Studies, 2017). Team Leaders will need more directive strategies—telling, explaining, advising—when the person they are developing has low readiness or is facing a highly complex or ambiguous task. These two conditions define the state of many new, inexperienced teachers. So, in a world where schools are onboarding greater shares of new, inexperienced teachers, we should expect Team Leaders to use more directive strategies often and effectively.

But Team Leaders don't stay in directive mode forever. They shift as they monitor the performance and progress of their Team Members. As Team Members learn and develop, the development moves can shift toward problem-solving or more facilitative coaching moves. If Team Members are regressing, the Team Leader needs to pivot. They may need to shift to problem-solving or facilitative moves to understand why the teacher is resisting the advice or direction they are receiving. Is there something they don't understand? Do they need a different kind of support to make progress? Or is there a breakdown in the relationship that is undermining their motivation or willingness to follow the direction they are receiving?

A RUDE AWAKENING: DON'T FOLLOW THE GOLDEN RULE

You have probably heard that the golden rule has been upstaged by the platinum rule. Treating other people the way you would want (or need) to be treated falls short—in life and in leadership—because other people are different from you in myriad ways. According to Linda A. Hill (2019), first-time managers are often "dumbfounded by their [Team Members'] diversity in talent, motivation, and temperament" (p. 117). In her research, she has found that first-time Team Leaders mistakenly assume that "they could use themselves as models" in understanding their Team Members (p. 118).

Team Leaders must get to know their Team Members—what motivates and inspires them, what frustrates and shuts them down, how their personal and professional experience shapes their approach and priorities—in order to tailor their approach to the strengths and needs of each individual. That's why building relationships was the first skill shift highlighted in this chapter. In general, Team Leaders who were consistently strong teachers and were elevated for their skill and motivation need to also learn to accept one key way in which their Team Members will not be like them. Inevitably, many Team Members will have lower levels of skill and some may have lower levels of motivation. The faster Team Leaders get past their surprise or dismay about this reality, the faster they can figure out how to do their job—to find a way to help each Team Member grow and succeed.

PAY ATTENTION TO YOUR TONE

No matter what move you are making to support a Team Member's development, no Team Leader wants to be perceived as disrespectful, patronizing, or harsh. Some might think that erring on the facilitative side of the spectrum is the key to avoiding sounding like a jerk. Yes, overrelying on directive moves can have risks. But sometimes, how a new leader is perceived is less about their moves and more about something more subtle—their tone.

Often, new Team Leaders learn about a tone problem abruptly, through feedback from their Team Members. They might hear that they are coming across as "bossy" or that they are being disrespectful. The feedback often comes as a slap in the face. These adjectives are the opposite of the Leader of Others' intention. This might be the first time they've ever received feedback like this. Where does this come from? What has changed?

Imagine if an experienced kindergarten teacher transitioned to teaching high schoolers. Would the tone, volume, and cadence that the teacher had established with young learners translate, without any modifications, to these new students? It's possible, if not likely, that some of the moves that they found very effective with young learners might feel disrespectful to older students. The teacher will need to pay attention to how the new students react to them and be open to making adjustments. In the same way, some new Team Leaders may find that the tone that served them well in the classroom doesn't translate perfectly to their new work with their colleagues, and they may need to experiment with new approaches.

EXERCISE 6.H

Honing Developing Others' Practices

Set the destination.

- Are you clear on your (school's) vision for excellent instruction? Can you describe concretely what you are looking for?
- Is each Team Member clear on the vision? If not, how might you make it more tangible?
- Is each Team Member motivated by the vision? If they are skeptical, why? Is it because they don't think it's possible? Because they don't believe it will lead to results? Something else?

(Continued)

(Continued)

"You are here."

- Where is each Team Member's practice compared to the vision? What are examples of things they consistently do well? Where are concrete areas where they need to improve?
- Can each Team Member provide a similar assessment of their practice? If not, how will you build alignment (direct feedback, co-teaching to model, opportunities to observe a peer)?

Navigate the journey.

- Do you have a clear personal preference for how you approach coaching and support? Are you more confident with directive strategies? Or do you prefer more facilitative approaches?
- Consider each Team Member, their development priorities, and context. Which Team Members may need more directive strategies (low readiness, underdeveloped skill)? Which Team Members may need more facilitative strategies (high readiness, high skill)?
- What personal preferences or habits might be making you less effective?

The platinum rule and tone.

- In what ways might you be making assumptions about your Team Members' motivations and mindsets, using yourself as a model?
- Have you gotten any direct or indirect feedback about your tone? (Differences of opinion that escalate into big or personal conflict may be about tone.) Who do you trust to be honest with you about sensitive areas like the impact of your tone?

SKILL SHIFT 3: BUILD A STRONG TEAM AND ENSURE MEMBERS WORK WELL TOGETHER

Think back on all the grade-level or department teams you've been a member of. For each team, remember how you felt when you walked into the room where your meetings were held. My guess is that some teams produced dread, resignation, or preemptive exhaustion. Those meetings felt cold and mechanical. Everyone suffered politely, but the interactions were guarded, maybe even standoffish. Does this sound familiar?

But you've also had experiences with teams that generated different emotions: joy, energy, motivation. When you walked into the room to work with these colleagues, there was a level of comfort, like being "home" at school. You knew and trusted each other. And when you worked together, you made each other better teachers and got a return on the time you spent together. As a Team Leader with time dedicated to supporting your Team Members individually and as a group, you play a critical role in which kind of team yours will be—energy enhancing or energy sapping.

BUILD TEAM CULTURE

Daniel Coyle's *The Culture Code* (2018) is an inspiring and practical guide to the art of building great teams—the kind of teams where "two plus two equals ten" (p. xv). Coyle's formula for strong teams is simple:

- Safety—Team Members feel like they belong, can be themselves, and are connected to each other.
- Vulnerability—Team Members aren't trying to impress each other or protect themselves. They take risks—asking questions, challenging each other, accepting feedback—which is essential to learning, cooperation, and collaboration.
- Purpose—Team Members are united by shared goals, values, and norms.

Effective Team Leaders will make early investments in building the group's culture. But that work is never complete. One of my mentors describes culture as perishable. You can't set it and forget it. It needs continual tending to stay fresh. When Team Members experience belonging, are willing to take risks, and are united by a shared purpose, it feels good. But that isn't the reason to invest in team culture; rather, it's a wonderful side effect. The reason for investing in team culture is because it makes teams more effective. It's the only way to maximize the impact of a team's collaborative work.

LEAD EFFECTIVE MEETINGS

In addition to a strong culture, you also need to identify the most important work to do together and be disciplined about how you use your precious time to get it done. As a Team Leader, it is now your responsibility to ensure that the precious time that your team has to meet, work, and learn together is purposeful, focused, and productive. It is your responsibility to maximize the opportunity to help your team get better and to improve results.

I recently talked with an experienced classroom teacher who had been named the grade-level lead who said, "I had no idea how I should approach our meeting time. I think it's because most teachers have never been a part of an effective meeting. And we have rarely been given the opportunity to play an active role in meetings. We are expected to sit there, passively receiving information." So, how do you get started? Let's start with some good "meeting hygiene"—components of a successful meeting.

First, Team Leaders need to make sure that everyone is on the same page about the purpose of each recurring meeting. Most meetings have one or more basic purposes: to share updates or information, to promote learning or build capacity, to make decisions, or to support problem-solving or collaboration. Any of these are fine purposes, but everyone needs to understand what the purpose of any particular meeting is. Then, it is your job as the person who plans and facilitates the meeting to ensure that the design of the meeting matches the purpose.

Within the broad purpose ("Why do these weekly meetings exist?"), you will define the objectives, goals, or outcomes for each individual meeting. Initially, you may be setting your objectives week-to-week as you try to get to know your team, grasp what's most important, and respond to emergent needs. Ideally, and eventually, your objectives for individual meetings are part of a broader scope and sequence—the overarching priorities you are working toward over the quarter or semester with your team. One of the biggest challenges you will have will be focusing—choosing a small number of priorities and sticking with them, even though you may have a long list of things that you want to improve over time. Describing the arc for these recurring meetings helps your Team Members understand where the work is going and how it will benefit them. Having a longer-term plan also allows Team Members to prepare in advance by completing prework, submitting their part of the work for review, eventually taking the lead for some parts, all of which will increase the value of these relatively short and precious meetings.

I use the word *precious* deliberately. One of the scarcest and most valuable resources in a school building is time, particularly classroom teachers' time. Compared to their international counterparts, on average U.S. teachers work longer days, deliver more instructional minutes, and have less planning time. Every hour that your team meets with you is a *precious* hour (multiplied by the number of participants) that they could spend preparing for their next lessons, reviewing data, communicating with students' caregivers, or supporting student success in some other way. You get it—you were recently in their shoes and still face similar trade-offs and tensions in your new role.

One of the most important things you can do to maximize, over time, your impact in team meetings is to evaluate them through what Morten T. Hansen (2018) calls an *outside-in view*, focusing on "the *benefits* our work brings to others" as opposed to "whether we have completed our tasks and goals, regardless of whether they produce any benefits" (p. 48) for our team. Do your Team Members find the meetings you lead valuable? Or do they dread them—spending the entire time thinking about the more productive things they could be doing (or actively multitasking)? In addition to asking them for their feedback along the way, you can ask for their input up front.

EXERCISE 6.I

Strong Team Checklist

- How would you rate your team's culture? Are members connected, willing to let their guard down, and united by a common purpose?
- What investments have you made in building the team's culture? What might you try?
- Do your Team Members find your team's meetings valuable? What do they value the most? What do they think could be more impactful? How do you get their feedback?
- How do you engage your Bridge Leader for support on your long-term planning? What routines do you have to prepare for or debrief individual meetings? What additional support do you need?

PRIORITIZE AND CHIP AWAY

Team Leaders play an irreplaceable role in the school leadership architecture. They are the ones who provide the coaching and support that our teachers deserve. They are the ones who will improve instruction to help the school move, month after month, toward its vision. This chapter outlined the key shifts in professional identity, time, and skills that Team Leaders need to make to thrive in their role and maximize their impact.

If you are a Team Leader or a Team Member preparing for a transition, thank you for your work and your commitment to the success of your colleagues and your students. As you dug into these shifts in professional identity, time application, and skills, what stood out to you? You will find a self-assessment at the end of this chapter and tools to prioritize and plan your next steps in Appendix D. If you completed the self-assessment as you read, you may have a list of things you want to dig into further. If you haven't looked at the self-assessment yet, I encourage you to complete it, using the descriptions of the shifts in this chapter as a guide. If your self-assessment produces a long list of areas you want to grow, don't be discouraged. Remember: this is about progress over time.

Big Ideas and Key Takeaways

- Most school-based Team Leaders are "player-coaches." The transition from player to player-coach requires big changes in professional identity, time applications and horizon, and skills.
- To succeed, new Team Leaders must adapt their professional identity: prioritizing others' success; valuing discussion, not just doing; and developing comfort with having authority.
- New Team Leaders must come to accept and embrace interruptions and the need to be responsive to the needs of their team.
- Over time, Team Leaders will work to extend the time horizon of their planning from weeks or months to semesters.
- Building trusting relationships is the foundation for helping individual Team Members grow and for facilitating teamwork and collaboration.
- This is also the critical period where new leaders develop their stance for coaching and feedback and learn to build productive, collaborative teams.
- Follow the platinum rule: Instead of using themselves as a model, team leaders must learn to tailor their approach to the strengths and needs of each individual.
- Expect to find areas where you will need to grow.

CHAPTER 6 SELF-ASSESSMENT

As you read through the chapter, use this tool to capture your observations on how you are navigating each shift. Use a 1–4 scale:

1 = Never or rarely

2 = Sometimes

3 = Often

4 = Almost always

	PROFESSIONAL IDENTITY
________	I prioritize others' success. I feel as proud about their growth and accomplishment as I do my own.
________	I have embraced the importance of discussing and being available to my colleagues, even when it takes away time from getting things done.
________	I feel comfortable with the authority that comes with my new role and how it changes my interactions with my colleagues.
	TIME
________	I spend at least 50% of my time on my Team Leader work.
________	I don't view interruptions from my colleagues as a distraction from my "real work." I've intentionally built my schedule so I can be responsive.
________	I am thinking and planning with a semester (or longer) view.
	SKILLS
________	I have strong, trusting relationships with all of my Team Members.
	DEVELOP TEAM MEMBERS
________	I have a clear vision of what excellent instruction looks like at my school.
________	My Team Members understand what excellent instruction looks like.

(Continued)

(Continued)

SKILLS	
______________	I have diagnosed where each Team Member is relative to the vision, and I have identified the highest-priority two or three things for them to focus on strengthening.
______________	Through conversations, feedback, and professional learning, each Team Member understands where they are relative to the vision and the most important focus areas.
______________	I am comfortable, confident, and effective in delivering feedback to my team members.
______________	Each Team Member has an action plan to support their improvement (observation/coaching, modeling, shadowing, professional learning).
______________	I have structured my calendar to be able to prioritize supporting each Team Member (i.e., time application).
BUILD STRONG TEAMS	
______________	My team has a strong culture. We are connected, open, and united by a common purpose.
______________	Each recurring meeting has a clear purpose (share information, promote learning or capacity-building, make decisions, collaborate/problem-solve). My team understands the purpose of each meeting.
______________	I have a long-term plan (scope and sequence) for each team meeting outlining specific objectives and priorities.
______________	Our meetings prioritize the most important work/learning for my team (including aligning to their individual needs and action plans).
______________	My Team Members view our meetings as valuable and a good use of their time. I know because they have told me directly or I have asked them for their feedback and ideas on how our time could be more productive.
______________	I have enough dedicated time to plan for our meetings (i.e., time application).

Once you've completed your self-assessment, turn to the tools for prioritizing and action planning in Appendix D.

CHAPTER 7

Team Leader to Bridge Leader

Bridge Leaders are a critical part of a strong and vibrant school leadership architecture. But they are often overlooked and underappreciated. Teachers (Team Members) are the lifeblood of the school, the people engaging students every day and making minute-by-minute decisions that advance student learning. Team Leaders are responsible for coaching and supporting teachers, helping them hone their craft, building their capacity, and guiding and supporting them to achieve excellent results. School Leaders set the vision and direction of the campus, defining clear goals and a strategy to get there.

Bridge Leaders are the U.S. Interstate Highway system. They keep everyone connected—to each other, to the vision, to the most important priorities for students. They build and maintain the structures, systems, and relationships that advance the mission and allow information and ideas to flow in all directions. As you make the shift from Team Leader to Bridge Leader, your job is to shift from working with individuals on the immediate work to improving the system and context at scale. You must deeply understand the vision, direction, and priorities for your school and proactively identify ways to advance them. You must broaden your view, by taking a wider lens and a longer time horizon, and learn how to work indirectly to achieve results. Like all shifts, this requires a change in your skills, time applications, and professional identity (Figure 7.1). Otherwise, you'll run around in constant reaction mode. You'll be exhausted, frustrated, and ineffective. And your team will be frustrated and ineffective too.

This chapter will help Bridge Leaders identify the shifts they need to make to succeed and thrive in this new role. We'll start with shifts in skills before turning to time applications and professional identity.

FIGURE 7.1 • Summary of Key Shifts for Bridge Leaders

<table>
<tr><th colspan="3">LEADERSHIP PASSAGE 2
Team Leader to Bridge Leader</th></tr>
<tr><td>Unique Leadership Mission</td><td>DELIVER RESULTS
• Track progress toward campus vision and successful execution of priorities.
• Build Team Leader understanding of campus vision and priorities.
• Ensure alignment between school-wide and team-specific priorities.
• Remove barriers and create supportive conditions (culture, systems, etc.) for teams to thrive.
• Support Team Leaders to achieve data-informed goals and close identified gaps.</td><td>BUILD CAPACITY
• Coach and develop Team Leaders (as coaches).
• Monitor Team Member results and development.
• Identify priorities for school-wide professional learning—in pursuit of campus vision and driven by needs/gaps.
• Drive school-wide professional learning (in partnership with Team Leaders and with input from School Leader).
• Train Team Leaders in consistent and effective use of protocols.</td></tr>
<tr><td>Shift in Skills</td><td colspan="2">• Establish and improve systems.
• Longer-term planning and prioritization.
• Empower delegation.
• Coach and support Team Leaders.</td></tr>
<tr><td>Shift in Time</td><td colspan="2">Time Application
• Managerial and system work will take 75% of your time.
• Adopt an organizational perspective vs. “own work.”
• Strategic and cultural issues are important.
Time Horizon
• Planning horizon will be one year or more.</td></tr>
<tr><td>Shift in Professional Identity</td><td colspan="2">• Become a connector and facilitator.
• Dial up trust, dial down control.</td></tr>
</table>

SHIFTING SKILLS

There are four key skill shifts that Bridge Leaders must navigate—two related to getting results and two related to building capacity. On the getting results side, Bridge Leaders' job is to translate the vision and direction established by the School Leader and facilitate the work that will bring it to life. To do this, they must build their muscle to establish and improve systems and to become effective long-term planners.

Then, they have to empower and deploy Team Leaders and their teams to drive execution. Bridge Leaders facilitate and oversee the execution of the plan, but they must become effective, empowering delegators and expand their skills to coach and support Team Leaders.

SKILL SHIFT 1: ESTABLISHING AND IMPROVING SYSTEMS

Response to Intervention (RtI) provides a strong metaphor for the work of a Bridge Leader. In a classroom, rigorous, engaging Tier 1 instruction is the foundation. Then, teachers use data to identify how to design targeted small group instruction (Tier 2) and identify the students who need more intensive individual support (Tier 3). If Tier 1 instruction is weak, the need for Tier 2 and Tier 3 interventions will multiply and may outstrip the school's capacity to deliver it. The success of the model depends on strengthening Tier 1 instruction.

Bridge Leaders must support Team Leaders to build *all* teachers' capacity to deliver engaging, rigorous instruction. Tier 1 support (the foundation) is establishing strong, consistent structures and systems: a clear definition of excellent teaching and learning, routines and protocols to guide teams' work, systems for analyzing and using data, protocols for coaching and feedback, and annual calendars that guide teams' scope and sequence. That list only scratches the surface. A school that lacks systems and structures will be overly reliant on individual intervention. Leaders will burn significant energy coaching each teacher toward a standard that hasn't been clearly defined and that they haven't been equipped to meet. No matter how hard they work, school leaders will never succeed at building teachers' capacity through Tier 3 interventions alone.

The Bridge Leader's role—working in close partnership with the School Leader—is to build the systems and structures that provide Tier 1 supports for Team Leaders to develop their Team Members. The systems aren't complete until Team Leaders understand them and have the skill to use them effectively and consistently. With the systems in place, the Bridge Leader can use data about teachers' performance and growth to help Team Leaders identify which team members need additional intervention and support. When a Bridge Leader is in a classroom or a professional learning community (PLC), their primary role is not to evaluate the teacher or lead the team's work. Their role is to assess how systems need to be strengthened and where the Team Leader needs coaching or support.

There are two basic lenses that Bridge Leaders can use to identify systems issues. The first is to ask, "What is the root cause of this issue/problem/opportunity?" Many school leaders will be familiar with root cause analysis as it has been embedded in many campus improvement planning processes. But, too often, these tools become rote exercises—worksheets that we complete and set aside—versus a way of looking at and seeing challenges and opportunities on our campuses.

The second lens Bridge Leaders can use to find systems issues and opportunities is to ask, "What tasks or activities are consuming significant time or energy? Which of these could be simplified, improved, or changed, requiring less time and energy while achieving the same outcome?" This second question is likely to reveal low-hanging fruit or quick wins for new Bridge Leaders. It can help them see opportunities to make life a little easier for their staff. By spending a few hours establishing or improving a system that saves staff time or energy, they can free up valuable resources to focus on thornier, more important questions.

EXERCISE 7.A

Establishing and Improving Systems

Foundation systems

- What systems, supports, and routines are already in place to facilitate Team Leaders' work of developing Team Members? Anything that you want to be consistent across all teams needs a system, protocol, or routine. Examples include the following:
    - Clear vision for excellent teaching and learning
    - Goal-setting and planning expectations and routines
    - Structures and routines for each standing meeting Team Leaders facilitate
    - Protocols and norms to guide team's work
    - Feedback and coaching protocols
- Are established systems, supports, and routines consistently and effectively used? How can you support Team Leaders to build their skill in using these tools (model, observe and provide feedback, shadow a peer)?

Addressing pain points and opportunities

- Identify a pain point. Use a 5-Whys protocol to try to find the systems issue. What role could you play in building or improving systems to address this issue?
- What are the top five things that Team Members or Team Leaders spend time doing? When you look at this list, are there any opportunities to build systems to make their work more efficient? (For example: If every Team Lead spends 10 hours formatting their data, is there a tool or system that could do some of that work?)

SKILL SHIFT 2: LONGER-TERM PLANNING AND PRIORITIZATION

As leaders move into larger roles, they often expect greater flexibility and autonomy. Many are surprised to realize that they are, in some ways, more interdependent and constrained in their new role. How can this be? Yes, there are fewer people telling them what to do and fewer layers of approval needed in decision-making. But anything that a Bridge Leader wants to accomplish or change involves a lot of people. To get it done, they need to communicate with and motivate many people, through many layers. They need to build shared understanding and skill. In short, getting anything done well takes time and effort.

To make matters more complicated, the rhythms of a school year define a small number of windows for leaders to initiate big change or improvement efforts. In these windows, teachers cannot be asked to focus on an infinite number of priorities. School leaders must prioritize. Bridge Leaders will be much more successful (and much less frustrated) if they learn to be great planners. Ideally, Bridge Leaders are consistently thinking and planning on a one- to two-year time horizon. Working backward from the vision and long-term strategy defined by the School Leader, Bridge Leaders start by asking, "What are the most important two or three things that my teams must change, do, or achieve in the next two years in order to move us toward that vision?"

Once decided, the task is to define when and how to initiate and drive the priorities. This is why understanding the school's rhythms and operating with more than a year's time horizon are both key. There are likely natural times to initiate new priorities or change initiatives. In many schools, major changes must be launched at the beginning of the school year, largely because it is the time when school leaders have the greatest opportunity to build their staff's knowledge and capacity and to be built into everyone's plans and tactics for the year. But those priorities aren't established in the weeks leading up to the new year. They require runway, foresight, and planning.

EXERCISE 7.B

Establishing Your Planning Cadence

Planning will be an iterative process. You need to think through key milestones for different streams of work and how they all fit together.

Step 1: Map organizational rhythms.

Map all major milestones on a calendar: staff development days, instructional leadership team meetings, formative and summative assessments, and any other key activities.

Step 2: Identify deadlines and milestones for recurring work.

- For each month, map out each team's priority recurring work:
  - What is the most important work they need to accomplish?
  - What do they need from you (during or in advance) to be able to accomplish that work?
  - What deadlines will you set for yourself? How can you protect time to meet those deadlines?
- For each month, what is your additional recurring work (in addition to supporting Team Leaders):
  - What are the most important one or two priorities you need to accomplish?
  - What deadlines do you need to meet?
  - To meet those deadlines, when should you initiate this work? How can you protect time to do it?

Step 3: Set dates for annual priorities and initiatives.

- When do annual school priorities get decided? When are they launched with staff?
- Working backward from those decision/launch dates, when do you need to invest time and energy in thinking and planning toward those deadlines? When are data available to inform your planning? On which days will you block time on your calendar to do this work?

Step 4: Iterate and refine.

- Once annual priorities are established, they will likely need to be mapped back to recurring work/rhythms:

- What do teams need to do?
  - How does this impact staff development?
  - What additional responsibilities do I need to focus on to ensure systems and structures are established?
- What might we need to stop in order to be able to prioritize our most important work?
- What, if anything, am I missing? Who could help me pressure-test this plan and offer feedback?

SKILL SHIFT 3: EMPOWERING DELEGATION

Inevitably, Bridge Leaders' planning will generate more work that needs to be done than they can (or should!) do on their own. Planning helps the Bridge Leader identify how they need to deploy and direct their teams, including what priorities they need to assign to Team Leaders. Bridge Leaders must master delegation. In the simplest version, delegation is a three-act play.

ACT I: IDENTIFY SOME OF YOUR WORK AND ASSIGN IT TO SOMEONE ELSE

Leaders can struggle with any (or all) of the three acts. Those who fail at Act I simply don't delegate. Leaders who don't delegate are busy and stuck in the weeds. They work furiously to (personally) deliver all their responsibilities, like a hamster on a wheel: running fast but standing in place. Leaders get trapped in this loop for a variety of reasons. Delegation is scary. *What if they do this differently than I would?* They probably will. That's OK. *What if I could do it better?* You might be able to. That doesn't mean you should. Follow Green and Hauser's (2012) rule of thumb that if someone else could do the work 70% as well as you could, you should delegate it.

Delegation can feel like more work, at least at first when you aren't very good at it. To get over the hump, try thinking longer term. Instead of looking at your responsibilities at 4:30 p.m. on a Thursday and trying to figure out what you can offload Friday morning, think about the work that you could delegate six months from now (i.e., You have to plan it. See prior section.)

There are two ways that you can identify work that is ripe for delegation. First, you might identify some tasks that you need to delegate because taking them off your plate will allow you to prioritize your *most* important work (or the work that only you can do). Seeing delegation through this lens can motivate us and alleviate some of our fears about delegation. Even if the work we delegate gets done a little less well, it's OK because we're dedicating our time and energy to something more important. The second way to identify work to delegate is to focus on your team: Is there work that you are currently doing that aligns with one of your team members' top strengths or would give them an opportunity to grow and develop? In either case, priority-driven or team-driven, identifying what you want to delegate several months down the road enables you to plan and prepare for how you will make it happen.

ACT II: PROVIDE INFORMATION, RESOURCES, AND CAPABILITIES FOR SUCCESS

In Act II, you've made the decision to delegate, but you aren't out of the woods yet. Being a "bad delegator" is almost as bad as not delegating at all. Bad delegation comes in many forms. The one you can avoid in Act II is vague or unclear delegation. In Act II, you clearly define what you are asking for—the goal, the outcome, the product, what success looks like. You might even define interim milestones or checkpoints that break down the task into smaller pieces and will help you both know if the work is on track.

The key is to focus on defining the what and the why but being flexible on the how. That's because flexibility in the "how" creates space for ownership. Before you close Act II, you want to confirm two things: Does the person you've delegated to understand what you've asked them to do? Do they have the resources (including time) that they need to be successful? Once you can answer "yes" to both of these questions, you're in Act III.

ACT III: PROVIDE ACCOUNTABILITY ALONG THE WAY TO ENSURE WORK IS ON TRACK AND SUCCESSFULLY COMPLETED

It is your responsibility to ensure that the work you've delegated is successful. Delegation isn't putting a message in a bottle, throwing it out to sea, and then walking away and hoping it gets where you intend it to go. It also isn't carefully planting a new fern in a pot and then ripping it out every other day to look at the roots to see if it's growing. Neither is effective, and your team doesn't want to be the bottle or the plant. Instead, you want to operate like a shepherd. Most of the time, you are monitoring from a distance, but you're also collecting information to know when it's time to step in and engage. But always remember: Your focus is on achieving the goal (the what), not on the details of the path (the how). If you are swooping in every time the path departs from how you would do it, you are in the territory of micromanagement. Micromanagement is annoying and demoralizing. It robs people of opportunities to develop and to demonstrate what they are capable of, and it keeps you wrapped up in the weeds. If you need to redirect the work regularly, you need to consider whether to reset on Act II—shared understanding on the clarity of the task.

EXERCISE 7.C

Empowering Delegation

ACT I: Identify work to delegate

- Think about how you want to be spending your time six months from now.
  - What work do you need to delegate in order to be able to focus on your top priorities?
  - Is there work that you're currently doing that either aligns to a team member's strengths or offers them opportunities to grow and develop?
- When will you delegate these things? It doesn't have to be immediate. Make a realistic plan.

ACT II: Initiate delegation

- As you prepare to delegate, concretely define what you are asking for:
  - What does success look like?
  - Are there any parameters or boundaries?
  - What is the deadline? Are there any interim milestones that need to be achieved or where you expect updates?
  - What resources does the delegee need to be successful?
- After you've communicated your expectations, ask your teammate to play back what they've heard and what they are committing to.
- Agree when you'll check in next and what progress you expect.

ACT III: Monitor and provide support and accountability

- Do you err toward not giving enough support and accountability (set it and forget it) or micromanagement? (You might ask your team members.) Why is that your tendency?
- As you define your cadence for checking in about the work, think about what information you need to monitor the work and know when more support is needed.
- As you get updates, how do you remain disciplined about giving your team member flexibility as long as they are achieving the goals and parameters?
- Consider updating your User's Manual to describe what kind of delegator you hope to be and naming what you're working on. You might even include a few requests for your team members that will help you move toward your aspiration.

SKILL SHIFT 4: COACHING AND SUPPORTING TEAM LEADERS

Most Bridge Leaders have risen through the ranks for their effectiveness at getting things done, solving problems, and guiding and developing others. But now, their success depends on their ability to build up Team Leaders to be excellent problem-solvers and people-developers. They must learn to coach and support leaders in ways that build their capacity and confidence. To do this, they will have to learn to tame what Michael Bungay Stanier (2016) calls the Advice Monster. Have you met them? They're probably with you right now and you've likely seen them in action before. They typically appear unannounced. Perhaps you're sitting in a meeting with one of your team members. They're telling you about some problem they're facing. They're not even halfway through, and, in your mind, you already know what's going on and what they should do about it.

Your inner Advice Monster has appeared. It belongs to a specific part of the monster family—the non-scary, adorable monsters we love, like the Cookie Monster. It feels *good* to give advice. We feel helpful and smart. We add value. Our team might even appreciate our advice (sometimes). After all, when they're following our advice, we're the one who is responsible for the problem. What a relief for them.

But here's the dark side of the Advice Monster. It doesn't uncover or build anyone's capacity. It keeps your team dependent on you, which ultimately keeps you entangled in the weeds and overwhelmed most of the time. It produces a strange, downward spiral: "The more you help your people, the more they seem to need your help. The more they need your help, the more time you spend helping them" (Bungay Stanier, 2016, p. 9). Even if you have effectively delegated a task or project, if you create a dynamic where your team is constantly checking in with you about every decision and event that they encounter, it will basically nullify your delegation. Yes, technically, you've assigned responsibility to a team member, but if they bring all decisions back to you, you are still doing the work. Plus, it will consume a lot of your time.

As a Bridge Leader you must work to expand and deepen your coaching stance. In general, you need to shift from what Bungay Stanier (2016) calls *coaching to performance*—which you did a lot of as a Team Leader, particularly with newer teachers—to more *coaching for development*. While coaching for performance "is about addressing and fixing a specific problem or challenge" (Bungay Stanier 2016, p. 40), coaching for development is focused less on the specific challenge and more on building the capacity of the person facing the challenge to have the skills, mindsets, and confidence to navigate it.

Of course, there is a role for advice—it is one move that leaders make to develop and grow their people, especially with novice or struggling team members. But it shouldn't be the only tool in your toolbelt, especially as Bridge Leader.

EXERCISE 7.D

Coaching and Supporting Team Leaders

- What do you notice about your instincts: How often is your first move advice or providing direction?
- If this is your first move most of the time,
  - Why do you lean on advice?
  - How might you start small in practicing coaching for development versus moving to problem-solving? Consider picking *one* problem that a Team Leader has been wrestling with and planning a short coaching conversation (no more than 30 minutes) to address it. Success for this conversation is building the Team Leader's skill, not solving the problem.
- If you sometimes jump to advice, but not always, are there any patterns?
  - Do you rely on advice with specific people or situations?
  - Why? Does this instinct reflect a lack of trust or confidence in the person you are supporting? Or, perhaps, advice-giving happens when you are tired or rushed?
  - What could you commit to practice?

SHIFTING TIME ALLOCATIONS

It is easy for schools to fall into a reactive pattern. The Bridge Leader has the opportunity and responsibility to help the school avoid it. This is why it is so critical that Bridge Leaders step back from spending most of their time reacting to day-to-day issues. If they don't, they won't be able to see the big picture and they'll miss opportunities to help the school improve over the long term. To escape the reactivity trap, prioritize your unique leadership mission, and maximize your impact as a Bridge Leader, you must navigate four shifts in how you spend your time:

1. Managerial and systems work (75%+ of the time).
2. Invest in organizational priorities, not just your area(s).
3. Spend time on the "soft" stuff.
4. Extend your time horizon—think and act with an eye to an annual cadence.

TIME SHIFT 1: MANAGERIAL AND SYSTEM WORK (75% OF TIME)

As you transition to Bridge Leader, your task is to deepen the shift you began as a Team Leader—to spend less of your time on individual contributor work so that most of your time is dedicated to coaching, managing, and supporting your team and diagnosing and improving systems. Take a look at your calendar. Roughly, what portion of your time is dedicated to individual contributor work? Individual contributor work is easy to spot. If you are working by yourself and you are producing or completing something but not planning or preparing for a meeting or conversation with one of your team members, then you are doing individual contributor work. Ideally, this work would comprise 25% or less of your time or less.

That's not because that work isn't important or is "beneath" you. (Many of us hold on to old duties to demonstrate our commitment to servant leadership, or we're afraid of looking out of touch. These motivations and concerns are genuine, but they don't serve us.) It's because your team and your school are counting on you to prioritize the things that only you can do—coaching, managing, and supporting and improving systems. This is where 75% or more of your time would ideally be spent. There will be days and even weeks when your time doesn't reflect this 25/75 split and when, frankly, there's nothing that you can (or should) do to change that. That's OK. It's the reality of working in a school. The goal is to achieve or move toward the 25/75 split most of the time and over long periods of time. And the goal is to move toward the 25/75 split where you have control and choice over how you spend your time. And you do this through the skills outlined above: delegating, coaching, and improving systems.

TIME SHIFT 2: ORGANIZATIONAL PERSPECTIVE VERSUS AREA/FUNCTION

In your prior roles, you have been rewarded for being laser focused on your goals—your individual results or the results of your team—and driving your time toward achieving them. As a Bridge Leader, you have a broader lens. The time that you spend sharing information with your boss and your colleagues, collaborating and problem-solving on school-wide or interdepartmental issues, and preparing for and participating in leadership team meetings isn't a distraction from your work—it *is* your work.

If you notice yourself shaving time off these responsibilities by skipping meetings or showing up unprepared or resenting them and viewing them as distractions, you are struggling with the shift to embracing organization-wide responsibilities. Your calendar should reflect this, and you must learn not to resent being asked to spend your time in ways that extend beyond your core responsibilities. You won't have the perspective and information you need to succeed without it.

TIME SHIFT 3: STRATEGIC AND CULTURAL ISSUES

In 1984, Lee Bolman and Terrence Deal published a leadership classic: *Reframing Organizations: Artistry, Choice, and Leadership*. It describes a four-frame model of leadership: structural, human resources, symbolic, and political. The structural frame is about logic, reason, and structures—the "hard stuff" of rules, goals, and policies. The human resources frame is about the people side of the equation—their skills, needs, and relationships. The symbolic frame is about culture and meaning, the rituals and stories that inspire and motivate. The political frame isn't about partisan politics or elections. It is about the reality that in any group of people there is conflict about what the goals should be or how they should be accomplished. Bolman and Deal (1984) argue that

- effective organizational leadership depends on all four frames,
- most leaders (and the people they lead) have one or two preferred frames—ways that they see and approach organizational challenges or opportunities—and a few neglected or underutilized frames, and
- everyone can become more balanced by learning to frame and address issues through all four frames, including their neglected or underutilized ones.

If they haven't already, Bridge Leaders must begin working on achieving greater balance across the four frames. In particular, they need to watch out for getting stuck in the structural frame—thinking or acting as if every challenge or opportunity can be addressed through updating goals, changing rules, or tweaking structures (or explaining the existing goals, rules, or structures again). They must value the "soft stuff": people, group dynamics, and culture. On the other hand, if you gravitate toward the soft stuff and have a tendency to neglect the structural frame, you will need to work on that balance too. It is likely to show up as a weakness in delegation and unclear goals. We tend to spend our time on the things we value, so your calendar will be telling here. What do you spend time doing? What do you spend time planning and thinking about? What do you spend time talking to your team members about?

EXERCISE 7.E

Bridge Leader Calendar Audit

STEP 1: Review your calendar: Does it reflect how you actually spend your time? If not, take a few minutes to reconstruct how you spent your time in the last week.

STEP 2: Color code your calendar.

- In blue, highlight all your time allocations that reflect your unique leadership mission as a Bridge Leader.
- In orange, highlight all your time allocations that are Team Leader responsibilities, other duties, or reactive.

STEP 3: What do you notice?

- **75% vs. 25%**
  - What's the ratio of your time? (To be clear, there is no expectation that you are going to spend 100% of your time on Bridge Leader work. We all have other duties.)
  - What's the root cause of your "orange" time? Are there one or two things that you are spending a lot of time on?
- **Organizational, strategic, and cultural investments**
  - Do you see evidence of where you are investing time taking an organizational perspective? If not, why not?
  - How are you investing time in the strategic and cultural needs of your school?

STEP 4: Action planning

- What could you do differently to spend more time operating as Bridge Leader?
- Where do you need to be more disciplined or build new habits?
- What aspects of your time allocation feel outside of your control? How might you get support from your School Leader?

TIME SHIFT 4: EXTEND TIME HORIZON TO A YEAR OR LONGER

Over time, your goal will be for the time horizon for thinking, planning, and acting to extend to a year or longer. Achieving this time horizon will depend, significantly, on the three shifts in time allocation outlined in this chapter. Increasingly, you must embrace organizational issues—observing, learning, and contributing—versus channeling all your time and energy into your areas of responsibility. You must prioritize strategic and cultural issues, the "soft" side of leading an organization. And you must continue to embrace spending time on getting work done through others versus through your individual contributions.

SHIFTING PROFESSIONAL IDENTITY

There are two professional identity shifts that new Bridge Leaders must navigate:

- Embrace being a connector and facilitator. Bridge Leaders are neither the driver of the day-to-day work nor the person who sets the overall vision, but rather the person who helps to mobilize the teams toward the vision.
- Dial up trust, dial down control. As they get out of the weeds, Bridge Leaders must learn how to cope with less direct control, playing their role in a way that empowers the people around them.

PROFESSIONAL IDENTITY SHIFT 1: CONNECTOR AND FACILITATOR

As a Bridge Leader, you are a connector and facilitator. Your job is to proactively bridge and close information gaps and to help ensure the big vision gets translated into the right day-to-day actions. Think of a significant decision or initiative on your campus, maybe one that is unpopular among some teachers. Imagine that you're talking to one of your team members about that initiative. They have questions or are expressing frustrations. You respond, "When that decision was made ___________, (school leadership/the people responsible for the decision) ___________." How do you describe the people who made that decision? Do you say "they"? Or do you say "we"?

As a Bridge Leader, you are officially part of the "we." This is a significant shift in your professional identity. As a Team Leader, you made a significant shift. You transitioned from measuring your success through your personal, direct contributions to the accomplishments and outcomes of your team members. You multiplied your scope and your impact four to eight times (the size of your team). But your focus was fairly narrow. You stayed focused on your sphere of control—what happened in the classrooms of your team members.

Becoming a Bridge Leader is more than just expanding your scope and impact as a manager—leading more teams and people. It requires you to broaden your understanding of your sphere of influence and your sphere of concern. Your job is to communicate and collaborate with your boss (School Leader) and your peers and teams to ensure the success of the school. If you identify a significant problem or opportunity, it is your responsibility to contribute to addressing it—even if it is not in your defined responsibilities. Most of the time, the actions you need to take are to share information about the problem you are seeing, to offer ideas or suggestions for how things could be improved, or to confirm that someone is taking action to address the problem. Sometimes, you may need to get more involved in the problem-solving process. But you can't be a bystander on your campus. You can't stand by passively observing missed opportunities or poor decisions thinking, "*Well, that isn't my responsibility*" or "*But no one asked me.*"

As a Bridge Leader, you have a unique perspective, and you have access to information that your peers and your boss need to make good decisions, solve problems, and implement change ideas effectively. If you are sitting on that information waiting to be asked, you are doing a disservice to your teammates and you are still navigating this transition in your professional identity.

EXERCISE 7.F

Embracing Your Role as Connector and Facilitator

Think of a time in the past few weeks when you noticed an opportunity or challenge at your school that was outside your formal scope of responsibility. How did you respond?

- Did you see it as a "we" issue or a "they" issue?
- Did you take any action (including gathering or sharing information), or were you passive?
- Why did you respond in this way? What does your response suggest about your orientation toward this shift?
- If this issue is still relevant, what will you do next?
- What do you commit to try the next time you face a similar situation?

PROFESSIONAL IDENTITY SHIFT 2: DIAL UP TRUST, DIAL DOWN CONTROL

As a Team Leader, you were in the details of the work. You had deep, specific knowledge of the work of your Team Members. If your boss asked, "What lesson is Mr. Lopez teaching on Thursday afternoon? And, if I stop by, what is he currently focused on in terms of improving his practice?" you could have answered in detail, from memory. You took great pride in knowing your stuff and being on top of things. This detailed knowledge helped you feel in command of your responsibilities.

Now that you are a Bridge Leader—working across a broader scope—you need to learn how to dial down your need for control and dial up the trust that you build with and extend to your team. If you are like most high-performing leaders, this shift is going to feel uncomfortable. You are going to have to make it before you are ready. Here's the (wrong) approach that many new Bridge Leaders take to trust:

> *I got this role because of my strong track record of results—first as an excellent teacher and then as a Team Leader. Now I have an opportunity to scale my impact, ensuring excellence across all the teams that I lead. I am going to get in there and evaluate how things are going. As my team members prove to me that they can deliver the results that I expect, that will build my trust, and I will give them more room to run. But until then, I'll do my part to make sure that we succeed.*

Unfortunately, this isn't how trust works—first you prove it and then I give it to you (Marquet, 2020). That's because the "prove it" mindset can unleash a vicious cycle. Your team knows you don't trust them—as demonstrated by your actions and words—which undermines their confidence and dampens their initiative. They are more tentative and deferential to you, increasingly seeking your advice, input, and direction. Subconsciously you think, *See! They don't know what they're doing. They need me to get more involved.* You tighten the screws of "support" (also known as micromanagement) and before you know it, you're basically doing their jobs for them.

Now, trust doesn't mean setting your team loose with no direction or no boundaries. That's bad management. Your job is to provide clear expectations on the front end, feedback and redirection when the work is off track, and accountability throughout. But, in between, you need to provide space for your team to navigate.

You need to pay attention to your inner monologue, to what Stephen Covey (2022) calls your foundational beliefs as a leader. To succeed, Bridge Leaders must operate from this foundational belief: *I am surrounded by a lot of talented and capable people. My job is to build their capacity, create conditions for them to succeed, and help unleash their potential.* If you still hear the voice, *I'm the only one who can ___________. No one else will be able to do it at the level I can,* you still have work to do to get comfortable with trust. Without making that shift in professional identity, you will likely struggle in your new role, trying to do too much, feeling overwhelmed, and struggling to get to your most important work.

EXERCISE 7.G

Dialing Up Trust and Dialing Down Control

- Do the people you lead believe that you trust them? Despite your intentions, what actions might communicate to your people that you don't trust them? (You can only answer these questions by asking your people.)
- Go back to your Leadership Point of View and your User's Manual exercises (6.B and 6.C) from Chapter 6. Does trust appear in either document?
  - If so, are you living up to the values you expressed, or is there room for growth?
  - If not, what do you want to be true when it comes to trust? How do you want your team to feel?
- If trust is hard for you, consider these questions:
  - How much time do you spend noticing your team's successes and wins versus dissecting their mistakes? How might this ratio impact your instincts to trust?
  - How is withholding trust hurting you, your team, and your results?
  - Where are there small opportunities to extend trust?

Embracing these new professional identities as a facilitator and connector and as someone who leads through trust is critical to succeeding and thriving as a Bridge Leader. But Bridge Leaders must also change how they spend their time—embracing their new unique leadership mission.

PRIORITIZE AND CHIP AWAY

What's on your mind as you finish reading this chapter? You may have a growing list of things you've noticed that you want to work on—maybe even some that you picked up in Chapter 6. That's great. And remember: Don't try to tackle everything at once. Pick one or two things to focus on—the things that will make the biggest immediate difference, the quick wins, or the things that will help you build some momentum and confidence. The self-assessment at the end of this chapter and the tools in Appendix D are designed to help you think through how to get started.

Don't forget to take the long view and to stick with it. Your Team Leaders are counting on you to be an excellent, empowering coach who brings out the best in them. They need you to see the big picture and the long view, to help prioritize and integrate the most important work. Your School Leader is counting on you to connect teams to the big vision and priorities and to build the systems and processes that the school needs to thrive. The shifts in professional identity, time application, and skills may seem small and subtle, but they can be the key to maximizing your impact and thriving in this role.

Big Ideas and Key Takeaways

- A Bridge Leader's job is to keep everyone connected—to each other, to the vision, to the most important priorities for students.
- As you make the shift from Team Leader to Bridge Leader, your job is to shift from working with individuals on the immediate work to identifying system issues and improving the system and context at scale.
- Bridge Leaders will be much more successful (and much less frustrated) if they learn to be great planners. Ideally, Bridge Leaders are consistently thinking and planning on a one- to two-year time horizon.
- Delegation is key, as is prioritization.
- Accountability will help keep work on track.
- Bridge Leaders must expand and deepen the coaching stance they established as Team Leaders. They need coaching moves that build capacity, not just solve problems.
- Bridge Leaders must deeply understand the vision, direction, and priorities for their school and proactively identify ways to advance them.
- As Bridge Leaders work across a broader scope, they need to learn how to dial down their need for control and dial up the trust that they build with and extend to their team.

CHAPTER 7 SELF-ASSESSMENT

As you read through the chapter, use this tool to capture your observations on how you are navigating each shift. Use a 1–4 scale:

1 = Never or rarely

2 = Sometimes

3 = Often

4 = Almost always

SKILLS	
______________	I effectively establish and improve systems (vs. reacting to one-off problems or opportunities).
______________	I am a strong planner. I have clear priorities and goals, and I have established clear milestones and deliverables to achieve them. My plans help me ensure I am spending time on the right things and proactively delegate and coordinate initiatives with other team members.
EMPOWERING DELEGATION	
______________	I actively identify work that can and should be delegated to a member of my team.
______________	When I delegate work, I am very clear about the "what" (the goal, the parameters, and the timeline) and give them flexibility in the "how." I ensure that team members understand what they're being asked to do and have the time and resources they need to succeed.
______________	I routinely monitor work that I've delegated. When something is off track, I provide coaching and support.
______________	Overall, most of the projects I delegate are accomplished successfully without me needing to get involved in the details.
COACHING TEAM LEADERS	
______________	My team does not need my advice or permission for every decision they need to make or at every step of their work.
______________	I prioritize using a facilitative/coaching stance as much as possible and avoid leading with telling or advice.
______________	I spend more time coaching for development than coaching for performance.

TIME	
______________	For each of my priority responsibilities, I have a long-term plan and approach. I see the key milestones a year or more out.
______________	I don't view spending time on organizational questions and issues—beyond my personal areas of responsibilities—as a distraction from my "real job."
______________	I invest time in strategic and cultural issues and opportunities.
______________	75% of my time is spent on managerial work (getting things done through others) or building and improving systems.
PROFESSIONAL IDENTITY	
______________	I have embraced my role as a connector and facilitator.
______________	I am comfortable trusting my team and not having control of all the details. I stay informed without getting involved in every element.

Once you've completed your self-assessment, turn to the tools for prioritizing and action planning in Appendix D.

CHAPTER 8

Bridge Leader to School Leader

Many School Leaders understand being an "instructional leader" as a long list of things that principals need to personally do. The school leadership architecture presented in this book sharpens what it means for School Leaders to provide instructional leadership, focused on their unique leadership mission. It is not their job to coach every teacher individually. When it comes to building capacity, the principal's primary responsibility is to operate as the coach of coaches.

The School Leader is also not monitoring every lesson plan or getting involved in every day-to-day or week-to-week decision. These, too, are the remit of Team Leaders with support from Bridge Leaders. The School Leader should not be designing and shepherding every significant initiative on the campus. The School Leader's role is to set and communicate the vision, establish priorities and define systems and routines, and cultivate and maintain a positive, supportive culture. Once their role is defined, Bridge Leaders have the time and responsibility to build and improve campus systems and to drive and facilitate continuous improvement. Then, School Leaders use data to monitor how the system is working and make adjustments.

Embracing this focused role and succeeding in it requires School Leaders to navigate shifts in their skills, time applications, and professional identity (Figure 8.1).

FIGURE 8.1 • Summary of Key Shifts for School Leaders

LEADERSHIP PASSAGE 3 Bridge Leader to School Leader		
Unique Leadership Mission	**DELIVER RESULTS** • Establish shared vision for the campus (including vision/ definition of excellent instruction).	**BUILD CAPACITY** • Coach and develop Bridge Leaders. • Monitor Team Leader results and development.

(Continued)

(Continued)

LEADERSHIP PASSAGE 3 Bridge Leader to School Leader		
	• Ensure and manage alignment with district vision and priorities, including advocating for campus needs. • Establish short- and long-term campus priorities. • Through regular, purposeful communication, build understanding and ownership of the campus vision and priorities to all members of the campus community. • Use data to monitor progress and identify areas requiring attention. • Allocate resources (people, money, time) in alignment with vision and priorities. • Establish and maintain school climate and culture.	• Establish protocols for feedback, team collaboration, etc. • Establish priorities for professional learning and ensure coherence of build-capacity efforts and deliver results.
Shift in Skills	• Define long-term strategy and goals for the school, balancing future goals (three- to five-year plan) with present needs and pressures. • Communicate clearly and effectively with all stakeholders. • Prevent and navigate crises.	
Shift in Time	*Time Application* • Shift from primarily internal to significantly external focus. • Protect time to think, reflect, and analyze. *Time Horizon* Adopt long-term thinking and strategy (two to three years).	
Shift in Professional Identity	• Accept attention/scrutiny that comes with being highly visible. • Own organizational culture. • Lead with confidence and humility.	

SHIFTING SKILLS

As School Leaders shift their time to embrace their unique leadership mission, they will need to develop and hone three skill shifts: setting long-term direction and strategy, clearly and effectively communicating, and navigating crises. Again, these are not the only three skills that a great School Leader needs. They will continue to use the skills and capabilities they developed as a Team Leader and Bridge Leader and will need a deep reservoir of instructional knowledge and skill. But these are three areas where new School Leaders' skills may be tested for the first time or in new ways.

SKILL SHIFT 1: SET LONG-TERM DIRECTION AND STRATEGY

School Leaders' top priority is establishing the vision and strategy for the school. This work starts with clearly articulating a vision for what effective instruction and engaged learning look like in your school. Every person on your team, especially your Team Leaders, must understand the vision that they are working toward. This clear, concrete vision of excellence is what enables you to share leadership.

Leaders who haven't articulated a vision will continue to feel the need to be personally involved in every aspect of instructional leadership. They don't have confidence that the work will move forward without them. In the absence of a vision, they are the glue that holds it all together. And they are right to be concerned. Without a concrete vision of excellence, each person will be guided by different ideas of the destination. The result will be misalignment, wasted energy, and slow progress.

Facing this reality, many School Leaders think they're confronted by two bad choices: share leadership and accept misalignment or hold leadership tightly and stay trapped in the cycle of an impossible job where there will always be more work to do than the School Leader can do well. There is another choice. The School Leader must do the work that only they can do—clearly defining a vision for effective teaching and engaging learning that aligns and orients the work of their leadership team.

Once the vision is established, the School Leader must decide what to prioritize and focus on how to get there. This work often feels like walking a tightrope. There are dangers on both sides. On your left is the risk of being too reactionary, of allowing short-term problems to become your highest goal. Leaders who take this approach to strategy and goals tend to think one year at a time—always focusing on the most urgent needs and opportunities. Year after year of short-term goal setting will likely result in leaders and schools who are working very hard but feel like they're not making much progress.

To your right, you face a different risk: focusing on lofty, long-term aspirations and neglecting the short-term work that needs to be done to create the conditions to achieve them. These are School Leaders who start with their end destination—what will be true in five years?—but don't work their vision backward. They can't answer the question, "What do we need to do *this* year to get there?" Or they articulate goals that ignore the pressing issues facing the school, as if they can just leapfrog over their current reality to a future state.

The way to walk the tightrope is to use both lenses for balance. Exercise 8.A invites you to start mapping out your long-term and short-term priorities. This will likely be an iterative exercise and one that will benefit from getting input, advice, and ideas from others. Odds are that you will list more ideas for how you can strengthen your school than you have capacity to take on. Overcommitting yourself or your team will not make you more successful or earn you any awards for commitment. It will exhaust you. It will frustrate your staff. And it will make everyone a little more cynical next time you go through a strategy or planning process. Before you put pencils down on your planning, make sure you confirm what you are going to *stop* doing to have resources to invest in new efforts.

The point of long-term planning and goals isn't to establish your every move in concrete, never to change. The point of long-term planning and goals is to improve the quality of your short-term goals and execution—to increase the likelihood that you will move toward your big aspiration. Effective long-term planning and goals also improve your ability to adapt to changing circumstances—responding to unforeseen challenges or opportunities without losing the path to your ultimate aims. You are able to flex because you are clear on what's most important and what it will take to get there if and when you need to adjust.

EXERCISE 8.A

Split-Screen View—Short-Term and Long-Term

Start with the long term. Grab some paper and make a list.

- What needs to be true in three years? Five years?
- What are all the things that need to be true to get there? What skills or capabilities do we need to develop? What needs to stop, start, or change?

- Realistically, how long would it take to develop those skills, capabilities, and conditions? (Hint: probably more than a year)
- Start mapping out what your goals and priorities would be, working backward.

Now, grab a fresh piece of paper and focus on the short term.

- What are the school's most pressing needs today?
- What are the results that you must deliver or the areas that you must address? Think about all your stakeholders—students, caregivers, staff, district leadership.
- What work do you need to start immediately because it's critical to where you're trying to go and it will take time to accomplish?
- Try to map out your short-term goals across the next two to three years.

Now, set them side by side.

- Do they connect or bridge to each other?
- What is missing?
- How might you re-sequence your priorities to both address short-term needs and make progress toward your long-term vision?

SKILL SHIFT 2: COMMUNICATE CLEARLY AND EFFECTIVELY WITH ALL STAKEHOLDERS

Communication is the engine of leadership—essential to mobilizing a group of people around a common purpose. Leaders communicate through their words *and* their actions, but the shift that new School Leaders experience is the weight of their words. Let's start with a basic formula: SAF-T. Your communication needs to be **S**imple, **A**udience-focused, **F**requent and repetitive, and **T**ransparent.

KEEP IT SIMPLE

There are two anti-simplicity errors. The first is the suspense movie error. We love a good thriller: a complex plot with lots of twists and turns that keeps you glued to your seat for the final reveal. The suspense that builds to the twist at the end is the reward of the genre. But your emails are not suspense movies. No one wants to read four paragraphs of anecdote or storytelling wondering where this is all going. They won't be thrilled by the surprise at the end; they'll just stop reading your emails. When writing or speaking, it is almost always best to lead with the bottom line. Say your conclusion and then make your case. You'll be surprised how much less explaining and case making you need to do when you just clearly state your point or big idea. And you'll be pleasantly surprised at how many more people get your message. The other perk of communicating this way? You'll have to make sure you know what your bottom line is before you communicate.

The second error is the temptation to "sound smart." This is the love of big words and long sentences. The more advanced degrees you get, the more you tend to love big, nuanced, beautiful words. Those of us who write and speak big and long can feel like calls for simplicity are calls for watering down our complex, nuanced ideas, but they are not. Pursuing simplicity is an opportunity to think creatively about how to share our ideas in ways that are easy for busy people to understand and remember. In addition to shorter words and simpler sentences, metaphors and analogies are your greatest tools in powerfully communicating big ideas in simple ways. When you get it right, you can condense paragraphs of explanation into one memorable sentence or phrase.

TO BE AUDIENCE-FOCUSED, MOVE BEYOND THE GOLDEN RULE

Most communicators dutifully follow the golden rule. As we prepare our communication, we start with what *we* know, and then we focus on communicating what *we* would want to know or understand. But we aren't the audience. We need to focus on who they are, what they need to know, and why they should care. And we need to be clear about how we want to make your audience feel. It might help you to get specific. Rather than thinking about a big group, zero in on one specific person. Can you confidently describe what they need to know and why they should care? If not, it might be time to do some listening before you start talking or writing.

Really knowing your audience can be a communication superpower. Too often, when we talk about "inspirational" communicators, we describe people's style or energy—the ability to entertain, to wow, to dazzle. Research has demonstrated that inspirational leaders are not marked by personality or charisma. Instead, they have exceptional self-awareness and cognitive empathy—the ability to "take other people's perspective, comprehend their mental" or "see through the eyes of others" (Goleman, 2015, p. 99). The better a leader understands their audience, the better they can select messages that will connect with and move them. But what sparks inspiration is when the audience senses that the message also comes from the leader's heart—aligned with their values and beliefs.

So, if you want to be a more inspiring communicator, in addition to sharpening your messages and delivery, focus on knowing your people and building your self-awareness. Remember: Communication doesn't happen when the message is sent—that is talking (or writing). Communication happens when the message is received.

DON'T BE AFRAID OF FREQUENCY AND REPETITION

If I wandered around your school, bumped into a teacher, and asked them what the school's mission, values, and most important priorities are for that semester or school year, could they tell me? If the answer is "no," then you need to be communicating a lot more frequently and you need to be repeating yourself more. In interpersonal relationships, repeating yourself is generally frowned upon. It might send the signal that you think the other person is dense or that you are too focused on your own ideas. But as a School Leader, it's different. Your team and community are drowning in messages and information.

You need to identify your most important messages—your vision, values, and priorities—and you need to repeat and reinforce them all the time. That's how you build alignment. And you need to assume that key stakeholders don't necessarily hear or read every message that you send. That's why you need higher frequency and to reinforce messages across different channels (in person, email, social media, etc.).

BE AS TRANSPARENT AS YOU CAN

Audiences can tell when someone is hiding something or is skirting around an issue. Particularly when facing pointed questions or delivering hard news, it can be easy to take a defensive posture. It's understandable. Sometimes pointed questions are just criticisms disguised in a question costume. And there are many situations where we don't have the answer, or we can't share it. But ultimately, leaders will do much better if they operate with a "there are no hard questions" mindset. When leaders walk around feeling nervous about hard questions, they will be guarded and defensive. Even if they're not, they will look like they are hiding information. And, if they consistently operate in this way, people will just stop asking questions (which is bad for the organization and the leader).

A "no hard questions" mindset shifts the leader from a defensive crouch to an open one. They focus on what they *can* share instead of what they don't know or can't share. And they look proactively for *opportunities* in hard questions. Every question is an opportunity to build context—to fill in gaps in shared knowledge and understanding and to share the *why*, even if they can't provide details on what or how.

LISTEN. LISTEN. LISTEN

We sometimes use communication as a synonym for talking. As leaders, we use this shorthand at our own peril, as it overlooks a crucial component of communication and of leadership: listening. Communication isn't the message we delivered; it is the message our audience received. Only by listening and engaging in real dialogue can we identify and close the gaps between what we intended to say and what people heard.

We all *know* that listening is important. And we all aspire to be good listeners. And yet, despite our good intentions, organizational leaders often build bad habits that make them bad listeners. We are perpetually in a hurry with too much on our minds. The volume of decision-making and problem-solving wears us down. The role can be isolating and we can start to think that "no one gets it." Yes, School Leaders have a unique perspective. They operate from the highest elevation, seeing the widest context better than most—a vantage point that positions them to lead the work of long-term vision and strategy. *But,* as leaders increase their elevation, they *lose* information and perspective too.

Teachers will be quick to point out, "My principal doesn't *really* know what it's like to be in the classroom." Hearing that pinches the heart of most principals. Though they usually have the good judgment to not say it out loud, in their minds, they start rehearsing their bona fides—all those years they spent in the classroom and how good they were. Or they think, "*I'll show them*" as they launch their latest campaign to be in classrooms all the time. They might even take on a few substitute teaching roles.

School Leaders: Your teachers are right. You will never know what it's like to be a teacher in this school at this moment in time the way that your staff does. You don't have to because *they know.* You just need to listen to them. Inevitably, you're not going to agree with everything you hear. But, even if what you're hearing is 90% "wrong," is there 10% that you can learn from? There might be one thing that was missing from your thinking. Or you learned how your staff feels or that something you are saying or doing is being widely misunderstood. All of that information is gold. It helps you change how you communicate your vision or ideas in ways that may make it easier for your team to understand and embrace the change you are promoting.

When you ask for or receive advice you don't have to do everything—or anything!—that you're told. You just have to listen and really consider what is being said. Your go-to response can simply be "Thank you for sharing that with me. I'm going to think about it. Can I come back to you if I have more questions about what you've shared with me?" If you do this consistently, your team will be more willing to share what they see and what they think. And you'll get the gift of expanding and deepening your self-awareness—a critical need for senior leaders.

Virtually everything the School Leader needs to accomplish depends on the quality of advice, perspectives, and ideas that the School Leader hears from their team, from students, and from the community. Don't overlook the importance being a great listener. And if you've drifted a bit, it's never too late to recommit.

EXERCISE 8.B

Practices for Improving Communication

- **Simplicity:** Calculate the Flesch-Kincaid score of a written message or draft speech. (Microsoft Word can calculate it for you—Review→Editor→Document Stats—or you can use online tools.) Texts are scored from 0 to 100 with higher numbers being easier to understand. Aim for a score of 60 to 80. You will get a higher score by using shorter words and simpler sentences.
- **Audience-Focused**
  - Before you share information, spend time writing down who your target audience is, how you want them to feel, and what you think you know about them. What do they know or think about this topic? How might their perspective be different than yours? How do they feel about this topic? What might they want or be concerned about?
  - Test your message with one or two people. See how they respond. Ask follow-up questions to confirm if you have a good understanding of their point of view, feelings, and interests.
  - After you deliver your message, ask for feedback. What did people understand or take away? Was there anything about your delivery that could have been better?
  - You won't have time to do this for every message you deliver. But if you make it a regular practice, you will notice patterns and themes that can benefit all of your communication.
- **Frequent and Repetitive:** Identify the most important two or three things that you need your team to know or do in the next three to six months. Make a plan for when and how you will repeat your key messages. (Note: Simple messages are easier to

(Continued)

(Continued)

repeat.) If you aren't bored of saying it yet, you probably need to repeat it.

- **Transparent:** Practice your "no hard questions" mindset, especially if you know you are about to get some. Invite your team to ask challenging questions and practice sharing what you know and building context versus reacting defensively (highlighting what you don't know or can't share). The side benefit of this approach is that it builds your team's context and skill too.
- **Listening**
    - What structures, systems, or routines do you have to proactively listen to staff and make it easy for them to share feedback with you?
    - How can you be present and engaged when you are listening to a Team Member? What might send the message that they don't have your full attention?
    - When a Team Member shares an idea or feedback that you disagree with or is hard to hear, say, "Thank you for sharing that with me" or "I never thought of it that way" and "I want to think more about that. Can I follow up with you if I have more questions about what you're saying?"

SKILL SHIFT 3: NAVIGATE CRISES

No matter how hard you work to proactively identify and manage risks, steering around and de-escalating avoidable problems, at some point, your school will experience a crisis—an acute period of heightened risk and escalated emotions. Your job is to act wisely and decisively to address the situation while responding to and managing the emotions that are in play. This isn't easy work.

When a crisis hits, you will quickly find your brain clicking into fight or flight mode, or what Leonard J. Marcus and colleagues (2019) call "the basement." This part of your brain is important for helping you react quickly in a car accident or for protecting a child who begins to dart into the road. But you don't want to navigate a crisis from the basement. You need to access what Marcus and colleagues (2019) call the workroom—the home of fast, instinct-based, routine thinking—or the laboratory—where your deliberate, creative thinking occurs.

So, in a crisis, your first job is to get yourself out of the basement. Doing so will enable you to think and act more clearly. And it will help your team get out of the basement too. During a crisis, all eyes are on leaders. As a result, our actions will reverberate more than usual. If we are panicked or frozen, the anxiety of the people around us will rise.

Then, you mobilize a team to respond to and resolve the crisis. Yes, this work is about strong decision-making and swift action. But communication is also critically important. Particularly during the early stages of the crisis response, people need to hear from you early, often, and predictably. Your communication grounds people in the facts that you have, provides information about what actions you are taking, and helps different stakeholders know what actions they need to take. Providing frequent, reliable information builds confidence and trust and helps to minimize anxiety and stress. Don't wait until you have all the information to begin communicating. Simple holding statements—here's what we know, what we don't know, and how we'll share more information—are better than silence and speculation.

As a School Leader, you won't navigate crises alone. Your district will partner with and support you. But as the School Leader, your team, your staff, your students, and your community will be looking to you. They will count on you to be calm, competent, and decisive. They will count on you to be visible, to be transparent, and to provide the information that they need to understand what is happening and to know what action to take.

EXERCISE 8.C

Navigating Crises

→ Crises will tax your energy. If you enter a crisis depleted and exhausted, your work will be harder. How well do you manage and maintain your physical, mental, and emotional resources? What is one thing you could do to invest in yourself?

→ When you are stressed, what is most effective in slowing down and regulating yourself?

→ Schedule a conversation with your manager to rehearse how you would respond to a crisis. Make sure you are clear on what your role is and where you should lean on your district for support.

SHIFTING TIME APPLICATIONS

To deliver their unique leadership mission, School Leaders will need to make three key shifts in their time applications and time horizon.

TIME SHIFT 1: LONG-TERM TIME HORIZON AND STRATEGY (TWO TO THREE YEARS)

Over time, School Leaders must operate with a multiyear vision and perspective—far beyond the required cycles of campus improvement planning and other compliance-related mechanisms. Big visions and big results won't be achieved on a continuous loop of one-year strategies.

One of the most intense pressures that School Leaders must navigate is the tension between the urgency of achieving results today and the need for longer-term, sustained improvement efforts to achieve a bigger, bolder vision of what is possible for students over time. Increasing your standardized test scores by a few points this year is a fine goal and one that will require focus and work to achieve. But this short-term, incremental gain doesn't get you out of bed in the morning. And it doesn't inspire your teaching staff. It doesn't unleash their motivation or discretionary effort. Ultimately, there's a huge disconnect between what we can realistically achieve in a year and what we, as educators, want our schools to be and to accomplish for our children. We have much bigger dreams for them and for us. But if all our dreams must be packaged into annual performance goals or quarterly benchmarks, they get sanded down. We are afraid to have one of our dreams played back to us as a goal that has the potential to make us a failure. That cycle makes us cynical and makes our dreams small.

Your job as a School Leader is to have the courage to hold bigger dreams over a long-term time horizon. It will take some practice and time in your role to build long-term muscles and skills. It will also take courage. Why? Because the bolder your vision and perspective of what is possible for your school, the bigger the gap between that vision and your current reality. Small dreams result in small gaps to close. Big dreams result in big gaps to close. The work of holding the tension between your vision and your current reality is not easy work. There will be days when you feel beat up by your own bold vision. You will feel discouraged that there is still so much work to do and that progress is slower than you would like. But the price of escaping that pressure is immense. You accept small, incremental progress toward less meaningful goals. And you lose the anchor that you need to drive toward a more meaningful destination over time. This isn't the kind of thinking that you can do in the shower or on your commute. To do it well, you will have to set aside time for it.

TIME SHIFT 2: PROTECT TIME TO THINK, REFLECT, AND ANALYZE

Former U.S. Navy captain David Marquet (2020) describes two types of work: *doing*, which he calls "redwork," and *thinking*, or "bluework." In most organizations, the default is doing—to execute, to perform, to continue whatever we have started. Change, improvement, and learning all happen during bluework—when we pause our execution to think. Contrary to what we might like to believe, it is very difficult—basically impossible—to dedicate your mind to the work of *doing* and *thinking* at the same time. Marquet argues that creating pauses for bluework is one of organizational leaders' most important jobs. Establishing these rhythms for a school starts with the leader protecting time and space for this kind of thinking for themselves.

Some School Leaders may think, *OK, I've protected the time—now what?* Over time, you will use your bluework time in two distinct ways, what Goleman (2015) calls selective attention and open attention. Selective attention—"the neural capacity to beam in on just one target while ignoring a staggering sea of incoming stimuli" (p. 14)—is used for problem-solving and is commonly associated with mathematicians. Open attention, where our minds "take in information widely in the world around us and the world within us and pick up subtle clues we'd otherwise miss" (p. 86), is what enables creativity and new ideas.

Protecting time to think isn't a luxury. It is essential for you to do your job. If you feel guilty taking this time while everyone else at your school is forced to run around with their hair on fire, maybe one of the things you can think about is how to deploy your Bridge Leaders to change building systems, structures, and schedules that allow all the adults in your building to have some time to think. Protecting time, what Goleman (2015) calls "a creative cocoon" (p. 46), is a crucial first step. But School Leaders also must learn how to ward off distractions, which come in two basic varieties: task monsters and emotion monsters. At any given time, there will be dozens of things competing for your attention as a School Leader. You must develop strong judgment to recognize which things warrant your immediate attention and response and which can be set aside for now. This may require sturdy scaffolding at first, but eventually, practice will strengthen this muscle.

Even if you can protect your attention from chasing task rabbits, the emotional monsters of worry and rumination will still lurk. And they are dangerous to our attention and focus. Goleman (2015) warns us, "Emotional reactivity flips us into a different mode of attention, one where our world contracts into fixation on what's upsetting us" (p. 54). Ultimately the ability to turn our focus away from distractions, to dial down emotions, is a skill. It's called executive attention. Like all skills, we each have a different baseline, but we can all improve. Mindfulness training is one of the most effective ways to build this muscle. For many of us, this kind of practice is uncomfortable. We feel awkward. We aren't good at it. It's hard to tell if we are getting better or if it is making a difference, especially in the short term. *"This just isn't who I am!"* There it is again: the excessive need to be me.

TIME SHIFT 3: FROM PRIMARILY INTERNALLY TO SIGNIFICANTLY EXTERNALLY FOCUSED

The final shift in time allocation is from a "down and in" focus—teachers, students, staff—to an "up and out" focus—parents and caregivers, community members, and the broader district. Prior to the transition to the School Leader role, for most of your career you have been focused on down-and-in leadership—driving effective execution by your teams within the four walls of your school. The transition to School Leader requires a shift to prioritize up-and-out leadership. Significant time needs to be spent with parents and caregivers listening to their ideas and concerns, with community leaders building relationships and recruiting partners, and generally being visible in your community. You have a unique role to play in representing your school in the community. These interactions aren't taking you away from your real job—they are your job. And the way that you orient to this work will set the tone for how every member of your team orients and interacts with your community.

EXERCISE 8.D

School Leader Calendar Audit

STEP 1: Review your calendar: Does it reflect how you actually spend your time? If not, take a few minutes to reconstruct how you spent your time in the last few weeks.

STEP 2: Color code your calendar.

- In green, highlight time that you have protected for deep thinking and planning.
- In yellow, highlight time that you invested in your broader community (not focused on staff or students).
- In blue, highlight time that is directly linked to your unique leadership missions.
- In purple, highlight unplanned or reactive time allocations.
- In orange, highlight all other time allocations that are *not* devoted to School Leader tasks.

STEP 3: What do you notice?

- What's the ratio of your time?
- Where do you see wins?
- Where are there opportunities to improve? What's the root cause of these issues?

STEP 4: Plan for action.

- What could you do differently to shift your time allocation?
    - Where do you need to be more disciplined or build new habits?
    - Where do you need to delegate or build capacity in your team?
    - How might new or improved systems shift your time allocations?

WHAT WILL YOU STOP DOING? AND HOW WILL YOU STOP?

Learning to direct your attention, harness your focus, and dial down distractions will be critical to your ability to lead at this level. You are never going to have time to do this kind of thinking if you continue to be involved in every detail of campus operations. It is just not possible—there are not enough hours in the day. School Leaders must be disciplined about what they are going to stop doing. To do so, they must get clear about who is responsible for that work.

Yes, this is partly about clearly defining roles and responsibilities. But if School Leaders empower their team to execute tasks but not make decisions, they will find themselves constantly sucked into execution. Who can make decisions on your campus? Let's get specific.

- What decisions can Bridge Leaders make without your involvement or participation—decisions that you have fully delegated? If someone asked them, would they know they are empowered to make these decisions?
- What decisions are Team Leaders fully empowered to make (without the involvement or participation of their Bridge Leader or you)? If someone asked them, would they know they are empowered to make these decisions?
- What is the ratio of decisions delegated to Team Leaders and Bridge Leaders compared to all the decisions made on your campus?

Most School Leaders are committed to shared decision-making. They value people's opinions and have a lot of formal and informal channels for people to have input and voice to campus decisions. Most School Leaders *want* to empower people to drive decisions. But, in most schools, even when other people are leading a decision-making process, they still need to get sign-off from the School Leader before they finalize the decision—either formally or informally (i.e., someone tells you before they do anything).

If this describes you and your school, here's the implication: Though you want to empower your team and are *committed* to inclusive decision-making, you are still participating in all or most of the decisions. Your attention continues to be focused on the more short-term, immediate work.

What if you actually released decisions to your Bridge Leaders and Team Leaders? They would keep you informed of the decisions that have been made, but you would spend less time tracking each step, weighing in, and providing your blessing. This could free up huge amounts of time and attention for you to do the work that *only you can do*. We know what you could gain. What would you lose?

Most School Leaders are worried about losing control or losing context. The first sounds like: *What if someone makes a bad decision?* They might. And if and when they do, you will coach them through it. But there are many decisions that you are more likely to get wrong than your team is, because you aren't the person with the most relevant information, expertise, or perspective. Fred Kofman (2018) provides a good rule of thumb: "decisions are best left to the people who know the most about [the relevant] circumstances, who understand the most about the changes that need to be made, and about the resources needed to make them" (p. 18). He argues that there are tactical decisions that benefit from "local knowledge"—people who are doing the work and closest to the problem—and then there are global decisions that impact many stakeholders and require a big picture view. Those latter types of decisions are yours. But the former will be decided correctly more often if they are decided by others, often by teachers.

But what if a parent or community member calls me with a question and I don't know the answer? This is the fear of losing context, of not having the information you need to do your job. But ownership and information are two different things. The fact that you won't make the decision doesn't mean that you shouldn't know about it. If a parent asks about something you don't have all of the information on, you will be fine. All you need to do is listen to the question and any underlying concerns, make it clear that you care about their perspective, and then gather the information you need to address their concern.

Creating systems, routines, and discipline to reorganize leadership responsibilities will be ongoing work, not a one-time event. Formally define (or clarify) leadership responsibilities, including decision-making rights, is a good place to start. Lockhart ISD called this "threading" leadership responsibilities (Chapter 3). What matters is that you have real, candid conversations with your team, and you hold yourselves accountable for what you agree to.

In addition to defining responsibilities for the important, recurring work of leading a school, you also have to deal with all the unplanned, unexpected events that occur on a daily basis in a school. There will be times when the unexpected demands your attention and leadership. That's why being flexible, visible, and available is important for School Leaders. But if you are the first responder to every unexpected event on your campus, it will make it difficult to invest your time and attention in strategic, long-term work. Consider mapping out the most common unexpected events on your campus and identifying a person who can be the first responder to each type of event, with clearly defined protocols for how and to whom events get escalated for more support.

EXERCISE 8.E

Protecting Time for Long-Term Thinking

A checklist of moves and strategies

→ Clearly define responsibilities, by level, for the most important, recurring work that happens on your campus.

→ As part of defining responsibilities, clarify who is the decision-maker. If you have a veto—if someone has to confirm that you support the decision before it is made—you are the decision-maker.

→ Identify the most frequent unplanned events (also known as interruptions or small emergencies) on your campus. Identify a first responder for each type of event and a clear protocol for escalating issues when they require more support. Ensure each first responder receives training and support so they can confidently respond.

→ Proactively share the way you have defined responsibilities and first responders with your principal supervisor or key members of the central office. Ask for their support sticking to these systems. Help them understand where you may need more support from the central office to prioritize your most important work.

SHIFTING PROFESSIONAL IDENTITY

Like each of the previous leadership passages, becoming a School Leader and embracing your unique leadership mission will require a shift in your professional identity. Part of this shift is simply releasing the work that you used to do to embrace the work that only you can do—the work of vision and direction of organizational communication of prioritizing and balancing short-term, urgent needs with long-term aspirations. But there are also three specific shifts in professional identity that School Leaders must make to succeed and thrive as the leader of the organization. New School Leaders must embrace the irreplaceable role they play in cultivating a healthy school culture, develop new inner dispositions to cope with the scrutiny that comes with the top job, and manage their ego, balancing confidence with humility.

PROFESSIONAL IDENTITY SHIFT 1: OWNING ORGANIZATIONAL CULTURE

Years ago, I encountered a metaphor for educational reform that has always stayed with me—the contrasting strategies of an animal trainer versus a horticulturalist. An animal trainer sets out to control an animal's behavior. They define a standard of excellence and, through repetitive practice, supported by reinforcing rewards and consequences, mold the trainee to conform consistently to the standard. A horticulturalist understands their job differently. Their goal is to cultivate a healthy, flourishing plant—tall, sturdy, vibrant. Their method is radically different from the animal tamer. They can't tell the plant what to do or provide structures that force it to grow. What they can do is create the conditions that will allow the plant to thrive: temperature, light, water, soil.

School Leaders are horticulturalists—they can accomplish more, over time, by creating supportive conditions versus trying to direct every detail of the work. In addition to vision, direction, systems, and structures, one of the most important conditions the School Leader must cultivate is a vibrant, positive, focused organizational culture. Culture is mostly invisible and can seem hard to change. It is difficult to trace the direct impact of time or energy invested in a school's culture. As a result, it's easy to neglect as we naturally drift to focusing on things where we can see the scoreboard of our impact more clearly.

But School Leaders play an irreplaceable role in establishing, enhancing, and improving a school's culture. Culture building is long-term work, not a one-time event. Kofman (2018) offers a four-step formula for building culture: define, demonstrate, demand, delegate. This is work that only School Leaders can do. They must guide the process of defining the culture and they must live it (demonstrate) or else it will never take root. If School Leaders neglect it, the culture will stagnate or erode.

EXERCISE 8.F

Organizational Culture

- As a School Leader, have you spent time understanding your school's culture and thinking about what kind of culture you need?
- Have you taken any intentional actions to shape, enhance, or change your school's culture?
- Does school culture inform your short- and long-term plans and priorities? Why or why not?
- If you haven't invested much energy in your school's culture, what competes for your time and attention instead (i.e., what's a higher priority)? Are any of those things something you could delegate to a member of your team?
- If school culture feels like a low priority, why is that?

PROFESSIONAL IDENTITY SHIFT 2: ACCEPTING ATTENTION/SCRUTINY THAT COMES WITH BEING HIGHLY VISIBLE

As the School Leader, you now represent the school—all that is right about it and all that needs to be improved—in the eyes of key stakeholders. There's a spotlight on you. With that attention comes a lot of scrutiny. Ultimately, you are responsible for everything that happens in your school: the way that students interact with each other, every lesson that is delivered, and every email that a member of your staff sends to caregivers. Because you are leading a big organization, things won't always go perfectly. Mistakes will happen. Sometimes the mistakes will be yours. And it will be your job to own them, address them, and fix them.

You must work to maintain a positive orientation toward this scrutiny: *People are watching me. That means that I have an opportunity to influence people through what I say and do.* But there will be moments when the scrutiny feels overwhelming, and you will struggle to see it as positive. In those moments it feels suffocating, the parsing unfair, the criticism personal and demoralizing.

School Leaders must build and deepen their capacity to deal with this pressure in a healthy way. They must develop thicker skin without becoming callous or cynical. They must take some of the commentary with a grain of salt while still taking the people—their hopes, motivations, concerns—very seriously. They must be compassionate toward themselves, including in the moments when they screw up, and remain compassionate toward others, even when they appear to be acting as adversaries or opponents. At the end of the day, Goleman (2015) warns, "It's not the chatter of people around us that is the most powerful distractor, but the chatter of our own minds" (p. 48). School Leaders must learn to contain the rumination and negative self-talk that can dominate their thinking. It is a recipe for heightened stress and lowered effectiveness. Three strategies will help.

DE-PERSONALIZE IT: YOU ARE NOT YOUR ROLE

"A conflict situation is the wrong place for a leader to look for love" (Bolman & Deal, 2014, p. 97). Part of the reason it is so hard to withstand scrutiny and criticism is because it can feel and sound very personal. You may encounter stakeholders who question your motives and intentions. To you, it may feel like people are questioning your character and are choosing to paint you in a negative light. This hurts and your first instinct may be to defend yourself.

But you must remember that people are often reacting to you as your role, not as an individual. Ron Heifetz and Marty Linsky (2002) admonish leaders, "Remember, when you lead, people don't love you or hate you. Mostly they don't even know you. They love or hate the positions you represent" (p. 198). Your team, your staff, your students, your families, and your community are often interacting with you as the principal of your school, not as __________ (insert your name here). Remembering this can protect your self-worth. You are a valued, worthy person regardless of whether you are an extraordinary principal or a mediocre one. Your family and friends are going to love you whether you succeed or fail. That's the truth in which your self-worth is anchored. It can also make it easier for you to withstand heat and pressure and to receive criticism openly and without defensiveness. Doing so will earn people's respect and trust. It will also allow you to hear what's true and useful to keep the organization moving toward the goal.

FOCUS ON WHAT YOU CAN INFLUENCE, NOT WHAT YOU CAN'T CONTROL

When facing sharp criticism, School Leaders may be tempted to feel sorry for themselves, complain to themselves about the unfairness of their circumstances, and focus on all the events and circumstances that are out of their control. This may feel comforting, but it won't help the leader respond to their circumstances effectively. Instead, School Leaders need to stay grounded in what Kofman (2018) calls the "response-ability" mindset:

> the ability to choose one's response to a situation. It's about focusing on the aspects of reality that you can influence instead of feeling victimized by circumstances that you cannot. It's about being the main character of

> your own life. Instead of asking "Why is this happening to me?," a person who is response-able asks, "What can I do when this happens?" (p. 171)

Kofman argues that this response is more empowering and more effective. Instead of getting distracted by what's not in your control, response-ability is about accepting accountability and staying focused on what you can do to move toward your goals and stay anchored in your values. Challenges and crises will come. You can decide in advance how you will respond to them.

ANCHOR IN VALUES

School Leaders must be deeply anchored in who they are, what they believe, and the values that guide them. Without a clear north star (or southern cross), School Leaders end up navigating by the lights of satellites. Chasing the approval of everyone and avoiding criticism or challenge may shield you from short-term pain, but it guarantees you won't lead your school toward a bolder vision or the outcomes students deserve.

Your values become a lens through which you use criticism to help you get better. Sometimes criticism is a reminder that you have drifted from your true north. Be grateful for the reminder, adjust, and get back on course. When criticism feels unhelpful, consider what you can learn from it—perhaps there are new strategies you need to deploy to communicate better and build coalitions—and move on.

EXERCISE 8.G

Dealing With Scrutiny

- When a decision you made or an event at your school is criticized, how do you react internally and externally?
- What is your inner narrative about having "all eyes on you" as the School Leader? Is that narrative serving you? If not, how might you rescript it?
- Think of a time when you felt personally criticized and it hurt. What would it look like to take the person's concern seriously, without taking the commentary personally?
- Which of the strategies in this section could help you navigate scrutiny in a healthier, more sustainable way?
    - De-personalize criticism—remember that you are not your role.
    - Find where you have influence.
    - Anchor in values.

PROFESSIONAL IDENTITY SHIFT 3: LEADING WITH CONFIDENCE AND HUMILITY

Sometimes, the demands of leadership are infuriating. You're often sandwiched between two completely contradictory demands: Be patient and move with urgency. Care for people and drive for results. It can feel like a lose-lose proposition. And in your low moments, you may throw up your hands thinking, *This is impossible*. In these moments, remember that learning to lead effectively requires learning to live with and embody paradox.

In our culture, we often treat confidence and humility as opposites. Confidence is believing in yourself and your abilities. It is trusting your instincts and taking your own counsel, particularly when facing difficult decisions and high-pressure situations. Humility, on the other hand, is often associated with having a low view of yourself, with doubt.

Excellent School Leaders demonstrate confidence and humility. A leader without confidence will be rudderless, chasing whatever is popular, or paralyzed, unable to commit to any path forward. Humility is a healthy recognition that you are imperfect and are still learning. You know a lot but not everything. You are doing your best, and you will make mistakes. It is their confidence that allows great School Leaders to operate with humility and without defensiveness. They aren't threatened by new ideas or being challenged by people they lead or serve. They know that they will make mistakes, and those mistakes won't be fatal because they will learn from them.

This ego balance is essential. And with all balances, we will each have a natural tendency to err in one direction or the other, like a car with a steering wheel that is slightly out of alignment. Your job is to recognize your lean, if you have one, and rebalance it.

PRIORITIZE AND CHIP AWAY

As a principal, you have an extraordinary opportunity—to shape the educational opportunities available to every student who walks through your door. It is an enormous responsibility and a demanding job. But it isn't something that you need to carry alone. What you must do is lean into the work that only you can do and unleash the talents and gifts of the people around you.

Big Ideas and Key Takeaways

- The school leadership architecture sharpens what it means for School Leaders to provide instructional leadership, focused on their unique leadership mission.
- School Leaders' top priority is establishing the vision and strategy for the school. Leaders who haven't articulated a vision will continue to feel the need to be personally involved in every aspect of instructional leadership.
- Communication is the engine of leadership. It is essential to mobilizing a group of people around a common purpose. School Leaders' communication needs to be simple, audience-focused, and frequent and repetitive.
- If school systems attempt to strengthen the school leadership architecture through addition only—adding people, adding salaries, adding work to be done—they will quickly find the math difficult to balance. The key is to rethink and repurpose—not just add.
- Virtually everything the School Leader needs to accomplish depends on the quality of advice, perspectives, and ideas that the School Leader hears from their team, from students, and from the community. Don't overlook the importance of being a great listener.
- In a crisis, your job is to act wisely and decisively to address the situation while responding to and managing the emotions that are in play.
- Over time, School Leaders must operate with a multiyear vision and perspective—far beyond the required cycles of campus improvement planning and other compliance-related mechanisms. Big visions and big results won't be achieved on a continuous loop of one-year strategies.
- Change, improvement, and learning all happen when we pause our execution to think. School Leaders must make time for this deep thinking.
- You have a unique role to play in representing your school in the community.
- If School Leaders empower their team to execute tasks but not to make decisions, they will find themselves constantly sucked into execution.
- School Leaders play an irreplaceable role in establishing, enhancing, and improving a school's culture.
- School Leaders must build and deepen their capacity to deal with pressure and scrutiny in a healthy way.
- Excellent School Leaders demonstrate confidence and humility.

CHAPTER 8 SELF-ASSESSMENT

As you read through the chapter, use this tool to capture your observations on how you are navigating each shift. Use a 1–4 scale:

1 = Never or rarely

2 = Sometimes

3 = Often

4 = Almost always

SKILLS	
LONG-TERM STRATEGY AND GOALS, BALANCING FUTURE GOALS WITH PRESENT NEEDS AND PRESSURES	
______________	We have developed a clear, bold vision for where we want to be as a school in five years or more that inspires and motivates our school community.
______________	My team has a clear, shared understanding of the school's strengths and areas that need improvement and have diagnosed root causes.
______________	Based on the shared vision and strategy, we have multiyear goals that help us prioritize our work and balance short-term and long-term needs.
______________	We use our planning and goals to make decisions about what to say "yes" and "no" to and to allocate resources (time, people, initiatives).
COMMUNICATE CLEARLY AND EFFECTIVELY WITH ALL STAKEHOLDERS	
______________	My written and verbal communication is simple—easy to understand, easy to remember, brief.
______________	I adapt my communication in response to what I know about my audience and what they care about.
______________	I repeat important messages via multiple channels and over time. I don't expect people to remember something I said one time.
______________	I err toward transparency and don't respond defensively when I get a question or am challenged.
______________	I seek out feedback and advice. I have formal and informal ways of hearing from different stakeholders.
______________	I am intentional about how I communicate with parents, staff, community members, and students. Stakeholders are highly satisfied with the frequency and quality of communication they receive.

PREVENT AND NAVIGATE CRISES	
______	I ensure that our school is rigorous in its emergency preparation. I have demonstrated through my words and action that emergency preparedness is a priority.
______	I have a strong understanding of my district's emergency protocols. I know what my role is and how I will receive support from the central office. I have rehearsed my understanding with my supervisor.
______	I routinely scan the environment, identifying issues that could escalate into something more significant and ensure they are resolved effectively.
______	I remain calm in stressful situations and put the people around me at ease. When I am off balance internally, I have habits and routines to regain my composure.
______	I have strong habits and routines for managing my physical, mental, and emotional resources. I am not usually working at the edge of exhaustion. (I am more likely to have "reserves" to meet a crisis.)
______	If I have already navigated a crisis in my role, I effectively provided frequent, simple communication that built confidence and trust, helped stakeholders know what action to take, and lowered anxiety.
______	If I have not already navigated a crisis in my role, I have planned for and rehearsed the types of communication I would provide, when, and to whom.
TIME	
______	I think about goals, priorities, and strategy for my school with a long-term view (two or three years).
______	I regularly (at least monthly) have time within my working day that is dedicated to thinking and reflection.
______	My calendar reflects the importance of spending time with and being responsive to caregivers, community members, and others who depend on and/or can support our school.
PROFESSIONAL IDENTITY	
______	I prioritize and value the work of actively and effectively building a strong, engaged, productive school culture.
______	I am comfortable with the attention and scrutiny that comes with being a highly visible community leader.
______	I trust myself and feel secure in my leadership (confidence). I know I am still learning, will make mistakes, and am open to others' perspectives (humility).

Once you've completed your self-assessment, turn to the tools for prioritizing and action planning in Appendix D.

CHAPTER 9

Rethinking Leadership Development

Districts must fulfill two critical responsibilities to create a strong school leadership architecture. They must improve the structures, and they must develop ready leaders. Without strong leadership development systems, individuals promoted to new leadership roles will struggle. Every leader must have the skills, capabilities, and mindset to lead at the right level. They have to shift how they spend their time and evolve their professional identities to embrace the work that only they can do.

Most districts are working hard to try to develop their people but find themselves trapped in a cycle where the need for strong leaders at every level outstrips the supply of people who are ready to step into the role. Leadership development systems can help districts address the three big reasons why individuals fail to succeed in a new leadership role:

- Expectations for the next leadership level are not clear and shifts are not named.
- Aspiring leaders are selected for a new role before they are ready.
- Development and support aren't available, aren't focused on the most important priorities, or aren't effective.

To build a bench of leaders ready to lead at every level, districts need to build systems that address each of these points of failure. They need to refine their selection processes, onboard and support new leaders, and proactively identify and develop future leaders at every leadership level from Team Member to School Leader.

FIGURE 9.1 • Leadership Development Systems, Grounded in Clear Role-Based Leadership Expectations

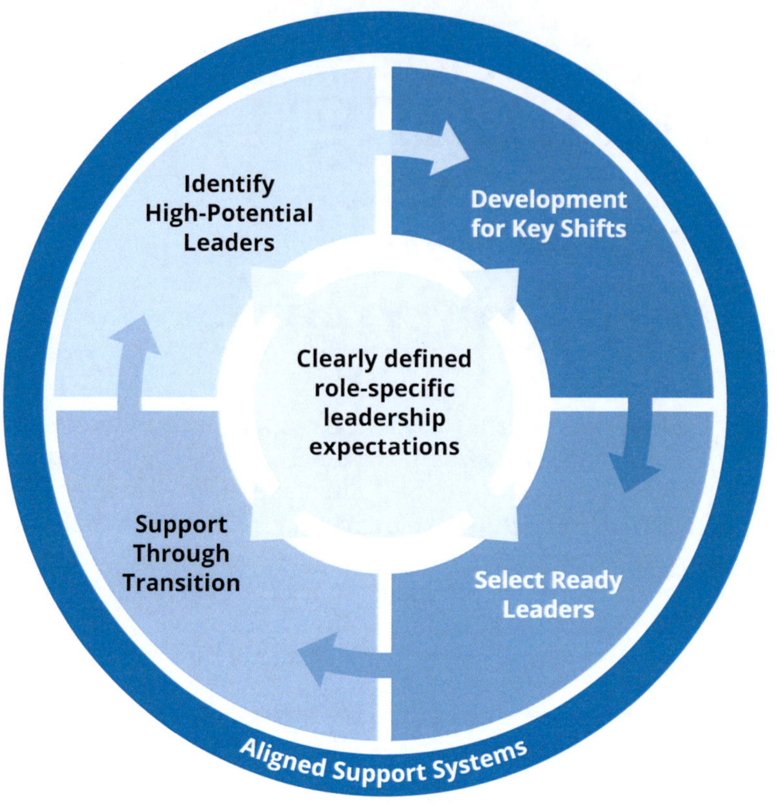

The foundation of all these systems is clearly defined expectations for leaders at every level (Figure 9.1). So, that is where we will start. The rest of the chapter will highlight key principles for building the other key leadership development systems. It will close by helping districts identify a path for tackling this work, including identifying the most important immediate priorities.

THE FOUNDATION: CLEARLY DEFINE LEADERSHIP EXPECTATIONS

The first step to building effective leadership development systems is to clearly define leadership expectations. A strong leadership definition

- provides clear expectations to aspiring leaders, allowing them to own their own development;
- anchors criteria for leader identification and selection;

- serves as the framework for all leadership development and training efforts; and
- ensures these efforts align and add up to something—that what we are selecting for matches what we are developing and, most importantly, aligns to what leaders need to know and be able to do to succeed in the role.

This can seem very basic, especially because most school systems (and the leaders within them) are confident that they all know what great leadership looks like. The problem is that, too often, the district hasn't clarified leadership expectations for anyone except the principal. The district can't explain how leadership expectations grow and change from level to level. In the absence of this clarity, individuals across the district are using different formal and informal definitions of leadership to guide their work.

Between the curricula of the leadership academies, the criteria guiding assistant principal and principal selection processes, and the leadership evaluation standards, most districts are juggling at least three or four different visions of what leaders need to know and be able to do. Without a clear, shared definition of the skills and capabilities leaders need, it becomes very difficult to align these efforts. Instead, there is a natural gravitational pull toward incoherence and silos. Fragmented systems waste and deplete district resources. Lots of people are working hard to develop and support leaders, but those efforts don't add up to anything—or as much as they could. Fragmented systems also confuse and frustrate aspiring leaders. They don't understand what to prioritize or how to improve.

Unique leadership missions describe the "what" of each leadership level. The leadership definition describes the "how": the competencies, skills, behaviors, and dispositions that leaders need to succeed at each level. We recommend that districts start by developing a broad leadership definition that applies to *all* staff in the district, before getting more specific about expectations at each level. Figure 9.2 offers an example. A strong broad leadership definition will meet three criteria:

- Clarity: It is simple and clear enough to be used frequently across the district.
- Ownership: Current and aspiring leaders say, "Yes, that's who I want to work to be as a leader."
- Rigor: It is supported and reinforced by relevant and forward-thinking research.

FIGURE 9.2 • Example of a Broad Leadership Definition

CATEGORY	COMPETENCY
Builds Capacity	**Demonstrates Personal Leadership:** Remains rooted in values. Reflects on self-practice. Pursues growth and improvement.
	Communicates for Impact: Listens well and expresses ideas clearly, demonstrating an understanding of the needs of the audience and ensuring transparency and collaboration.
	Builds Relationships: Knows the people served. Demonstrates respect and compassion. Shows appreciation.
	Develops Others: Coaches and supports every individual to grow and maximize their full potential.
	Shares Leadership: Encourages collaboration and shares power to make decisions and advance the mission and vision.
Delivers Results	**Inspires Excellence:** Models a pursuit of excellence that challenges and inspires others. Celebrates success.
	Creates Strategy and Planning: Sets a vision and defines priorities. Builds and implements a plan to achieve short- and long-term goals.
	Facilitates Change: Leads innovation and is open to new ideas and strategic risk-taking.
	Is Data-Driven: Uses data to identify opportunities for growth, drive decision-making, and support student success.
	Knows Core Knowledge: Continuously develops knowledge and expertise to deliver results.

Let's start with clarity. Achieving it is harder than it sounds. As you do this work, there are going to be many details that you want to include. There will be words that you love that you can't let go of and nuanced, rigorous competency frameworks that you want to fully incorporate. Adding layers of detail will make your system more complicated. You may think it is more nuanced, more rigorous. But every level of complicatedness that you add will make your system harder to operate. Your job is to build a *simple* system that addresses complexity without becoming complicated. We recommend your leadership definition have no more than four categories, broken down into fewer than 15 competencies with short, easy-to-understand descriptions. A longer, wordier leadership definition may move you closer to perfection, but it also takes longer to read and is harder to remember. It increases the likelihood that it will sit on the shelf, unused. In almost every case, shorter is better.

Having supported dozens of districts to develop leadership definitions, we have found that there are significant similarities among them (because they build from a shared research base). But the differences are important. Figure 9.2 is illustrative, not a recommendation. You can use it as a jumping-off point. But we strongly encourage you to not just adopt our template like an off-the-shelf product. Why? Because having conversations about the leadership competencies and level-specific behaviors is an opportunity to build shared understanding of the school leadership architecture and ownership of the level-specific behaviors. The words and the framing in your leadership definition need to reflect your context: state leadership standards, district priorities, language that resonates with your culture and values. So, if you have critiques of Figure 9.2, great. You may dislike the language, disagree with how key behaviors are clustered, or think one or more competencies are missing or underemphasized. Build a leadership definition that reflects your district. Exercise 9.A outlines the basic steps.

EXERCISE 9.A

Establishing a Broad Leadership Definition—Basic Steps

You will develop your leadership definition through six basic steps. The challenge will be keeping the focus on rigor, ownership, and simplicity. This will be an iterative process and there isn't one right answer. You can find a few additional examples in Appendix E. They are simple and united by a common research base. If you drill into the competencies, you will find significant overlap. Their differences in framing and language reflect district values and priorities in order to generate ownership.

1. **Identify your key stakeholders:** The most likely way leaders will feel ownership of the definition is if they had a role in shaping it.
    a. Steering Group: Though you want to collect broad input, you will need a smaller group (typically four to eight people) to make decisions that prioritize simplicity and rigor. This group is also responsible for leading workshops with the design group and facilitating any broader input.
    b. Design Group: This group of 20 to 40 people will be highly engaged in shaping the districts' definition through input and feedback. We generally encourage districts to prioritize principals in this process because they are (1) experienced leaders and (2) will play a big role in building ownership with their teams once the definition has been established.
    c. Broader input (optional): Some districts may choose to engage more stakeholders through surveys or other ways of providing input.

(Continued)

(Continued)

   d. Each of the subsequent steps will involve iterating between the Design Group (input/feedback) and Steering Group (decision-making/synthesis), including any broader input.

2. **Synthesize district values and priorities:** Through workshops, listening sessions, or surveys, identify stakeholders' expectations and hopes for their leaders, the qualities they value, and the leadership skills that are most important for advancing the district's goals and priorities at *this* time.

3. **Cross-walk what you heard with research on effective school leadership:** Identify the two or three research-based sources that your Steering Group and Design Group will ground their work in (including any state-adopted competency frameworks). What are the common themes? What, if anything, is missing from the priorities your district identified? What did you elevate in importance? To facilitate this conversation, you might produce a crosswalk of the definitions in an Excel spreadsheet.

4. **Synthesize and narrow to 9 to 12 key competencies:** Using your cross-walk from Step 3, look for themes and groupings in the data. Are there overlapping ideas you can combine without losing anything essential? Focus on language that makes it clear what leaders need to do—short headings, with brief descriptions to capture the nuance.

5. **Group the competencies under two to four categories:** How do the competencies cluster and reflect your district priorities and values? Develop titles that are simple, clear, and memorable. These categories will be the first thing that your staff will internalize, so make sure they paint a complete (if high level) picture of your expectations.

6. **Over time, test and iterate to fine-tune.** Once you're confident, use a communications campaign to drive understanding, alignment, and ownership.

Then, the broad definition can be further specified for each leadership level. The level-specific definitions are where expectations become more concrete and where there are opportunities to align and connect to professional standards. By engaging principals and leaders from each leadership level, this process is an opportunity to continue to build alignment around and help leaders internalize what it means to lead at each level. Using the unique leadership missions of each level and the key shifts, get concrete about how the competencies from the broad leadership definition apply to Team Members, Team Leaders, Bridge Leaders, and School Leaders.

Though these will be more detailed than the broad leadership definition, simplicity is still critically important. One way to keep these level-specific behaviors as simple as possible is to write them so that each level includes but does not need to repeat the behaviors of the previous level.

BUILDING AND RENOVATING: ALIGNED, PROACTIVE LEADERSHIP DEVELOPMENT

Equipped with the general and level-specific leadership definitions, it is time to build or renovate key leadership development systems: identification, development, selection, and support. The choice to visualize these systems as a circle was intentional (Figure 9.1). There is no natural starting point as the district is perpetually working at each stage of the cycle as it works to elevate new leaders today and invest in strong leaders for tomorrow. As we discuss in the final section of this chapter, where you start will depend on your system priorities and needs. But for simplicity, in this section, we will introduce key principles in the order we would expect a district to tackle them if they are introducing a new role in the district—for example, a new Team Leader role. In this scenario, the district's priorities are to:

1. Select the strongest leaders for the role today.
2. Support and onboard those leaders to the new role today.
3. Build systems to identify future leaders.
4. Proactively develop future leaders.

LOOK FOR THE RIGHT THINGS WHEN SELECTING LEADERS

Too often, selection processes are primarily focused on an individual's current performance or how they perform in an interview and not focused enough on their demonstrated potential for the skills, time applications, and professional identity required in the next role. Let's focus on one example—an individual moving from Team Member to Team Leader. A Team Member succeeds through their individual work, their ability to develop high-quality, timely work products. Exceptional Team Members are often distinguished by their above-and-beyond knowledge and skill, their ability to work independently, and their proactiveness and ownership of their work. But to succeed at the next level, a former Team Member needs more than individual skill and competence. They need to be effective in working with others to deliver results. They need new skills, time applications, and professional identities. When selecting an individual to make the shift to Team Leader, you are looking for more than a high-performing Team Member. You are looking for an effective Team Member who demonstrates potential to be a great Team Leader. Do they seek out collaboration with their peers? Are they good at building relationships? Are they the person Team Members seek out for advice when they're stuck on a tough problem? Do they *enjoy* providing support in these scenarios?

A Team Member who actively dislikes and resists collaborating with others is probably not the right person for the job, no matter how exceptional they are in their current job. When we select individuals based on their performance in their current role without any consideration for the demands of the next leadership level, we increase the risk that they will fail to shift their behavior to lead at the right level. The level-specific leadership definitions, which clearly define the expectations of each leadership level, provide an anchor for this work.

EXERCISE 9.B

Selection Process Audit

- For each role, have you clearly defined what you are selecting for?
- Which of the following are evaluated through your selection process?
  - Universal criteria valued in all leaders (see Figure 4.3)
  - Skill, competence, and effectiveness in their current role
  - Demonstrated skill and potential for the required competencies of the new role, which focus on key shifts
- Are these criteria rooted in your leadership definition? (You can find a sample of criteria aligned to leadership definition competencies in Appendix E.)
- How are each of the three categories weighted? Are you overemphasizing current performance?
- How are your criteria assessed? For each of the following, assign a weighting:

  ____% Authentic performance tasks

  ____% Data and evidence from current/past roles

  ____% Interview questions that focus on concrete examples (what the leader has actually done, in practice)

  ____% Interview questions that focus on philosophy/ hypothetical future situations

- How can you shift more weight away from philosophical or hypothetical questions and toward the first three modes of assessment? *Note: There are two challenges with hypothetical questions. First, many leaders know what they* should *do but may not consistently operate in that way. Second, hypothetical questions may reward communication skill over leadership skill and habits.*

ONBOARD AND SUPPORT NEW LEADERS

No matter how well prepared and ready a leader is for a new role, they will need intentional onboarding and ongoing support as they transition. It is especially important for districts to be intentional about their strategy for onboarding and supporting leaders who are taking on newly created or redesigned roles. We should expect leaders in these roles to face higher than normal levels of ambiguity. There aren't established role models for them to look to. The system may still be building a shared understanding of leadership expectations, which could result in mixed signals. So, districts should prioritize building onboarding and support systems for leaders in new roles even if they need more time to revamp the process for all leaders.

The common mental model for onboarding is an informational session where leaders receive a lot of information—often about new systems and processes. That may be important to do but isn't what we're talking about here. We're talking about a system of supports that help leaders understand the shifts they will experience in their new role, prioritize their growth and development, and monitor and support their transition. The new leader's manager will play a key role. (Chapters 5 through 8 can be a resource.) And there's a simple, but powerful first step—naming the shifts required at the new leadership level. It can be as simple as saying,

> *I know that you used to spend a lot of time doing X and you were really good at it. In this role, you'll need to do less of X and really prioritize Y. It's going to feel a little weird at first—I know, I've been there! You may miss doing those things you've been so good at. But I promise you in six months you are going to love the impact you are making in this role. I know that you can do it, because I've seen you _______. And I'm here to support you along the way.*

The district's role is to set consistent expectations for how managers support new leaders. Over time, they might build just-in-time modules to help leaders navigate this passage. Some of these learning supports may lean more heavily on classroom learning that's focused on helping the leader internalize role expectations, including shifts in professional identity and time applications, and to practice new skills in a low-stakes environment. But any concepts taught in the classroom must be reinforced through coaching and mentorship during the leader's first few months on the job. Once the leader has mastered the basics of the leadership passage, development focuses on how they can deepen their knowledge or master other skills and competencies in this role to become an exceptional performer (core development) and accelerate their readiness for the next role (high-potential development), discussed below.

EXERCISE 9.C

Planning Onboarding and Support

- What are your onboarding priorities (what knowledge do you want to build and what skills do you want to support each leader to prioritize) for the new leader's
    - first 30 days?
    - first 90 days?
    - first semester?
    - first year?
- Quick check: Do these priorities reflect the key competencies and shifts that these leaders need to make? Or are they primarily focused on technology knowledge, systems, and role expectations?
- For each of these priorities, which are best achieved through
    - direct support from the new leader's manager?
    - information, training, or support provided by the district?
- In any areas where the new leader's manager is the primary support, how will the district equip these managers to provide strong, consistent coaching and support?
- How will you monitor new leaders' growth and development through their first year?

INVEST IN LEADER IDENTIFICATION

Robust, structured leader selection processes are important. But if there are weak or underdeveloped candidates going through strong selection processes, the outcome will still be unprepared, new leaders being thrown into roles. Spending 80% of your energy on selection would be like a teacher spending 80% of their time writing the test, with 20% allocated to designing and delivering instruction. Tacking on a strong selection process to the back end of a passive process is too little too late.

Districts need to look for leaders earlier. They need to develop systems to identify high-potential leaders. To understand the distinction between identification and selection, consider the U.S. Soccer Federation, the entity that is responsible for building successful men's and women's national teams to represent the United States in international competition, from the World Cup to the Olympics. The most prominent decision it makes is *selecting* the players, deciding which combination of eligible players will give the team the greatest opportunity to win championships tomorrow. But the federation's most impactful work begins much earlier. It is also responsible for developing systems to *identify* promising, high-potential young players, often as young as 13 years old and sometimes even younger. These players drive the team's long-term future success. Once these players are identified, the organization can develop their potential and make them more skilled and ready for international competition and success.

The same is true in a school district. Selection focuses on picking someone to move into a leadership role tomorrow. Identification is about spotting future talent or what we call "high potentials." Selection is important, but identification is far more powerful. Identification creates opportunities to recruit high-potential individuals for leadership positions. Selection is focused on identifying the one best candidate who is ready to fill a vacancy immediately. Identification is focused on finding multiple individuals who have the potential to become—with focused development and support—a great leader in the future, often years down the road (Figure 9.3).

FIGURE 9.3 • Selection Versus Identification

	SELECTION	IDENTIFICATION
Purpose	To find and place an excellent leader	To find promising individuals in order to develop them into strong future leaders
Time Horizon	Immediate—position open now	Multiple years away—anticipating vacancies to be filled in the future
Level of Readiness	"Ready now"—evaluating candidate's ability to succeed in the new role tomorrow	"High potential"—evaluating a candidate's ability to grow into a strong leader in the future
Number of Candidates Selected/ Identified	Selecting the *one* best candidate	Identifying *all* high-potential candidates; goal is to identify at least three or four high-potential candidates for each anticipated vacancy

(Continued)

(Continued)

	SELECTION	IDENTIFICATION
Criteria	*Universal Criteria (see Figure 4.3)* • Student-centered "why" • Embodies organizational values • Growth mindset • Track-record of listening and relationship building • Learns quickly *Role-Specific Criteria:* • For instructional leadership roles, track record of effectiveness • District-defined competencies for the (new) role with a focus on key shifts	

Districts that focus only on selection need to reprioritize some of their energy to proactively identify promising future leaders. To be clear, identification is not the "tap on the shoulder" system. There's nothing wrong with people putting their hand up for leadership. But by relying solely on self-identification—or principals to "tap on the shoulder" using their own varied "know it when I see it" instincts—the district misses out on all the capable future leaders who need a nudge or a little bit of encouragement or who don't match implicit mental models. Like selection processes, identification should be a consistent, structured approach guided by specific, shared criteria and rooted in the district's leadership definition (see Exercise 9.D).

In the status quo, too many individuals with leadership potential don't pursue leadership roles because no one has ever highlighted their potential and encouraged them to consider them. Early identification can change that. And, it gives the district the opportunity to proactively develop them and get them ready for the next role (discussed in the next section).

EXERCISE 9.D

Simple Protocol for Leader Identification

Before You Start

- Clarify which leadership level you are focused on. *In this example, we will focus on identifying future School Leaders, but the same process could be followed to identify future Team Leaders.*

- Identify the people who will participate in identification conversations.
    - Who has the most concrete information about the performance and potential of these future leaders? *For future School Leaders, this will most likely be sitting School Leaders.*
    - Who else needs to participate to support next steps? *School Leaders' supervisors, individuals who will execute development strategies, etc.*
- Anchor in your criteria—the level-specific leadership behaviors you outlined in your leadership definition. Do you want to prioritize any of these behaviors in your identification conversations (because you have evidence that they are stronger predictors of high-potential leaders)?
- Gather relevant data. What information do you have about leaders' skills, results, and experiences that may contribute to more robust conversations?

When You Meet

- You have two goals for talent identification meetings:
    - To identify the highest-potential candidates for future vacancies. (Note: if you want to estimate your future vacancies, we have found taking your five-year vacancy average to be a reasonably strong forecast. Use that number to challenge yourself to invest in building two or three strong candidates for each vacancy.)
    - To increase calibration and alignment about leadership expectations among all participants, decreasing the likelihood that strong future leaders will be overlooked and increasing the likelihood that all leaders will receive consistent coaching and feedback.
- As pre-work, ask each *sitting School Leader* to do the following:
    - Review all of the individuals who are in *School Leader pipeline* roles (i.e., one or two positions away based on your career pathway) and assign them to one of four categories, using the criteria and any supporting data:
        - Still onboarding to current role: Too new to place or still learning to consistently demonstrate the competencies associated with the current leadership level.
        - Well-placed: Solid performance in current role. Not interested in expanding leadership influence at this time and/or not yet demonstrating skill or potential.

(Continued)

(Continued)

        - Potential (two years or more): Some evidence of skill or potential to succeed at the next leadership level. May have several areas where they need development or experience to increase their readiness.
        - High potential (<one or two years): Strong evidence of skill or potential to succeed at the next leadership level.
    - Come prepared to offer evidence or specific examples in support of each leader's placement. For potential and high-potential leaders, come prepared to discuss specific growth opportunities.
- At the identification meeting
    - Each *School Leader* spends time briefly presenting each individual. In general, more time should be spent on potential and high-potential leaders, getting clear on their development priorities.
    - The facilitator should probe for evidence and calibration throughout the process.
    - After all leaders have been presented, spend time considering whether any leaders have been overlooked or misplaced.
    - Before concluding, summarize any themes in potential and high-potential leaders' development priorities.

PROACTIVELY DEVELOP HIGH-POTENTIAL LEADERS

Most districts need to rethink *how* they approach leadership development and *who* they focus on. They need to shift from a sit-and-get default to a job-embedded approach to development. And they need to focus more of their energy on their highest potential leaders.

THE HOW: SHIFT FROM A SIT-AND-GET TO A JOB-EMBEDDED APPROACH TO DEVELOPMENT

When you hear "leadership development," what picture pops into your mind? Many people see a group of people in a room receiving information from an expert or having discussions with their colleagues. Their first thought is classroom learning—it's information acquisition. There is a role for this kind of learning, but it's a supplemental form of leadership development. The Center for Creative Leadership has made the case for decades that we've confused a side dish for the main course. The 70/20/10 principle is like the food pyramid for leadership development—helping us keep healthy proportions across leadership development strategies:

- The main course, comprising 70% of how leaders develop, is on-the-job learning: the development that comes from real-life practice, stretch assignments, and tackling new, challenging work.
- The next biggest driver, 20% of a leader's development, is coaching and mentorship.
- Classroom learning matters, but it's the smallest driver—10% of a leader's development.

Too often, the first thing that an organization does to develop leaders is create a classroom-based program. But we need to remember that the highest impact development opportunity that we have is not what we read in a book or discuss in a classroom; rather, it is the work we do each day. Future leaders get better from tackling challenging work, from opportunities to practice and to refine their craft. And we know that individuals master challenging work faster when they have support and frequent, high-quality feedback and coaching.

How can a school district move away from sit-and-get and toward job-embedded development? First, they need to flip the model. Instead of starting with the curriculum for classroom learning, start by identifying the job-embedded practice opportunities. Then, plan how coaching and support can be provided to leaders as they practice. In this flipped model, the classroom sessions become targeted opportunities to build knowledge and reflect on leaders' practice together.

Second, they should focus on improving the quality and quantity of coaching that every leader in the system receives. We aren't talking about a new coaching or mentorship program. Those add-ons are hard to sustain. We are talking about strengthening the support every leader receives from their manager. Managers are the ones who ensure that each leader understands their strengths and growth opportunities and has clear priorities for areas they are working to improve. Managers can help each person identify and lean into opportunities for practice—in their core responsibilities or through special assignments. And they help each individual identify resources and supports—the 10%—that can support their learning. This is the power of the school leadership architecture: It bakes coaching and development into the structure versus trying to provide it through one-off mentorship or coaching initiatives. School Leaders mentor Bridge Leaders who coach Team Leaders who develop Team Members. As a result, the coaching and feedback individuals receive should be meaningful, sustainable, and embedded into their day-to-day work. But we should never take the quality of this support for granted. Districts must continually set expectations for coaching and feedback and support leaders to meet them.

THE WHO: INVEST IN HIGH-POTENTIAL LEADERS

When we talk about leadership development, we are often talking about three distinct audiences: development for *everyone*, which we call core development; development for *the interested*; and development for *high potentials*. The purpose of core development is to support people in all roles to grow and get better at their current job. The district's role is to provide a base of resources that are available to everyone with support from their current manager. This is important work. High-potential development has a different purpose. It exists to support identified high-potential leaders to develop the skills, time allocations, and mindsets to be ready for future leadership roles. Unlike core development, which is primarily facilitated by an individual's manager, the district plays a big role in designing, facilitating, and monitoring the development of a small number of high-potential leaders. Districts need to invest in high-potential development if they want to increase the number of future leaders who are ready to step into new roles. Neglecting it is a big mistake and a missed opportunity.

FIGURE 9.4 • High Potential Versus Core Development

	CORE	HIGH POTENTIAL
Target Audience	Everyone (including the interested)	Identified high-potential future leaders
Purpose	Support growth, development, and success in current role	Build skills, mindsets, and capabilities to succeed in future roles
Content and Focus	Job-based competencies and targeted technical knowledge and skills	Key leadership shifts of next/future roles
Responsibility	• Individuals own/drive development • The manager is significantly responsible for coaching/guiding • District is responsible for building resources and systems of support	• Individual ownership and manager coaching continues to be significant • District is more proactive in driving development experiences and monitoring growth and progress

And yet, many districts dedicate upward of 90% of their development resources to everyone, or what we'll call "core development." The remaining 10% goes to the interested (leadership academies, etc.), with little focus on high-potential leaders. Why? To start, you can't systematically invest in high-potential leaders if you aren't identifying them. But there may be other reasons districts overlook high-potential development. In egalitarian cultures, it is easier to treat everyone the same. To increase the number of leaders ready to step into critical leadership positions, districts must dedicate significantly more time, energy, and resources to high-potential development—closer to 30% or 40% of their total leadership development effort.

What does high-potential leadership development look like? First, it focuses on key shifts. It isn't a one-size-fits-all survey course or one-off trainings that aren't connected to an overarching framework of leadership skills or are not relevant to immediate job challenges. By focusing on the *targeted* shifts that individual leaders need to make to succeed, we can unlock more effective leadership development.

Second, high-potential leadership development is 70/20/10, turbo-charged. Like core development, the 70% is buoyed by the high-potential leader's day-to-day work, including portfolio design and stretch assignments. But the district may want or need to do more to accelerate the leader's development by giving them opportunities that wouldn't be available in a traditional assignment. One strategy is to implement a more formal residency program where high-potential leaders rotate through multiple campuses over a year. Each assignment tests their skills in a different area. In each assignment, the high-potential leader is matched with the strongest sitting leader in that domain, increasing the quality of coaching and mentorship that they are receiving (the 20%).

Or the district could work with the high-potential leaders' manager to design stretch assignments in their current role. These experiences both build their skills and demonstrate their readiness for leading at the next level, providing data to the district about the leaders' readiness and informing the next steps in their development. Though classroom learning is only 10% of the pie, it is most powerful when a leader learns something they can immediately apply in their work and when the learning focus is a top priority for them. The district's job is to shift away from informational survey courses toward learning opportunities that are timely or connected to the job-embedded learning leaders are experiencing. When high-potential development has done its job—increasing the readiness of future leaders—the baton is passed back to core development, which also benefits from a just-in-time approach.

The 70/20/10 principle reminds us why districts must take ownership of high-potential leadership development. They cannot view it as an activity outsourced to universities or other partners. Only school districts have the power to harness the factors most significant to a leader's development—the work they do daily and the coaching and mentorship they receive from their supervisor, peers, and others in the organization.

EXERCISE 9.E

Development Audit

How much of your leadership development investments are currently focused on each of the following groups?

- ____% Everyone
- ____% The interested
- ____% High-potentials

How do you approach leadership development, particularly for high-potential leaders? What percentage of your leadership development investments fall into each mode of learning?

- ____% Knowledge-building (book clubs, information sessions, trainings)
- ____% Coaching and mentorship
- ____% Job-embedded experience and practice

Are there any bright spots you could build on? Do you have any leadership development efforts (even if they are small) that use job-embedded experience or coaching effectively?

- What can you learn from these efforts? How can they inspire others?
- How might you scale or copy some of these efforts?

How do you support managers and supervisors to be strong coaches, especially for their highest potential leaders?

- How do you monitor the coaching and support they provide?
- What simple things might you try to improve the quality and consistency of coaching across your district?

PRIORITIZE AND CHIP AWAY

As you have read through this chapter, you may have accumulated notes and ideas about work you need to do in your district. It may feel like a lot of work. For every leadership level, you need to build systems and structures to identify, develop, select, and support excellent leaders—all aligned to a clear definition of leadership expectations. You may not have the capacity to build or revamp all the systems at once. So how do you prioritize? And how do you decide where to start?

Though all districts are working toward a common destination—a strong, capable leader ready for each vacancy—the path to get there, and the right first steps, will depend on each district's context. Your decisions will be based on your assessment of both your needs (where are our systems the weakest and most in need of attention?) and your capabilities (what strengths do we have to leverage?). It is impossible to map the infinite variations and combinations. Figure 9.5 attempts to sketch two possible paths. The first column highlights the priorities for a district that is going through a major revamp of the leadership architecture. In these districts, they need to prioritize new investments to help leaders thrive in the new model. Then, they will scale and expand these systems over time. The second column shows the path for a district that has strong role structures in place but wants to tighten the leadership development systems. In this scenario, it may make sense to tackle this work one leadership level at a time, in phases.

FIGURE 9.5 • Prototypes for Prioritizing Leadership Development Systems

	MAJOR RESTRUCTURE	ONE-ROLE AT A TIME
Profile	District is implementing major changes to leadership architecture, first on pilot campuses and then district-wide	District is not implementing major changes to leadership architecture but needs to improve leadership development
Foundation Building	Leadership definition establishes clear expectations for each leadership level	
First Phase	For pilot campuses: • Selection processes for new (or reposted) roles • Effective onboarding for new (or reposted) roles • Core development for individuals and leadership teams to operate at the right level	Identify your highest-need leadership level: Which roles are the hardest to fill? Revamp systems focused on this role: • High-potential identification • High-potential development • Leader selection • Onboarding and support

(Continued)

(Continued)

	MAJOR RESTRUCTURE	ONE-ROLE AT A TIME
Second Phase	• Scale selection, onboarding, and core development practices to new campuses • Identify your highest-need roles district-wide: For which leadership level are you most worried about your leadership bench strength? • High-potential identification for highest-need roles • High-potential development for highest-need roles	Choose your next priority leadership level and revamp systems: identification, development, selection, onboarding
Third Phase	• Expand high-potential leader identification and development across all levels (prioritized by need and impact) • Implement strong practices for selection and onboard across all levels (prioritized by need and impact)	Choose your next priority leadership level and revamp systems: identification, development, selection, onboarding

In all scenarios, these are big investments of time and capacity. But this work is worth it because it creates different outcomes. Too many School Leaders struggle due to a weak school leadership architecture and a system that doesn't do enough to prepare them to succeed. Too many leadership development systems are passive, focused on selecting candidates but not doing much to actively identify or develop them. Leadership expectations aren't clearly communicated and as a result leaders are less prepared than they could be to make the shift to a new role.

It doesn't have to be this way. With strong systems to identify, develop, select, and support future leaders, they are more likely to be ready to move to a new leadership level and to thrive. Guided by their leadership definition, districts will identify leaders early in their careers, while there's time to invest in and develop them. When identification is a system—not just based on the instincts of individual principals—high-potential leaders are less likely to fall through the cracks. Identification is connected to and drives development, which is personalized and job embedded. The district dedicates resources to the development of high-potential individuals. As a result, future leaders may spend time in residencies or rotations building key skills with the coaching and support of excellent principals. These experiences also offer exposure to different grade levels and different strategies and approaches.

In this revamped system, district selection is still important. But selection outcomes are much stronger when the district invests more of its energy and focuses upstream—identifying and developing future leaders. When they do this well, school districts are more likely to have two or three ready leaders for every vacancy. A 2:1 or 3:1 ratio will ensure that a district has choices between strong candidates, allowing them to prioritize "fit"—matching principal strengths to the needs of specific schools. And ultimately, this increases the likelihood that each school in a district is led by an excellent principal and team of School Leaders—today, tomorrow, and five years from now.

Big Ideas and Key Takeaways

- A strong school leadership architecture requires districts to improve both how roles are structured and how leaders are developed for them.
- Too often, leadership development efforts are like pieces of a puzzle that don't fit together. They aren't unified by a common vision of the skills and capabilities that leaders need.
- A strong leadership definition will be characterized by clarity, rigor, and ownership.
- Selection processes are often focused on a leader's current performance and how well they interview. They need to be focused on evaluating whether the leader has the skills and capabilities for the *next* role.
- Districts need a system of supports that help leaders understand their new role, monitor and support their transition, and focus on their most important development priorities. Managers will play a key role in this process. A district's job is to set expectations and provide scaffolding.
- Selection focuses on picking someone to move into a leadership role tomorrow. Identification spots future leaders to proactively develop them. Districts need to make bigger investments in identifying leaders.
- Most districts need to rethink *how* they approach leadership development and *who* they focus on. They need to shift from sit-and-get learning to job-embedded development using the 70/20/10 model. And they need to focus more on developing high-potential leaders.

Conclusion

Educators are heroes. They deserve our admiration and respect. They demonstrate stamina, persistence, strength, and courage. Becoming great at their craft requires a unique combination of superpowers: deep knowledge, wide-ranging skill, creativity, and emotional intelligence. No matter how schools change, one thing will remain the same: Educators will be their heartbeat. Technology will continue to get better at helping students master technical knowledge and skills. But educators will play an irreplaceable role in supporting students to learn to think deeply and critically, to collaborate, to care about and build strong relationships with others, and to make effective, ethical decisions rooted in their values. Anywhere you find a great school, you will find great, talented, mission-driven people.

Every child deserves to have access to an excellent education that helps them realize their full potential and sets them up to live with agency, autonomy, and purpose. We will never get there if we do not create schools that enable teachers to grow and thrive. We will never get there if we ask educators to be lonely superheroes—tackling impossible jobs, receiving limited support and coaching, and working in isolation.

In the last four years, we've witnessed leaders—of our classrooms, schools, and districts—stretched beyond their limits. It feels like we are approaching a breaking point. Each month, we get new data—measured in statistics and stories—of educators leaving the profession, of low morale and high discouragement, of unsustainability. Anyone who cares about the future of our schools and the students who depend on them should be worried by these trends. I am worried. Concern about the challenges facing the education profession, the unmet needs of our students, and fear of where our current trajectory is headed drove me to write this book.

But I am also fueled by hope. I am encouraged by the doggedness and courage of so many educators. Despite the challenges they face, they persist, driven on by a sense of calling, purpose, and responsibility to their students. I see these mission-driven people giving themselves to an all-encompassing job. Their efforts and commitment draw my admiration and gratitude. These educators—these heroes—deserve to work in schools where their efforts are matched with an equal measure of support. They deserve to know that the outcome of their effort will be growth—their personal growth, their students' growth, and their schools' growth.

We need a school leadership architecture that allows the heroes working in our schools every day to work together, as a team. A strong leadership architecture can achieve the following results:

- Teachers would receive strong, effective coaching, improving their practice and satisfaction.
- Educators would find their jobs challenging but also meaningful and sustainable.
- Educators would see a path for growing their impact and their careers.
- New teachers would be more likely to grow into excellent, experienced ones. Excellent, experienced teachers would be more likely to stay in the profession.
- Schools would have the capacity they need to drive key initiatives and tackle their most important priorities.
- Schools could prioritize long-term vision, strategy, and planning—driving bold changes that respond to the needs of their students and communities.

From a classroom teacher to a campus principal to a district leader, we can each play a role in moving toward this new vision.

DISTRICT LEADERS

Districts are responsible for ensuring an effective leadership architecture—investing in multiple levels of leadership and moving away from a structure that is overreliant on principals. This work can't be offloaded to individual schools. The central office must play a leading role and ensure consistency in how roles are defined across all schools. Though this work is ultimately the responsibility of district leaders, they must approach it as a partnership with schools, principals, and teachers. Changing the school leadership architecture is something the district does *with* schools, not to them. And district leaders must be on the lookout for ways that a new school leadership architecture demands that they change too.

But improving the structure of the school leadership architecture is only half of the work. The districts' other, equally important, responsibility is to systematically identify, develop, place, and support ready, capable leaders at every level. As districts improve the structure of school leadership roles, this work is more than simply developing new leaders for new roles. Districts cannot overlook the important work of supporting *sitting* leaders to learn the new behaviors that they need to lead in the new structure.

CURRENT SCHOOL LEADERS

To School Leaders in a district committed to improving the school leadership architecture: Your leadership of this work will be critical. You know the needs of your campus better than anyone and will be able to identify the opportunities faster than anyone. Be proactive in sharing your perspective, including helping your district colleagues understand what you need from them.

In addition to helping to build the system and structures, the new architecture will require you to lead in new ways—releasing work that used to be yours to embrace work that only you can do. Don't underestimate this change. I hope that this book provides you with tools, resources, and provocations to identify the shifts that you need to make to thrive in this new architecture and to support and unleash the talents of the leaders around you.

To School Leaders in a district that hasn't (yet) tackled the work of improving their school leadership architecture: Yes, I believe that this work is best tackled with district leadership and support. But that doesn't mean that there aren't steps that you can take in the meantime. How can you use the diagnostics in Chapters 2, 3, and 4 to identify changes that are within your sphere of influence to strengthen your school's leadership capacity? How can you use Chapters 5 through 8 to identify opportunities for you and members of your team to lead differently within your current structures?

ASPIRING LEADERS AND THOSE WHO MENTOR, COACH, AND SUPPORT THEM

Aspiring leaders, you must lean into opportunities to deepen your leadership, including practicing the new skills, time applications, and professional identity shifts that will be required of you at the next leadership level. Inevitably, no one will be perfectly prepared for every aspect of their next leadership opportunity. But I hope that the key shifts help you know what to expect and build your confidence and help you identify work you can do *now* to prepare yourself. Remember: Embrace and accept discomfort, be kind to yourself, pick a place and chip away, commit to practice, recognize and name your triggers, watch out for the excessive need to be me, recognize what's temporary, and stay anchored in purpose.

Coaches, mentors, and supporters: You play an irreplaceable role in building strong future leaders. Your role is to define and clarify the leadership expectations, help the leaders you support to focus and prioritize, to encourage and elevate them, and, when they need support, to scaffold but not rescue.

Together, we can build the schools that teachers need and students deserve. I look forward to seeing what you build and to continuing to be inspired by your tenacity and creativity.

Appendix A
Typical High School Answer Key

TYPICAL HIGH SCHOOL ANSWER KEY

Based on the information we have available, here is a sample analysis of Typical High School:

- The principal is not operating as a School Leader. Instead, the principal is currently operating like a Team Leader or Bridge Leader.
- Despite common titles, assistant principal (AP) roles operate at different leadership levels. The associate principal and the two APs who supervise and coach teachers are operating at the Team Leader level. The other three APs are operating as Team Members. The dean of culture also operates as a Team Member.
- Though there are many titles that imply leadership roles (department head, specialists, facilitator), these roles are not utilized as true Team Leader roles.

TEAM MEMBER	TEAM LEADER	BRIDGE LEADER	SCHOOL LEADER
Teachers	AP		
Department Head	AP		
Specialists	Associate Principal		
Facilitator	Principal	Principal	
Dean of Culture			
AP (operations)			
AP (operations)			
AP (testing)			

Appendix B
Tools and Templates for Testing and Scaling New Structures

All of the tools and templates for Appendix B can be found on this book's companion website.

B.1 DEFINE LOOSE AND TIGHT PARAMETERS

ESTABLISHED CONDITIONS
How (de)centralized are decisions about instructional vision, curriculum, benchmark assessments, supplemental curriculum, and educational technology?
How (de)centralized are decisions about staffing and budget?
What implications do these established conditions have for how you tackle this work?
MONEY
Does the campus model need to be budget neutral? Or is the district willing to invest additional funds? If so, how much and for how many years?
Who will set salaries or stipends for new roles? When will those decisions be made? (Note: tightest approach is to establish a menu.)
Any other parameters you want to establish about funding?

(Continued)

(Continued)

POSITIONS
Which of the following recommended parameters are you adopting? *(Check all that apply.)* ☐ All teachers receive coaching and support from a Team Leader. ☐ Team Leaders have at least 50% release time relative to their full-time teacher colleagues. ☐ Team Leaders support between 6 and 10 teachers with a common goal. ☐ Team Leaders should not be used as emergency substitutes or interventionists. ☐ Because Team Leaders are responsible for the results produced by their team (typically a grade level or content area), they should have influence over all the supports that produce team success (paraprofessionals, aides, tutors, specialists, and coaches).

Are there any recommended parameters that you are modifying? ☐ ☐
Are any campuses tasked with building a three-level architecture instead of a four-level architecture? If so, what are the criteria?
How much flexibility does the campus have to tailor duties? For example, are there any responsibilities that must be assigned to a Team Leader (vs. Team Member), etc.?
Are there any parameters on who is the evaluator (of teachers, of Team Leaders, etc.)?

Are there any positions that a campus cannot *eliminate or repurpose? Are there any positions that a campus* must *eliminate or repurpose (including central office positions)?*
How will (new) leadership roles be filled? Is a formal selection process required? What role, if any, will the district play in the selection process?
Are there any other tight parameters related to positions?
OTHER FACTORS
Are there any upper or lower limits on class size?
Are there any non-negotiables regarding the master schedule?
Any other parameters?

B.2 PLANNING TO IDENTIFY AND SELECT PILOT CAMPUSES

HOW WILL YOU IDENTIFY PILOT CAMPUSES?

- ☐ Share information with all campuses, invite campuses to express interest, and run a formal selection process.
- ☐ Hand-pick campuses.
- ☐ Use some other method.

WHAT ARE YOU LOOKING FOR IN PROSPECTIVE PILOT CAMPUSES?

What are your ready, willing, and able criteria, and what evidence will you look for? The following tables start from the recommended criteria, but you are encouraged to edit these and add your own.

READY	
CRITERIA	***WHAT WE WILL LOOK FOR***
The principal's leadership approach demonstrates a comfort with and willingness to share power and empower others.	• • •
Principal has credibility and influence with peers and colleagues.	• •

WILLING	
CRITERIA	***WHAT WE WILL LOOK FOR***
The principal and their team are enthusiastic about the opportunity to change the school leadership architecture.	• •
The principal and their team have a demonstrated track record of embracing change. They are hungry to try new things.	• •

ABLE	
CRITERIA	***WHAT WE WILL LOOK FOR***
The principal and their team have demonstrated their skill and capacity to lead complex change on their campus.	•
The school has the capacity to invest time and energy in the change process. They are not engaged in too many other major change initiatives.	•

HOW WILL YOU EVALUATE?

Note: Even if you choose to handpick, what evidence or information will you use to confirm campuses are ready, willing, and able?

What data or information will you review?	
What information will you gather through an application?	
What information will you gather through an interview or conversation?	

B.3 TEMPLATE FOR CREATING PROTOTYPES

For each prototype, include an organizational chart, the progression of roles by level, and a summary of the roles.

Organizational Chart

[Note to reader: Add your own organizational chart here.]

Progression of Roles by Level

	ACADEMIC	OPERATIONS AND SUPPORT	SPECIALIST
SCHOOL LEADER			
BRIDGE LEADER			
TEAM LEADER			
TEAM MEMBER			

Summary of Roles—Team Member

PROPOSED TITLE	LEADERSHIP RESPONSIBILITIES	RELEASE TIME (%)	POSITIONS REPLACED, IF ANY (% ABSORBED)
	• •		• *Department head (100%)* • *New teacher mentor (250% = 2.5 positions)*

PROPOSED TITLE	LEADERSHIP RESPONSIBILITIES	RELEASE TIME (%)	POSITIONS REPLACED, IF ANY (% ABSORBED)
	• •		•
	• •		•
	• •		•

Summary of Roles—Team Leader

Note: Modify the percentages if positions are more than 50% focused on delivering results through others.

PROPOSED TITLE	LEADERSHIP RESPONSIBILITIES	TEACHING RESPONSIBILITY (OR OPERATIONS, ETC.)	POSITIONS REPLACED, IF ANY (% ABSORBED)
	___% (at least 50) • •	___% (no more than 50) • •	•
	___% (at least 50) • •	___% (no more than 50) • •	•
	___% (at least 50) • •	___% (no more than 50) • •	•

Summary of Roles—Bridge Leader and School Leader

PROPOSED TITLE	COACHES AND MANAGES	AREAS OF FOCUS FOR BRIDGE LEADER	POSITIONS REPLACED, IF ANY (% ABSORBED)
Principal	• •		•
	• •	• •	•
	• •	• •	•

B.4 DEFINING CAREER PATHWAYS

		ACADEMIC	OPERATIONS AND SUPPORT	SPECIALIST
SCHOOL LEADER				
BRIDGE LEADER				
TEAM LEADER				
TEAM MEMBER	Expert			
	Proficient			
	Developing			
	Emerging			

B.5 IDENTIFY LEGACY ISSUES AND BUILD AN ACTION PLAN

ELIMINATED POSITIONS		
POSITION	TIMING	NEXT STEPS/ CONSIDERATIONS

PHASE OUT		
POSITION	START/END	NEXT STEPS/ CONSIDERATIONS

LEVEL UP		
POSITION	START/END	NEXT STEPS/ CONSIDERATIONS

Appendix C
Key Shifts Case Study

CASE STUDY: LAURA'S TRANSITION FROM TEAM MEMBER TO TEAM LEADER

Laura joined the district as a teacher seven years ago right after she graduated from college. She faced the same growing pains that all new teachers confront—establishing a strong classroom culture and mastering classroom management, deepening her teaching skills while internalizing the standards and curriculum, and just getting comfortable with the pace and pressures of life as a teacher. But she stood out right away for her creativity, ability to connect quickly with students, and her work ethic. Five years in, she established herself as one of the strongest teachers in the school. The principal often highlighted her classroom as a model for others to emulate.

When Laura encountered a problem, she was tenacious and creative in troubleshooting it. One of the things that everyone in the school really appreciated about her was that she didn't need a lot of support or handholding. Laura acted independently and got things done.

She was also a voracious learner. Often she was the earliest to adopt and successfully implement new strategies or curricula. She was a good colleague and happy to share advice or resources with others. But she often showed frustration that others weren't as quick to understand as she was.

Last year, the school created a new Team Leader position in each grade level. The role was designed to enable a strong teacher to dedicate more time to coaching, mentoring, and supporting their colleagues and the effectiveness of the grade-level team. Team Leaders still taught but only 50% of the time, with the rest of their time dedicated to coaching and supporting other teachers.

Given Laura's stand-out performance as a Team Member, her principal encouraged her to consider applying. Initially, she had mixed feelings about it. She really liked being a teacher. She loved designing and delivering lessons and spending time working directly with students. Grade-level meetings were her least favorite part of the job, and the thought of spending more time focused on them wasn't appealing to Laura. But the thought of someone else in the role wasn't appealing to her either. She believed she was the strongest teacher on her team and if anyone should be coaching their colleagues, it should be her.

She applied and got it. Laura was confident in assuming the new role. She knew her stuff, had strong relationships with her team, and, frankly, thought the role sounded sort of cushy. What was she going to do with all her extra time?

Six months in, things weren't going as smoothly as she had hoped. Several members of her team needed a lot of support. They were really struggling and were expecting a lot from her. Immediately, she was disappointed that their teaching practice wasn't as strong as she hoped. (After taking the job, she realized that she had never actually seen them teach.) When she observed them teaching, she had to fight the urge to just take over the lesson. She knew that was not the right thing to do, but it was stressful to sit there and watch things go so poorly.

Over time, she started visiting classrooms less and less and began replacing that time with one-on-one meetings. But those were challenging too. Her colleagues often had a lot of basic questions. She expected them to know this kind of stuff and was hoping to spend her time planning and facilitating more interesting conversations about teaching and learning. Laura tried explaining what they should do, but they just didn't seem to get it.

Laura soon found that the fastest way to solve the problems was just to fix them herself. It was just too tiresome to coach her team on the details of lesson planning. It took forever and what they produced still wasn't as good as what Laura expected. She decided she would just use her release time to draft all the lessons plans and instructional materials for the team. She shared them in team meetings and gave people an opportunity to ask questions or make suggestions, but nobody said much. Her team members seem discouraged by her approach, but she just didn't see any other path for them to learn and to make sure the team's work was high quality.

The only problem was that she kept getting interrupted. Every time she settled into a flow to finally get some work done, a team member stopped by with a question or she needed to go to a meeting.

Sometimes Laura wondered if she did the right thing by accepting the promotion. She seemed to be doing less of the work she was good at and enjoys and isn't finding working with her team to be as gratifying as she thought it would be.

DISCUSSION QUESTIONS

1. Why do you think Laura is struggling? What might be a root cause?
2. Review Figure 5.1, focusing on the key shifts in skills, time applications, and professional identity that new Team Leaders navigate. Which of these feel relevant to Laura?
    - How is she spending her time?
    - Where might she have some underdeveloped skills?
3. In what ways does this feel familiar (or unfamiliar) to you?

(You can find our analysis of the shifts on the next page.)

ANALYSIS OF LAURA'S CASE

SKILLS

As a Team Member Laura relied on the strength of her technical skills and knowledge and the quality and timeliness of her work. As a Team Leader, she needs to hone her skills to monitor, coach, problem-solve, and provide feedback to her direct reports so that *they* can tackle problems, learn, and deepen their skills. She hasn't yet demonstrated comfort or competence with the skills associated with this passage: coaching, monitoring, planning, and building relationships to facilitate the work.

TIME APPLICATIONS

As a Team Member, Laura spent most of her time doing individual work and responding to immediate, short-term needs. As a Team Leader, she needs to spend more time coaching and supporting team members versus executing work directly. And she needs to think and act with a longer time horizon in mind. But she was struggling with this change. She consistently reverted back to time allocations that were comfortable to her as a Team Member. She constantly reallocated time for individual work versus making time for others. She found it faster and easier to do things herself. As a result, this sucked her down into day-to-day execution and problem-solving versus prioritizing the longer-term work.

PROFESSIONAL IDENTITY

As an individual contributor (Team Member), Laura's job was all about the work that she produced directly. She was recognized for, and grew to value and take pride in, her personal competence and expertise. This old identity continued to shape how she approached her work as a Team Leader. Her story contains clear examples of preferring to do the work versus supporting others to do the work. She struggled to value "discussing" over the work of "doing." She needed to make the shift to prioritizing the capacity and success of her colleagues, even if it was slower going and required more patience.

Appendix D
Tools for Prioritizing and Action Planning

All of the action plans for Appendix D can be found on this book's companion website.

PRIORITIZING

Remember what we discussed in Chapter 5. Our goal is to tackle these shifts over time, not overnight. You may have a number of areas to work on. Your job is to prioritize one or two.

STEP 1: WHAT DO YOU THINK?

If you have identified a number of areas that you want to work on, you may be unsure where to start. Here are a few ways to think about prioritizing:

- If you are new in your role, a few of the shifts that may make sense to focus on first because they set you up for success in other areas are building relationships, prioritizing managing over individual work, establishing your instructional vision, and diagnosing where team members are (a subset of developing others).
- You might want to focus on a quick win: which of these feels like an easy one to take on first or an area where you're especially motivated? That may help you get some positive momentum going.
- Or there might be one shift that is a higher priority than others because you know that it will unlock the rest (time will often unlock others), and you recognize that one shift is the key to your team-making progress or you feeling more comfortable in your role.

Circle or highlight the shifts that you think are your top priority. Ideally, you'll narrow this down to one or two, but three is your max!

STEP 2: GET SOME FEEDBACK AND ADVICE

If you have a manager/supervisor/coach who works closely with you, walk through your self-assessment and draft priorities with them. Get their reactions.

- Does your overall assessment of your strength and growth areas align with theirs? Where might you be overlooking something?
- What's their reaction to your priorities? Do they have advice on how to narrow it further or a different way of thinking about where to start?

STEP 3: PICK A PLACE TO START

Don't worry if you aren't sure if you have the most important priority identified. What matters more is picking a place to start and chipping away at the work of growing and improving.

Where will you start?

PRIORITY 1: ____

____

PRIORITY 2: ____

____

STEP 4: USE THE ACTION PLANNING TEMPLATES TO COMMIT TO ACTION

D.1 ACTION PLAN FOR SKILLS

MY PRIORITY: ______________________________

____

WHAT I NEED TO LEARN (KNOWLEDGE):

HOW I WILL LEARN IT:

- ☐ Read a book: ______________________________
- ☐ Attend a training: ______________________________
- ☐ Observe an expert: ______________________________
- ☐ Other: ______________________________

My realistic, committed deadline: ______________________________

HOW I WILL PRACTICE (FOR SKILLS):

- ☐ When, with what frequency: ______________________________

  ____

- ☐ How I will receive feedback and coaching (who, when, how frequently): ______________________________

  ____

  ____

I will commit to this practice, and we will review how I am doing on this date: ______________________________

____

D.2 ACTION PLAN FOR TIME

MY PRIORITY: ______________________________

____

WHAT I NEED TO LEARN (KNOWLEDGE):

HOW I WILL LEARN IT:

- ☐ Read a book: ______________________________
- ☐ Attend a training: ______________________________
- ☐ Observe an expert: ______________________________
- ☐ Other: ______________________________

My realistic, committed deadline: ______________________________

WHAT PRACTICES I WILL USE TO SHIFT MY TIME:

- ☐ Calendar audit (retroactive)
- ☐ I commit to spending ________ hours per week/month, prioritizing the following leadership activities: ______________________________.
- ☐ What I need to delegate to others in order to be able to change how I spend my time:

  ____
- ☐ How I will build others' capacity so I can delegate more effectively:

  ____

HOW I WILL SEEK ACCOUNTABILITY AND SUPPORT FOR THESE CHANGES:

- ☐ Who: ______________________________
- ☐ How frequently: ______________________________
- ☐ Starting (date): ______________________________
- ☐ End date: ______________________________

D.3 ACTION PLAN FOR PROFESSIONAL IDENTITY

MY PRIORITY: ____

____

WHAT PURPOSE MOTIVATES ME IN THIS WORK?

WHAT ARE MY VALUES? WHAT ARE MY BELIEFS ABOUT LEADERSHIP AND WORKING WITH OTHERS?

HOW CAN I USE MY PURPOSE OR VALUES TO REFRAME HOW I APPROACH THIS ROLE (OR SPECIFIC RESPONSIBILITY)?

Here are a few ideas to get you started:

- *It may never be my favorite part of my job, but I am motivated to do it, because it helps me advance my purpose ________________ (or live my values).*
- *I will stop viewing ________________ as a responsibility that I dislike and instead see it as a way that I advance my purpose ________________.*

HOW CAN I REFRAME MY THINKING ON A DAILY OR WEEKLY BASIS?

COMMITTING TO A TRIAL PERIOD

How long of a trial period I will commit to (recommend months not weeks):

____

____

What will it look like for me to do my best during this period (in terms of my actions, how I spend my time, and my inner narrative)?

How will I seek accountability and support during my trial period?

- ☐ Who: ____________________________
- ☐ How frequently: ____________________________
- ☐ Starting (date): ____________________________
- ☐ End date: ____________________________

Appendix E
Tools and Resources to Support Leadership Development Systems

All of the tools and templates for Appendix E can be found on this book's companion website.

E.1 BROAD LEADERSHIP DEFINITION EXEMPLARS

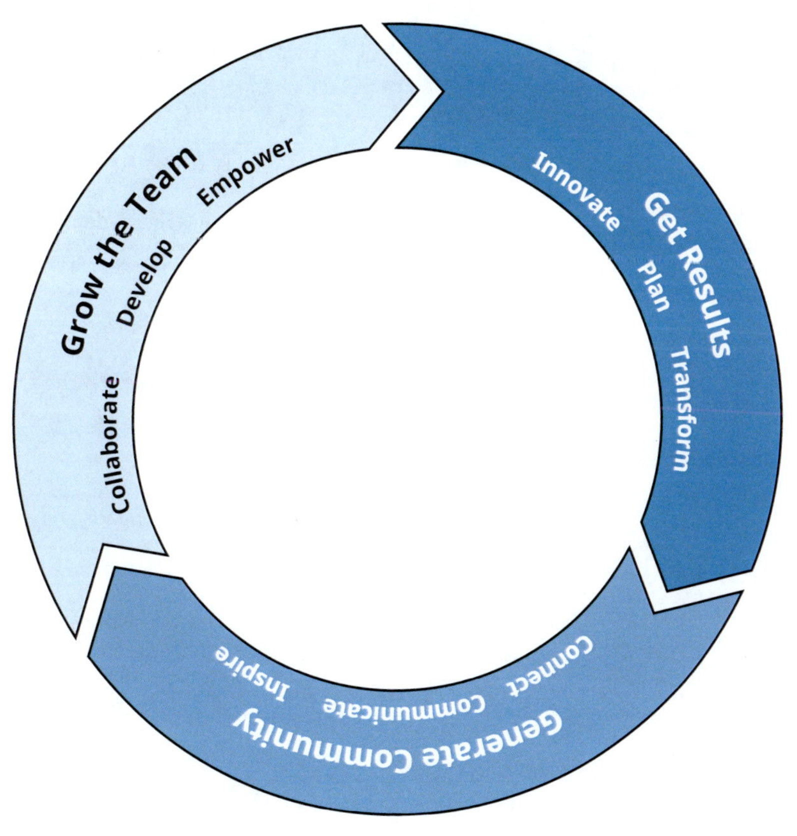

CHAMPIONS EVERY STUDENT	LEADS WITH COMPASSION	GALVANIZES A VISION	SUPPORTS OTHERS TO SUCCEED
Accountability	Cultural competence	Clear and compelling communication	Delegation
Instructional expertise	Trust-based relationships	Strategy setting	Coaching and development
System-building	Conflict resolution	Change management	Inspires and motivates

E.2 SAMPLE SELECTION/IDENTIFICATION CRITERIA, ALIGNED TO LEADERSHIP DEFINITION COMPETENCIES

	HAS IT	NEEDS IT	HAVE THEY HAD THESE EXPERIENCES?	HAVE THEY DEMONSTRATED THIS BAR OF COMPETENCY?
Results and improvement driven			☐ Led a content or grade-level team ☐ Responsible for delivering school-wide results that are critical to the school's success or standing with the community, state, or district	☐ Ability to manage a team working toward improved outcomes for students ☐ Continuous learner who protects time to strategize, reflect, and review outcomes in service of students, families, teachers, and the community
Strategy and long-term thinking			☐ Led an important change effort or new initiative implementation ☐ Has exposure to setting budget ☐ Has participated in master schedule and calendar	☐ Balances short- and long-term thinking with present needs and pressure ☐ Can set goals and milestones to help the team/organization move toward an ambitious vision

	HAS IT	*NEEDS IT*	HAVE THEY HAD THESE EXPERIENCES?	HAVE THEY DEMONSTRATED THIS BAR OF COMPETENCY?
Organizational mindset			☐ Has set a collaborative vision for something important ☐ Has had a responsibility that requires balancing competing/varying priorities within the school or district	☐ Ability to connect individual goals, initiatives, or teams with the broader vision of the school ☐ Consistently anticipates the impact of individual decisions on the school and prioritizes the whole school over smaller units
Communication			☐ Has been responsible for consistent internal communication that teachers and staff rely on for information	☐ Communicates clearly with individuals and groups ☐ Ability to communicate through layers of the organization and through various channels/modalities
			☐ Has managed large-scale external communication (parents, community, etc.)	☐ Has mindset and strategies to listen and gather input
Emotional intelligence and maturity			☐ Has managed challenging one-on-one parental or community relationships ☐ Has managed challenging one-on-one or team dynamics with teachers	☐ Has the diverse experience and emotional intelligence required to meet the stress/needs of and adapt to a variety of scenarios and stakeholders
Team culture and cohesion			☐ Has experience with supervision and performance management ☐ Has been responsible for the culture/ engagement of a group	☐ Ability to build strong relationships and bring out the best in others ☐ Has skills to build a strong team culture and a track record of supporting other adults to work together to achieve results

E.3 SAMPLE: MAPPING CRITERIA TO SELECTION PROCESS

Use the template to align on which criteria are screened at each stage of the process.

	APPLICATION	***PRE-SCREEN***	***PERFORMANCE TASK AND WORK SAMPLE***	***COMMITTEE INTERVIEW***	***FINAL INTERVIEW***
Results and improvement driven					
Strategy and long-term thinking					
Organizational mindset					
Communication					
Emotional intelligence and maturity					
Team culture and cohesion					

References

Bennet, M., & Cox, L. (2024 September). *Revolutionizing the principalship: Bold bets to elevate school leadership*. Aspen Institute Education & Society Program. https://www.aspeninstitute.org/wp-content/uploads/2024/10/Aspen-Ed-Soc-Revolutionizing-Principalship-093024.pdf

Berg, J. M., Dutton, J. E., & Wrzesniewski, A. (2008). *What is job crafting and why does it matter?* Center for Positive Organizational Scholarship. https://positiveorgs.bus.umich.edu/wp-content/uploads/What-is-Job-Crafting-and-Why-Does-it-Matter1.pdf

Bierly, C., Doyle, B., & Smith, A. (2016). *Transforming schools: How distributed leadership can create more high-performing schools*. Bain. https://www.bain.com/insights/transforming-schools/

Bierly, C., & Shy, E. (2013). *Building pathways: How to develop the next generation of transformational school leaders*. Bain. https://www.bain.com/insights/building-pathways-to-school-leadership/

Blanchard, K. (n.d.). *Developing a leadership point of view*. Retrieved August, 29, 2024, from https://resources.blanchard.com/leadership-skills/developing-your-leadership-point-of-view

Bolman, L. G., & Deal, T. E. (2014). *How great leaders think: The art of reframing*. Jossey-Bass.

Bungay Stanier, M. (2016). *The coaching habit: Say less, ask more & change the way you lead forever*. Page Two Books.

Center for Leadership Studies. (2017). *Situational leadership: Relevant then, relevant now*. https://www.situational.com/content/uploads/2017/10/FINAL_CLS_History_CaseStudy_Digital.pdf

Charan, R., Drotter, S., & Noel, J. (2011). *The leadership pipeline: How to build the leadership powered company* (2nd ed.). Jossey-Bass.

Charan, R., Drotter, S., Noel, J., Jonasen, K. (2024). *The leadership pipeline: Developing leaders in the digital age* (3rd ed.). Wiley.

Charles Butt Foundation. (2020). *2020: A survey of Texas teachers*. charlesbuttfdn.org/wp-content/uploads/2022/01/2020_A-Survey-of-Texas-Teachers.pdf

Covey, S. M. R. (2022). *Trust and inspire: How truly great leaders unleash greatness in others*. Simon & Schuster.

Coyle, D. (2009). *The talent code: Greatness isn't born. It's grown. Here's how*. Bantam.

Coyle, D. (2018). *The culture code: The secrets of highly successful groups*. Bantam.

Darling-Hammond, L., Burns, D., Campbell, C., Goodwin, A. L., Hammerness, K., Low, E., McIntyre, A., Sato, M., & Zeichner, K. (2017). *Empowered educators: How high-performing systems shape teaching quality around the world*. Jossey-Bass.

Denver Public Schools. (2019). Denver Public Schools' Teacher Leadership & Collaboration Model [PowerPoint slides].

De Smet, A., Mugayar-Baldocchi, M., Reich, A., & Schaninger, B. (2023 April 20). *Gen what? Debunking age-based myths about worker preferences*. mckinsey.com/capabilities/people-and-organizational-performance/our-insights/gen-what-debunking-age-based-myths-about-worker-preferences

Diliberti, M. K., & Schwartz, H. L. (2023). *Educator turnover has markedly increased, but districts have taken actions to boost teacher ranks: Selected findings from the sixth American school district panel survey*. RAND Corporation.

Doan, S., Steiner, E. D., & Pandey, R. (2024, June 18). *Teacher well-being and intentions to leave in 2024*. RAND Corporation.

Education Resource Strategies. (2013, May). *Promising practices in professional growth & support: Case study of achievement first.* erstrategies.org/wp-content/uploads/2023/12/CaseStudy-Achievement_First.pdf

Gallwey, W. T. (1997). *The inner game of tennis: The classic guide to peak performance.* Random House. (Original work published 1974)

Garcia, E., & Weiss, E. (2019, March 26). *The teacher shortage is real, large and growing, and worse than we thought.* Economic Policy Institute. epi.org/publication/the-teacher-shortage-is-real-large-and-growing-and-worse-than-we-thought-the-first-report-in-the-perfect-storm-in-the-teacher-labor-market-series/

Goldring, E., Rubin, M., & Herrmann, M. (2021). *The role of assistant principals: Evidence and insights for advancing school leadership.* The Wallace Foundation. www.wallacefoundation.org/sites/default/files/2023-10/the-role-of-assistant-principals-evidence-insights-for-advancing-school-leadership.pdf

Goldsmith, M. (2007). *What got you here won't get you there.* Hachette Books.

Grant, A. (2023). *Hidden potential: The science of achieving great things.* Viking.

Green, A., & Hauser, J. (2012). *Managing to change the world: The nonprofit manager's guide to getting results.* Jossey-Bass.

Hansen, M. T. (2018). *Great at work: How top performers do less, work better, and achieve more.* Simon & Schuster.

Hargreaves, A. (2017). Introduction. In *Building a lattice for school leadership: The top to bottom rethinking of leadership development in England.* University of Pennsylvania, Consortium for Policy Research in Education.

Heifetz, R., & Linsky, M. (2002). *Leadership on the line: Staying alive through the dangers of leading.* Harvard Business Review Press.

Hill, L. A. (2019). *Becoming a manager: How new managers master the challenges of leadership* (3rd ed.). Harvard Business Review Press.

Holdsworth Center. (2022). *District talent assessment* [Unpublished raw data].

Holdsworth Center. (2024). *District talent assessment* [Unpublished raw data].

Ingersoll, R., Merrill, E., Stuckey, D., Collins, G., & Harrison, B. (2021, May). The demographic transformation of the teaching force in the United States. *Education Sciences, 11*(5), 234. https://doi.org/10.3390/educsci11050234

Instruction Partners. (2024, November). *Principal role clarity: What does "principals need to be instructional leaders" mean in practice?* https://instructionpartners.org/wp-content/uploads/2024/10/Instruction-Partners-Principal-Role-Clarity.pdf

Johnson, S. M., & Donaldson, M. L. (2004). Sustaining new teachers through professional growth. In S. M. Johnson, *Finders and keepers: Helping new teachers survive and thrive in our schools.* Jossey-Bass.

Johnson, S. M., Marietta, G., Higgins, M. C., Mapp, K. L., & Grossman, A. (2015). *Achieving coherence in district improvement: Managing the relationship between the central office and schools.* Harvard Education Press.

Kena, G., Musu-Gillette, L., Robinson, J., Wang, X., Rathbun, A., Zhang, J., Wilkinson-Flicker, S., Barmer, A., & Dunlop Belez, E. (2015). *The condition of education 2015* (NCES Report No. 2015-144). U.S. Department of Education, National Center for Education Statistics. https://nces.ed.gov/pubs2015/2015144.pdf

Kofman, F. (2018). *The meaning revolution: The power of transcendent leadership.* Crown Currency.

Kraft, M. A., & Blazer, D. (2017). Individualized coaching to improve teacher practice across grades and subjects: New experimental evidence. *Educational Policy, 31*(7), 1033–1068.

Kraft, M. A., & Gilmore, A. (2016). Can principals promote teacher development as evaluators? A case study of principals' views and experiences. *Educational Administration Quarterly, 52*(5), 711–753.

Kraft, M. A., & Lyon, M. A. (2024). The rise and fall of the teaching profession:

Prestige, interest, preparation, and satisfaction over the last half century. *SSRN Electronic Journal*. https://doi.org/10.2139/ssrn.4810601

Kraft, M. A., & Papay, J. P. (2014). Can professional environments in schools promote teacher development? Explaining heterogeneity in returns to teacher experience. *Educational Evaluation and Policy Analysis, 36*(4), 476–500.

Learning Policy Institute. (2024, July 31). *The state of the teacher workforce: A state-by-state analysis of the factors influencing teacher shortages, supply, demand, and equity*. https://learningpolicyinstitute.org/product/state-of-teacher-workforce-interactive

Marcus, L. J., McNulty, E. J., Henderson, J. M., & Dorn, B. C. (2019). *You're it: Crisis, change, and how to lead when it matters most*. Public Affairs.

Marder, M., Torres, L., & Martinez, C. (2024). *Beyond the tipping point: Rise of uncertified teachers in Texas*. University of Texas at Austin.https://issuu.com/texaseducation/docs/ttp_riseofuncertifiedteachers_report_design_17x11_

Marquet, L. D. (2020). *Leadership is language: The hidden power of what you say and what you don't*. Portfolio Penguin.

McRaven, W. H. (2019). *Sea stories: My life in special operations*. Grand Central Publishing.

Merriam-Webster. (n.d.). Architecture. In *Merriam-Webster dictionary*. Retrieved August 29, 2024, from www.merriam-webster.com/dictionary/architecture

MetLife. (2012). *The MetLife survey of the American school teacher: Challenges for school leadership*. https://files.eric.ed.gov/fulltext/ED542202.pdf

Natale, C. F., Bassett, K., Gaddis, L., & McKnight, K. (2013, July 5). *Creating sustainable teacher career pathways: A 21st century imperative*. https://sep4u.gr/wp-content/uploads/pearson_edu.pdf

National Association of Secondary School Principals. (2022). *NASSP's survey of America's school leaders and high school students*. https://survey.nassp.org/2022/#leaders

National Center for Education Statistics. (n.d.). *Fast facts: Educational institutions*. nces.ed.gov/fastfacts/display.asp?id=84#:~:text=How%20many%20educational%20institutions%20exist,in%202019%E2%80%9320%20was%2030%2C492. Retrieved November 26, 2024.

National Center for Education Statistics. (2022, April 20). Changes in pupil/teacher ratios in 2020: Impacts of the COVID-19 pandemic. *NCES Blog*. https://ies.ed.gov/learn/blog/changes-pupilteacher-ratios-2020-impacts-covid-19-pandemic#:~:text=Since%20fall%202020%2C%20public%20school,in%20more%20than%204%20decades.

National Center for Education Statistics. (2022–2023). Common core of data (CCD): *Public elementary/secondary school universe survey* (2022-23 v.1a). https://nces.ed.gov/ccd/elsi/tableGenerator.aspx?savedTableID=651540

National Institute for Excellence in Teaching. (2018). *Unleashing teacher leadership: How formal teacher leader roles can improve instruction*. www.niet.org/assets/ResearchAndPolicyResources/464376c9ff/unleashing-teacher-leadership.pdf

Organisation for Economic Co-operation and Development. (2022, October 3). *Education at a glance 2022: OECD indicators*. https://doi.org/10.1787/3197152b-en

Papay, J. P., & Kraft, M. A. (2016). The myth of the performance plateau. *Educational Leadership, 73*(8), 36–42.

Partelow, L. (2019, December). *What to make of declining enrollment in teacher preparation programs*. Center for American Progress. https://cdn.americanprogress.org/content/uploads/2019/12/04113550/TeacherPrep-report1.pdf

Schleicher, A. (2018). *World class: How to build a 21st-century school system*. Paris OECD. https://www.oecd.org/en/publications/2018/05/world-class_g1g8d583.html

Senge, P. M. (2006). *The fifth discipline: The art & practice of the learning organization* (Revised and updated). Doubleday.

Suppovitz, J. (2017). Teacher leaders' work with peers in a quasi-formal teacher leadership model. *School Leadership & Management, 38*(1), 1–37.

Tan, T. S., Arellano, I., & Patrick, S. K. (2024). *State teacher shortages 2024 update: Teaching positions left vacant or filled by teachers without full certification*. Learning Policy Institute.

Templeton, T., Gregory, C., Lowrey, S., Mairaj, F., & Horn, C. L. (2024). *The Texas teacher workforce*. University of Houston Education Research Center. https://infogram.com/1p1qnpyq7klmmqfmz66k3qnz2zt626z3e57?live

Tooley, M. (2017). *From frenzied to focused: How school staffing models can support principals as instructional leaders*. New America. https://na-production.s3.amazonaws.com/documents/From-Frenzied-to-Focused.pdf

Walker, T. (2022, February 1). *Survey: Alarming number of educators may soon leave the profession*. National Education Association.

Wrzesniewski, A., & Dutton, J. E. (2001). Crafting a job: Revisioning employees as active crafters of their work. *Academy of Management Review, 26*(2), 179–201.

Index

Zeitfracht Medien GmbH
Ferdinand-Jühlke-Straße 7
99095 Erfurt, Deutschland
produktsicherheit@kolibri360.de